INSCRIPTIONS OF ASOKA

CORPUS
INSCRIPTIONUM INDICARUM

VOL. I.
INSCRIPTIONS OF ASOKA

PREPARED BY

ALEXANDER CUNNINGHAM, C.S.I.,

GYAN

Published by

Gyan Publishing House
5, Ansari Road
Daryaganj, New Delhi-110002
Phone: 011-47034999, 9811692060
E-mail: books@gyanbooks.com

Distribution Network
gyanbooks.com
India, USA, Canada, UK, Australia, France

ISBN : 978-81-212-2480-2 (HB)
First Published, 1877

2nd Impression 2021

Printed at: Gyan Press, Delhi.

Inscriptions of Asoka
Author: Alexander Cunningham

CORPUS INSCRIPTIONUM INDICARUM.

VOL. I.

INSCRIPTIONS OF ASOKA.

PREPARED BY

ALEXANDER CUNNINGHAM, C.S.I.,

MAJOR-GENERAL, ROYAL ENGINEERS, BENGAL, RETIRED;
DIRECTOR-GENERAL OF THE ARCHÆOLOGICAL SURVEY OF INDIA;
HONORARY MEMBER OF THE BENGAL ASIATIC SOCIETY;
MEMBER OF THE ROYAL ASIATIC SOCIETY, THE ANTHROPOLOGICAL INSTITUTE,
AND THE NUMISMATIC SOCIETY OF LONDON;
CORRESPONDING MEMBER OF THE ORIENTAL SOCIETY OF GERMANY,
THE IMPERIAL ACADEMY OF SCIENCES OF BERLIN,
AND THE ETHNOLOGICAL SOCIETY OF BERLIN,

"In the scarcity of authentic materials for the ancient, and even for the modern history of India, importance is justly attached to all genuine monuments, and especially to inscriptions on stone and metal."—*Colebrooke's Essays*, II, 213.

CALCUTTA:
OFFICE OF THE SUPERINTENDENT OF GOVERNMENT PRINTING.
1877.

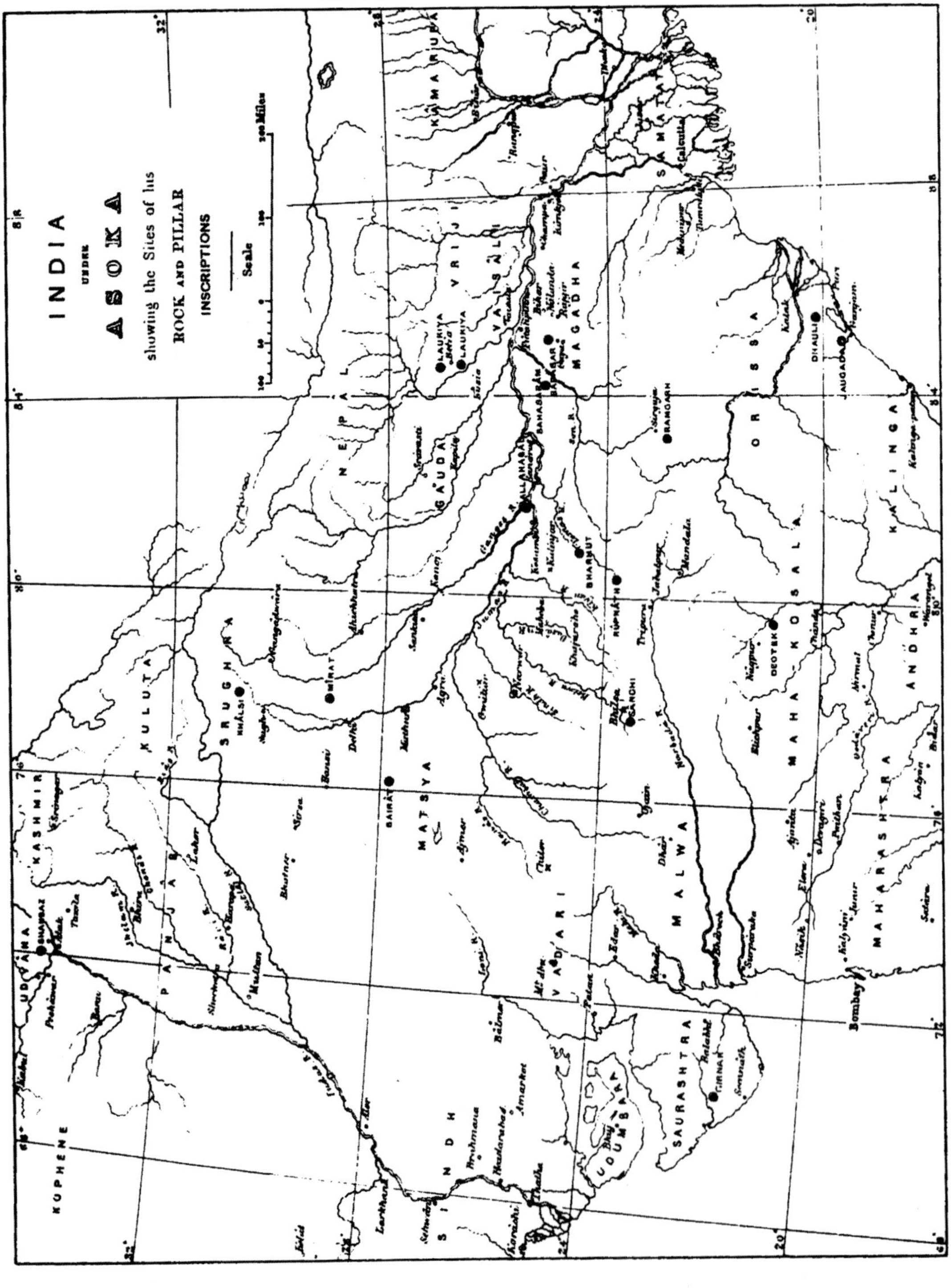

A. Cunningham del.

Lithographed at the Survr. Genl's. Office, Calcutta, April 1876.

CONTENTS.

	Page.
Preface	i
General Account of the Inscriptions	1

1.—ROCK INSCRIPTIONS.

1.— Shahbâz-garhi Rock, Great Inscription of Asoka	8
2.—Khâlsi Rock " "	12
3.—Girnâr Rock " "	14
4.—Dhauli Rock " "	15
5.—Jaugada Rock " "	17
6—7.—Two Separate Edicts on Dhauli and Jaugada Rocks	20
8.—Sahasarâm Rock, dated Edict	20
9.—Rupnâth Rock "	21
10.—Bairât Rock "	22
11.—Second Bairât Rock	24
12.—Khandagiri Rock	27
13.—Deotek Slab	28

2.—CAVE INSCRIPTIONS.

1—3.—Barâbar Caves	30
4—6.—Nâgârjuni Caves	31
7—15.—Khandagiri Caves	32
16—17.—Râmgarh Caves	33

3.—PILLAR INSCRIPTIONS.

1.—Delhi Pillar from Siwâlik (Firuz Shah's Lât)	35
2.—Delhi Pillar from Mirat	37
3.—Allahabad Pillar	37
4.—Lauriya Ararâj Pillar (Radhia)	39
5.—Lauriya Navandgarh Pillar (Mathia)	41
6—7.—Two additional Edicts on the Delhi Siwâlik Pillar	38
8.—The Queen's Edict on the Allahabad Pillar	—
9.—The Kosâmbi Edict on " "	—
10.—The Sâuchi Pillar	42

Part II.—LANGUAGE AND ALPHABET.

1.—Language of the Inscriptions	43
2.—Alphabetical Characters	49

CONTENTS.

Part III.—TEXTS.

1.—ROCK INSCRIPTIONS.

	Page.
At Shahbâz-garhi, Khâlsi, Girnâr, Dhauli and Jaugada	65
First Separate Edict—Dhauli and Jaugada	89
Second Separate Edict „ „	92
Sahasarâm, dated Inscription	94
Rupnâth „	95
Bairât „	96
Second Bairât Rock	97
Khandagiri Rock	98
Deotek Slab	102

2.—CAVE INSCRIPTIONS.

At Barâbar and Nâgârjuni	103
At Khandagiri	104
At Râmgarh in Sirguja	105

3.—PILLAR INSCRIPTIONS.

At Delhi, Allahabad, Lauriya Ararâj, and Lauriya Navandgarh	106
Edict VII on Delhi Pillar	114
Edict VIII on Delhi Pillar	115
Allahabad Pillar Separate Edict	116
Sânchi Pillar	116

Part IV.—TRANSLATIONS.

1.—ROCK INSCRIPTIONS.

Shahbâz-garhi, Khâlsi, Girnâr, Dhauli and Jaugada	117
First Separate Edict, Dhauli and Jaugada	127
Second Separate Edict „ „	129
Sahasarâm, dated Inscription	130
Rupnâth „	131
Second Bairât Rock	131
Khandagiri Rock	132
Deotek Slab	—

2.—CAVE INSCRIPTIONS.

Barâbar and Nâgârjuni	134
Udayagiri	135
Râmgarh in Sirguj a (not translated)	—

3.—PILLAR INSCRIPTIONS.

Delhi, Allahabad, Lauriya Ararâj, and Lauriya Navandgarh	137
Edict VII on Delhi Pillar	139
Edict VIII on „ „	139
Allahabad Pillar Separate Edict	140
Sânchi Pillar	141

PLATES.

No.
I.—Shahbaz-garhi Rock, Front or East Face Inscription.
II.— „ „ Back or West „ „
III.—Khalsi Rock, Front or East Face Inscription.
IV.— „ „ Side or South „ „
V.—Girnar Rock, Edicts 1 to 5.
VI.— „ „ „ 6 to 11.
VII.— „ „ „ 12, 13, 14.
VIII.—Dhauli Rock, First Separate Edict.
IX.— „ „ Edicts 1 to 6.
X.— „ „ „ 7 to 10 and 14, and Second Separate Edict.
XI.—Jaugada Rock, Edicts 1 to 5.
XII.— „ „ „ 6 to 10 and 14.
XIII.— „ „ Two Separate Edicts.
XIV.—Sahasaram, Rupnath, and Bairat Inscriptions.
XV.—Bairat, Ramgarh, and Deotek „
XVI.—Barabar and Nagarjuni, Cave „
XVII.—Khandagiri Rock and Khandagiri Cave Inscriptions.
XVIII.—Delhi Siwalik Pillar, Edicts 1 to 4.
XIX.— „ „ „ „ 5 to 7.
XX.— „ „ „ Inscriptions round the Pillar, Sânchi Pillar.
XXI.—Delhi Mirat Pillar, Edicts 2, 3, 4, 5.
XXII.—Allahabad Pillar, collected Edicts, Queen's Edict, and Kasâmbi Edict.
XXIII.—Lauriya Araraj Pillar, Edicts 1 to 4.
XXIV.— „ „ „ „ 5 and 6.
XXV.—Lauriya Navandgarh Pillar, Edicts 1 to 4.
XXVI.— „ „ „ „ 5 and 6.
XXVII.—Alphabets of the Inscriptions, Ariano-Pali and Indo-Pali.
XXVIII.—Origin of the Indian Alphabet.
XXIX.—Views of the Inscribed Rocks.
XXX.—Asoka Pillars.
XXXI.—Map of India under Asoka, showing the sites of his Inscriptions.

PREFACE.

THE object of the present work is to bring together in a few handy and accessible volumes all the ancient inscriptions of India which now lie scattered about in the journals of our different Asiatic Societies. As some of these publications are very costly, and at the same time not easy to procure, the present publication will be the means of placing in the hands of all scholars, who are interested in the history and antiquities of India, a complete collection of authentic copies of all those precious records on stone and copper which have been discovered up to the present time.

As fresh discoveries are constantly being made, it would now be almost useless to draw up any details of the contents of future volumes. But as the accessions of old inscriptions are comparatively few, I think it not premature to announce that the first three volumes will contain three distinct series of inscriptions, named respectively after the persons or periods to which they belong. The names and contents of these volumes will be as follow :—

Vol. I.—Inscriptions of Asoka on Rocks and Pillars.
,, II.—Inscriptions of the Indo-Scythians, and of the Satraps of Surashtra.
,, III.—Inscriptions of the Guptas, and of other contemporary dynasties of N. India.

The present volume contains the Inscriptions of Asoka. The gathering together of revised and authentic copies of these important records in a single volume has long been wanted for the purpose of collation and of re-translation by competent scholars.[1] This want will, I hope, be met by the collection which I now present to the public. No effort has been spared to render it complete, and at the same time to present the most perfect and authentic copy of each inscription that can now be made. To secure the latter important object, the whole of the inscribed rocks and pillars, as well as the caves, have been visited, either by myself or by my zealous assistant, Mr. J. D. Beglar. I have myself visited all the pillars and most of the caves, as well as the rocks of Shâhbâz-garhi, Khâlsi, Bairât, Rupnâth and Sahasarâm, and Mr. Beglar has visited the Dhauli and Jaugada rocks and the Râmgarh caves in Sirguja.

The original impressions have been carefully reduced under my personal superintendence by my draughtsman, Babu Jamna Shankar Bhat, who has a very correct eye, and is now conversant with the true shapes of these ancient characters. Every doubtful letter was brought to notice and jointly scrutinised and compared with photographs and former transcripts. Every single letter of the reduced pen-

[1] "These interesting monuments which, in spite of the investigations of Prinsep, Wilson, Burnouf and others, still remain incompletely translated."—Edwin Norris, M. S. Note.

cilled copy was then examined by myself while transcribing the different texts into Roman characters; and, lastly, the pencilled letters were all inked in by my own hand, so as to ensure the requisite accuracy in the shapes of the ancient characters. As the plates now published are mechanical copies by photozincography of my originals, any errors that exist must be solely due to my own oversight. That some remain I have no doubt; but I can truly say that I have done my best to make the present copies as perfect as possible.

Of the Khandagiri inscription I possess several large photographs taken from a plaster cast of the original made by Mr. H. H. Locke.

Of the Girnâr inscription I have had the use of the Bengal Asiatic Society's impression taken by Sir Legrand Jacob in 1838 for James Prinsep, as well as a separate copy of the 13th Edict examined by the General himself. These have been carefully compared with Norris' excellent lithograph prepared by himself from an impression forwarded to the Royal Asiatic Society by Sir Legrand Jacob. I have detected a few small differences, of which the chief is the occurrence of the compound letter *my*, which has been copied in the lithograph as *mn*, and read in the transcript as a simple *m*. The same compound is employed in the Jaugada text, where it is more clearly formed after the beautiful exemplars of the pillar inscriptions. This compound is used in the 9th and 11th edicts in the word *Samyapatipati*. I may mention also that the name of *Nâristika* does not occur in the 5th Edict. The first syllable belongs to the previous name *Gandhârânâm*, and the curtailed name is correctly *Râshtika*, which is one of the known appellations of Surashtra.

The *Shâhbaz-garhi* version of the edicts is particularly valuable, from being written in the Ariano-Pâli character, which possesses all the three sibilants of Sanskrit, and also approaches nearer to Sanskrit in the use of the sub-joined *r* as in the name of *Priyadarsi*. But it is of special value in giving certainty to many doubtful readings of the Indian Pâli texts, as in the case of similar Indian letters, such as *p*, *h*, and *s*, which are easily mistaken for one another in a mutilated inscription, but which in the Ariano-Pâli alphabet are widely different in form.

In PART I I have given a general account of the sites and dimensions and present condition of all the inscribed rocks, caves and pillars, which is illustrated by a map showing the exact position of each inscription. Then follows a detailed account of the inscriptions which are naturally divided into three classes according to the positions which they occupy, whether on rocks, caves or pillars. I have here added a few notices of any peculiarities or marked differences of reading which I have observed during my examination of the texts. An attempt has also been made to fix the date of each separate inscription.

PART II deals with the language and alphabets of the edicts. With respect to the first I have confined myself to extracts from Prinsep and Wilson, to show in what degree it approaches the Pâli of the Buddhist books of Burma and Ceylon. But the subject of the alphabetical characters is treated at much greater length. I have given a plate of the two alphabets side by side, containing three specimens of each, to show the changes that took place in some of the letters between the times of Asoka and Kanishka. With regard to the Indian Pâli alphabet, I have ventured to claim for it a local origin quite independent of all other alphabets. If my views be correct, the alphabetical characters of India must have passed through a pictorial stage of writing, similar to that of the early Egyptian hieroglyphs. It is true that no specimens of this kind of writing have yet been *found* in India, but it is quite possible that some may still exist, although they have hitherto escaped notice. I have myself published one early specimen of writing on a seal which was found in the Panjâb. The only difficulty about such a small and easily-transportable article as a seal is the possibility that it may have been imported from the west. But opposed to this objection is the strong fact that the cuneiform alphabets of the countries to the west of the Indus, which are now known to us, offer no affinities whatever with the characters of the seal.

In PART III I have arranged the texts of all the inscriptions in Roman characters one under the other for ready reference and comparison. The readings are my own, made from my new copies of the inscriptions; but all the principal variations from previous readings are given in the foot-notes of each page.

Amongst the *Rock Inscriptions*, the greater portion of the Khâlsi version and the whole of the Jaugada version are now published for the first time. But the most interesting addition is the newly-found dated edict in its three variant texts at Sahasarâm, Rupnâth and Bairât. For the able readings and translations of these important records I am indebted to the friendly pen of Dr. G. Bühler.

Of the *Cave Inscriptions*, only one is absolutely new; but the whole of them have been made from fresh copies and impressions taken by Mr. Beglar and myself.

Similarly, the *Pillar Inscriptions* have all been made from fresh impressións taken by myself. There are no less than five different texts, all of which were known to Prinsep. There are comparatively few variations in the pillar readings, as the characters are all of the same size and very symmetrically formed, and, where not injured by the abrasion of the stone, are particularly distinct and legible. The only difference in my reading that is worthy of special notice is in the last paragraph of the long edict, engraved around the Delhi Pillar, in which I find the word *Sila-phalakâni*, "stone tablets," instead of Prinsep's *Siladharika*.

In PART IV I have collected together all the translations of Asoka's Inscriptions which were published by Prinsep, Wilson and Burnouf. Where there is more than one translation available, I have placed the two versions side by side for ready reference.

As the Asoka inscriptions are exclusively Buddhistical, I take this opportunity to make a few observations on the Buddhist era of the Nirvâna. According to the Pâli books of Ceylon and Burma, Buddha's death took place in 544 B. C., a modest amount of antiquity which would no doubt have met with general acceptance had not the same chronicles assigned A. B. 162 for the accession of Chandra Gupta Maurya, and A. B. 218 for the inauguration of his grandson Asoka.[1] Now the dates of these two Princes can be fixed within very narrow limits, the first having been identified by Sir William Jones with Sandrokoptus, the ally of Seleukus Nikator, and the second having furnished his own date by the mention of no less

[1] A. B. stands for Anno Buddhæ, "in the year of Buddha."

than five Greek Princes who were his contemporaries. The date of Chandra Gupta's accession, therefore, is now assigned to B. C. 316, and consequently Asoka's inauguration will thus fall in B. C. 260, and his accession, which took place four years earlier, in B. C. 264. But if the Nirvâna occurred in B. C. 544, the date of Chandra Gupta's accession in A. B. 162 would be raised to 382 B. C., or 66 years too early, while the accession of Asoka would be placed in B. C. 330, just 66 years before Antiochus II succeeded to the throne of Syria, and 58 years before his contemporary Alexander II succeeded to the throne of Epirus. It seems certain, therefore, that there is an error of about 66 years in these two dates, and, as the succession of Buddhist teachers from the death of Buddha to the time of Asoka is natural and unbroken, while the succession of the Ceylonese Rajas in the same period is equally unobjectionable, the same correction must be applied to the date of the Nirvân itself, which will thus be brought down from B. C. 544 to B. C. 478.

But here it may be urged that, if the accession of Vijaya to the throne of Ceylon be lowered by 66 years, the whole of the later Ceylonese chronology will be disturbed to the same amount. But in reply I am prepared to point to a fault or disruption in the later strata of Ceylonese chronology which requires about the same amount of correction to make it straight. This period embraces the reigns of Mutasiwa and his nine sons, that is, of *two generations only*, who are said to have ruled over Ceylon from A. B. 176 to A. B. 338, or for the incredible period of 162 years. But as the longest period yet covered by two successive generations has very rarely exceeded one hundred years, while the average period of the six longest pairs known to me is only 96⅔ years, it is quite clear that there must be an error in the duration of these ten reigns of about 66 years.[1] By applying this correction to the date of Mutasiwa, we get A. B. 176—478 = 302 B. C. for his accession, which would make his *second son*, Devenipiatissa, a contemporary of Asoka, in perfect agreement with the Ceylonese history itself.

This later date for the Nirvâna of Buddha was first proposed by me in 1852,[2] as a result of the correction which was found to be necessary in the dates of Asoka and Chandra Gupta on the testimony of their Greek contemporaries. I have since added the almost equally strong evidence of the Ceylonese history itself, which, as I have shown above, requires an equal amount of correction in the very period contemporary with Asoka. I will now give a third reason for the adoption of this later date, which bears directly on the age of Buddha himself.

According to the Jains, the chief disciple of their Tirthankar, *Mahâvira* was named *Gautama Swâmi*,[3] or *Gotama Indrabhûti*,[4] whose identity with Gotama Buddha, the founder of the Buddhist religion, was suggested by both Dr. Hamilton and Major Delamaine, and was accepted as highly probable by the cautious and

---

[1] The longest pairs of reigns, of father and son, known to me are the following: Henry III and Edward I reigned 91 years; Louis XIII and Louis XIV reigned 105 years. Two Chalukya Rajas are said to have reigned 102 years; two Rajas of Bikaner 100 years; two Rajas of Kashmir 86 years; and two Rajas of Handur 96 years. These six pairs give an average of nearly 97 years per pair, which, applied to the Ceylonese chronology, would show an error of 65 years.

[2] See Bhilsa Topes, p. 74, and Bengal Asiatic Society Journal, 1854, p. 704.

[3] Ward's Hindus, II, 247, *and* Colebrooke's Essays, II—279.

[4] Stevenson's Kalpa Sutra, p. 92.

judicious Colebrooke. His clear statement of the case raises this probability almost to certainty.[1]

"In the Kalpa Sutra and in other books of the Jainas, the first of Mahâvira's disciples is mentioned under the name of Indrabhûti, but in the inscription under that of Gautama Swâmi. The names of the other ten precisely agree; whence it is to be concluded, the Gautama, first of one list, is the same with Indrabhûti, first of the other.

"It is certainly probable, as remarked by Dr. Hamilton and Major Delamaine, that the Gautama of the Jainas and of the Buddhas is the same personage, and this leads to the further surmise that both these sects are branches of one stock. According to the Jainas, only one of Mahâvira's eleven disciples left spiritual successors, that is, the entire succession of Jaina priests is derived from one individual, Sudharma Swâmi. Two only out of eleven survived Mahâvîra, *viz.*, Indrabhûtî and Sudharma: the first identified with Gautama Swâmi has no spiritual successors in the Jaina sect. The proper inference seems to be that the followers of this surviving disciple are not of the sect of Jaina, rather than that there have been none. Gautama's followers constitute the sect of Buddha, with tenets in many respects analogous to those of the Jainas, or followers of Sudharma, but with a mythology or fabulous history of deified saints quite different. Both have adopted the Hindu Pantheon, or assemblage of subordinate deities; both disclaim the authority of the Vedas; and both elevate their pre-eminent saints to divine supremacy."

Now, if we admit the identity of *Gotama Swâmi*, the chief disciple of Mahâvîra, with *Gotama Buddha*, the founder of the Buddhist religion, the date of the Nirvâna of Buddha can be determined within one or two years with absolute certainty by the following facts:—

(1) Mahâvira, the last Jaina Tirthankara, died in B. C. 527, according to the concurrent testimony of the Jains in all parts of India.

(2) If Gotama Buddha was Mahâvira's disciple, his term of pupilage must have been during the short period of his early monastic life before he began his long abstraction under the Bodhi tree at *Uruvilwa*, or Bodh Gaya.

(3) Prince Siddhârtha was 29 years old when he left his father's house to become an ascetic, and 80 years of age when he died in B. C. 478. He would, therefore, have joined Mahâvira in B. C. 478 + 51 = 529 B. C., just 2 years before that teacher's death, B. C. 527. His stay with the Jaina teacher could not, therefore, have been more than 2 years complete. This would place his birth 31 complete years before B. C. 527, or in B. C. 558, and his death 49 complete years after B. C. 527, or in B. C. 478.

Now it will be remembered that I was fortunate enough to discover at Gaya a Sanskrit inscription dated in the year 1813 of the Nirvâna of Buddha, on *Wednesday*, the 1st of the waning moon of Kârttika.[2] Here the week day being given, we have a crucial test for determining whether the Northern Buddhists reckoned the date of the Nirvâna from B. C. 544, in accordance with the Ceylonese calendar, or whether they had a separate and independent chronology of their own. According to the former reckoning, the date of the inscription would be 1813 less 544 or A. D. 1269, in which year the 1st of *Kârttika badi* fell on Sunday, the 27th October. But by adopting my proposed correction of 66 years, the date of the

---

[1] Colebrooke's Essays, Vol. II, p. 276.

[2] Archæological Survey of India, Vol. I, p. 1. I then read the date as 1819, and so it was read by learned men in Bengal, but the publication of the numerals preserved in the old manuscripts of Nepal shews that the unit figure is beyond all doubt a 3.

inscription will fall on the 4th October 1335 A. D., which day was Wednesday, as stated in the inscription.

The date of Chandra Gupta's accession offers another means of ascertaining within very narrow limits the true era of the Nirvâna. Dr. Bühler has already pointed out that "the two outside termini for the beginning of Chandra Gupta's reign are B. C. 321 on the one side, and B. C. 310 on the other."[1] As Chandra Gupta's accession is placed 162 complete years after the Nirvâna, the limiting dates for the death of Buddha will be 321 plus 162, or B. C. 483, and 310 plus 162, or B. C. 472. Now, within these limits there are only three years, which, taken as a starting point, will give *Wednesday* for *Kârtik badi* 1 in A. B. 1813. These three years are B. C. 319, 316, and 309.[2] The last is certainly too late, as it would place Asoka's accession in 257 B. C., his inauguration in 253, and his conversion to Buddhsim in 250. But his treaties with the Greek Kings, which followed his conversion, must have been made before the death of Alexander II of Epirus in B. C. 254, even if we admit that they were drawn up in ignorance of the death of Magas in B. C. 258. In these inscriptions also we find mention of the 10th and 12th years of Asoka's reign, which, if we take the year 309 for the accession of Chandra Gupta, would fall in B. C. 242 and 240, which is quite impossible, as Antiochus Theos died early in B. C. 246. It is certain, therefore, that the 12th year of Asoka must be placed before B. C. 246. We have thus only two years left which will suit the respective requirements of Asoka's history and the week-day of the Gaya inscription. These two are 316 and 319 B. C. for the accession of Chandra Gupta, which will give the following dates for Asoka:—

Accession	...	...	...	B. C. 267 or 264.
Inauguration	...	...	...	„ 263 or 260 1st year.
Conversion	...	...	...	„ 260 or 257.
10th year	...	...	...	„ 254 or 251.
12th year	...	...	...	„ 252 or 249.

Each of these dates seems unexceptionable so far as Asoka's own history is concerned. But I feel a preference for the later date of B. C. 316 for the following reason: In another place I have suggested that the *Kanwâyanas*, or *Kanwa* dynasty of the Purânas, were most probably the Indo-Scythian Turushkas of Northern India, and that the period of their rule should be corrected from 345 or 45 years to 145 years.[3] Accepting this suggestion as not improbable, the period of the Kanwas rule must be backwards from 79 A. D., which would place their accession in B. C. 67. By adding 112 years to this date we get B. C. 179 for the accession of the *Sungas*, and by adding 137 more years we get B. C. 316 for the accession of Chandra Gupta Maurya.

Regarding Asoka's own reign there is now no doubt that it extended to 41 years altogether, the shorter period of 37 years as stated in the Mahâwanso being

---

[1] Indian Antiquary, 1877, p. 154.

[2] I have made the calculations myself for every year from A. D. 1329 to 1344, corresponding to Chandra Gupta's date from B. C. 321 to 306.

[3] Objection has been taken to the longer period of 345 years as being impossible, but the objectors, who have all adopted the lesser period of 45 years, have failed to see that their smaller number is equally impossible for *four generations*.

the official reckoning from the date of his inauguration or *abhisheka*. That this was the initial point of the years of his recognised reign is made quite certain by the statements of the Mahâwanso regarding Mahindo. Thus Mahindo is said to have been ordained a priest in the 6th year of Asoka, and to have proceeded to Ceylon after he had been *twelve* years a priest, when 236 years had passed since the Nirvâna of Buddha, and in the 18th year of Asoka's reign. As the inauguration took place when 218 years had elapsed, this reckoning of 236 years as his 18th year shows that his recognised official reign was counted from his *abhisheka* or coronation, which did not take place until four years after his actual accession. The following table gives all the principal dates of Asoka's reign :—

B. C.		A. B.	Regnal years.
478	Nirvâna of Buddha Sâkya Muni	1	...
316	CHANDRA GUPTA, Maurya, 24 years	163	...
292	BINDDUSARA, 28 years	187	...
277	„ Asoka, Governor of Ujain	203	...
276	„ birth of Mahindo*	204	...
264	ASOKA, struggle with brothers, 4 years	215	...
260	„ inauguration	219	1
257	„ conversion to Buddhism	222	4
256	„ treaty with Antiochus	223	5
255	„ Mahindo ordained	224	6
251	„ earliest date of Rock edicts	228	10
249	„ second „ „	230	12
248	„ Arsakes rebels in Parthia	231	13
246	„ Diodotus rebels in Bactria	233	15
244	„ Third Synod under Mogaliputra	235	17
243	„ Mahindo goes to Ceylon	236	19
242	„ Barâbar Cave Inscriptions	237	19
234	„ Pillar edicts issued	245	27
231	„ Queen Asandhimitta dies	248	30
228	„ Second Queen married	251	33
226	„ Her attempt to destroy the Bodhi tree	253	35
225	„ Asoka becomes an Ascetic	254	36
224	„ issues Rupnath and Sahasaram edicts	255	37
223	„ dies	256	38
215	DASARATHA's Cave Inscriptions, Nagarjuni	264	...

* This date is derived from the statement of the Mâhâwanso that Mahindo was 20 years of age at his ordination. But the Burmese Life of Buddha makes him only 18 years old, and consistently states that Asoka ruled at Ujain for 9 years, which would place Mahindo's birth just two years later than given above, or in B. C. 274.

In the foregoing argument I have confined myself to the chronology of the southern Buddhists of Ceylon. I will now attempt to show that the discrepancy which exists between their date of the Nirvâna and that of the northen Buddhists may be reconciled by adopting the correction of 66 years which I have proposed for the Ceylonese date.

In the *Asoka Avadâna* of the northern Buddhists a prediction is attributed to Buddha that 100 years after his Nirvâna there would be a king of Pâtaliputra named Asoka, who would distribute his relics.[1] The same period of 100 years is also mentioned by the Chinese pilgrim Hwen Thsang.[2] But in another Buddhist work, the *Avadâna Sataka*, the date of Asoka's accession to the throne of Pâtaliputra is stated at 200 years after the Nirvâna of Buddha. This is not, of course, the exact

[1] Burnouf, Introduction à l' Histoire du Buddhism Indien, p. 370.

[2] Julien's Hwen Thsang, II., 170.

period elapsed, but only the nearest round number, which is therefore in strict accordance with the interval of 214 years assigned by the southern Buddhists.

But a still nearer approach to perfect agreement may be obtained by adopting the extra ten years of the Tibetan and Mongolian reckonings which place Asoka 110 years after the Nirvâna.[1] The corrected northern date for Asoka according to the Avadâna Sataka will then be 210 years after Buddha's death, which is the nearest decimal round number to the southern period of 214 years. That the period of 200 years given by the Avadâna Sataka is the correct one may be shown from the northern chronology itself. Thus Hwen Thsang repeatedly mentions that Kanishka ascended the throne 400 years after the Nirvâna of Buddha.[2] According to the Tibetan books this interval was "*more* than 400 years."[3] Here then we see that the northern Buddhists, who had two different dates for Asoka, were unanimous in placing the Nirvâna of Buddha at 400 years *or more* before the time of Kanishka. Now the age of Kanishka can be fixed with some certainty by the dates of the Roman silver coins that were extracted by General Court from a Stûpa at Mânikyala which was built during Kanishka's reign. The latest of these is one of Marcus Antonius the Triumvir, which cannot be older than B. C. 43, when the famous triumvirate was formed. A period of *upwards* of 400 years reckoned back from this time would agree very well with the corrected date of B. C. 478, which I have proposed as the probable era of the Nirvâna according to the northern Buddhists.

If this date be accepted, some explanation is required regarding the two discrepant dates assigned to Asoka by the northern Buddhists. The only explanation that I can suggest is, that at some very early period a difference of 100 years in the age of Asoka had been established, which it was found impossible to reconcile. Afterwards when Buddha Ghosa, or his predecessors, arranged the southern chronology, the discrepancy was forcibly reconciled by accepting two Asokas, the first being placed exactly 100 years after the Nirvâna, and the other upwards of 100 years later, or more than 200 years after the Nirvâna.

Whether this explanation be true or not, it at least has the merit of getting rid of the second synod under the fabulous Kalasoka, as well as of bringing the two conflicting chronologies of the northern and southern Buddhists into perfect harmony with each other.

I am aware that Professor Kern has published a special essay on the era of the Nirvâna of Buddha, which he refers to B. C. 388.[4] This date he obtains by raising the year of Asoka's accession from B. C. 263 to 270, and by taking the interval between it and the death of Buddha as 100 years, according to one of the two reckonings of the northern Buddhists. He thus gets B. C. 380 (it should be 370) for the date of Nirvâna, and then remarks that this date approaches so near to 388 B. C., the year in which Mahâvira *is said* to have died, that "it is difficult to

---

[1] Sanang-Setsen, as quoted in Fo-kwe-ki, p. 249, and Csoma de-Körös in Asiatic Researches, XX 297.

[2] Julien's Hwen Thsang, I., 95; II., 106, 107, 172.

[3] Csoma de-Körös in Asiatic Researches, XX., 297.

[4] See Dr. J. Muir's summary of Dr. Kern's dissertation "on the era of Buddha and the Asoka inscriptions," in the Indian Antiquary, 1874, p. 79.

think the coincidence can be accidental." He accordingly adds eight years more to the interval, by which he gets 118 years, the period elapsed between the death of Buddha and the accession of Asoka, which he takes to have been "the oldest Ceylonese tradition," instead of the 218 years as recorded in all their books.

I need hardly say that I dissent from this conclusion altogether, as it ignores, not only the existence of my Gaya Inscription with its Nirvâna date of 1813, but also the northern reckoning of 200 years for the interval between Buddha and Asoka, as recorded in the Avadâna Sataka. The first gives us an actual date in the reckoning of the northern Buddhists, and as it adds the week-day Wednesday, it offers a ready means of testing the accuracy of any proposed date. Now the year 478 B. C. which I have proposed has stood this test, and is moreover in perfect accordance with the date assigned to the era of the Nirvâna by one class of the northern Buddhists as well as by all the southern Buddhists. According to the detailed numbers of the latter, the interval between the death of Buddha and the accession of Asoka is 214 years. In the Avadâna Sataka of the northern Buddhists this interval is stated as 200 years, which is the nearest round number to the reckoning of the southern Buddhists. I conclude accordingly that the early chronology of both the northern and the southern Buddhists was originally the same, and that the actual interval between the Nirvâna and the accession of Asoka was 214 years, as stated in the Ceylonese chronicles. The true date of Buddha's death will, therefore, be B. C. 478, or just 66 years later than the date given in the Mahâvanso.

The foregoing discussion regarding the date of Buddha's Nirvân was written just before I had seen the first copy of the Sahasarâm inscription. The three symbols which form its figured date at once arrested my attention, and I suspected them to be cyphers, but the copy of the inscription was imperfect in this very part, and it was not until I visited Sahasarâm myself, and thus obtained several excellent copies of the edict, that I was satisfied that these three characters were real numerical symbols. The figure on the left hand I recognised at once as that to which I had already assigned the value of 200 in one of the Mathura inscriptions, while the value of the middle figure was conclusively determined as 50 by a second Mathura inscription, in which the date of Samvat 57 is expressed in words as well as in figures. The value of the unit I at first thought was 6, but on hearing that the late Dr. Bhau Dâji had found a somewhat similar figure as a variant form of 2, I adopted the latter as its probable value. I was the more ready to adopt this value, as it just brought the Sinhalese date of Asoka with respect to Buddha's Nirvâna into accordance with the date of the inscription.

From the new inscriptions of Sahasarâm and Rupnâth, we now gain a complete confirmation that the full reign of Asoka extended to 41 years, as it agrees exactly with the difference between the two extreme dates of A. B. 215 and 256. The same length of reign may also be deduced from the statements of Asoka himself in these two inscriptions. Thus the two periods of upwards of 32 years, say 32½, during which he did not strenuously exert himself, and of more than one year, say 1½, during which he had exerted himself strenuously, amount to 34 years, which being counted from the date of his conversion to Buddhism seven years after his accession, make up a total of 41 years.

I may add here that the Sahasarâm inscription of Asoka was first brought to notice so long ago as 1839 by Mr. E. L. Ravenshaw, who had received a copy of it from Shâh Kabîr-ud-din. It is described as being incised "on a stone at the summit of a hill near Sahásarâm called *Chandan Shahíd*. It is in the ancient character of the Allahabad and Bettiah pillars." It was then pronounced to be "so imperfect and confused as to baffle Pandit Kamalakanta."[1]

---

[1] See Journal, Bengal Asiatic Society, 1839, p. 354.

ERRATA.

Page 1, line 9, *for* 253 *and* 251, *read* 251 and 249.
„ 3, „ 7, „ 251 „ 244, „ 249—242.
„ 3, „ 10, „ 218, *read* 215.
„ 3, „ 37, „ 236, „ 234.
„ 4, „ 29, „ 315 „ 316.
„ 4, „ 30, „ 291 *and* 263, *read* 292 *and* 264.
„ 4, „ 31, „ "thirty-seven," *read* "forty-one."
„ 4, „ 32, „ 226, *read* 223.
„ 5, „ 8, „ 253 *and* 251, *read* 251 *and* 249.
„ 17, „ 9, „ 272 „ 263, „ 275 „ 264.
„ 17, „ 11, „ 271, *read* 274.
„ 17, „ 12, „ 251, „ 255.
„ 17, „ 14, „ 241 and 251, *read* 244 *and* 249.
„ 17, „ 16, „ 251, *read* 249.
„ 17, note †, „ "Dipamanso," *read* "Dipawanso."
„ 22, line 23, „ 56, *read* 256.
„ 22, „ 25, „ "omission," *read* "value."
„ 22, „ 26, „ "not uncommon in Indian inscriptions," *read* "entirely due to Dr. Bühler."
„ 30, „ 19, „ 251, *read* 249.
„ 30, „ 29, „ 251, „ 249.
„ 31, „ 31, „ 218, „ 215.
„ 31, „ 40, „ 218, „ 215.
„ 39, „ 19, „ "the" *read* "this."
„ 117, „ 8 of note, *for* "Pirate," *read* "*Piratæ*."
„ 117, „ 10 of note, „ "in 13th," „ "in the 13th."

N. B.—The numerous alterations in figures noted above are solely due to the alteration in the date and duration of Asoka's reign made since the translation of the Sahasarâm and Rupnâth dated inscriptions.

INSCRIPTIONS OF ASOKA.

PART I.—GENERAL ACCOUNT OF THE INSCRIPTIONS.

THE earliest Indian inscriptions that have yet been discovered are the Edicts of Asoka. These are of two distinct classes, which are generally known as Rock Inscriptions, and Pillar Inscriptions, to which may be added a few Cave Inscriptions in Bihâr and Orissa.

The five *Rock Inscriptions* hitherto known present us with five different texts of the same series of edicts which were published by Asoka in the 10th and 12th years of his reign, or in 253 and 251 B. C. These five inscribed rocks have been found at far distant places, of which four are on the extreme eastern and western borders of India, thus showing the wide extent of Asoka's rule, as well as the great care which he took about the promulgation of his edicts in the most remote parts of his dominions.

The five famous rocks on which these edicts are engraved are at the following places:—

No. 1.—At *Shâhbâzgarhi* in the *Sûdam* valley of the Yusufzai district, 40 miles to the east-north-east of Peshâwar, and 25 miles to the north-west of Attak on the Indus. Its version of the text in the transliteration is indicated by the letter S.

No. 2.—Near *Khâlsi* on the west bank of the Jamna, just where it leaves the higher range of mountains to pass between the *Dûns*, or valleys, of Kyârda and Dehra. Its version of the text is indicated by the letter K.

No. 3.—At *Girnâr*, near Junagarh in Kathiâwâr, 40 miles to the north of Somnâth. Its version of the text is distinguished by the letter G.

No. 4.—At *Dhauli* in Katak, 20 miles to the south of the town of Katak (Cuttack), and the same distance to the north of the famous temple of Jagannâth. Its version of the text is marked by the letter D.

No. 5.—At *Jaugada* in the Ganjam district, 18 miles to the west-north-west of the town of Ganjam, and about the same distance to the north-north-west of Berhampur. Its version of the text is indicated by the letter J.

Nos. 6 and 7.—In addition to these five texts of Asoka's collected series of edicts, there are two separate edicts at Dhauli and Jaugada, which agree so closely with each other as to form two independent but slightly variant texts of the same edicts. As the two separate edicts at Dhauli are addressed to the rulers of *Tosali*, they may be named very appropriately the *Tosali* Edicts, while those at Jaugada, being addressed to the rulers of *Samâpâ*, may with equal fitness be named the *Samâpâ* Edicts.

Of the five inscriptions above noted, three only were known to Prinsep and Burnouf, the *Khâlsi* and *Jaugada* versions having been discovered many years later.

Within the last three years, also, three new inscriptions have been brought to light, which on examination I find to be only slightly variant texts of a single edict; but it is a very important one, as all three texts are dated in an era which I take to be that of the Nirvân of Buddha. These three inscribed rocks are at the following places:—

No. 8.—At *Sahasarâm*, at the extreme north-east end of the Kaimur range of hills, 70 miles to the south-east of Benares, and 90 miles to the south-west of Patna. This inscription was found by Mr. Davis, and brought to notice by Mr. S. S. Jones, Assistant Magistrate of Sahasarâm. The date was discovered by myself.

No. 9.—At *Rûpnâth*, a famous place of pilgrimage, situated at the foot of the Kaimur hills, and near the extreme south-west end of the range, and thirty-five miles nearly due north from Jabalpur. This inscription was originally discovered by a servant of Colonel Ellis, who furnished a very imperfect and quite unreadable copy, which I found in a box in the museum of the Bengal Asiatic Society. A meagre endorsement in Nâgari letters merely stated that it was found at "Rûpnâth, in Parganah Salimabad." As there is a Salimabad Parganah between Gaya and Mongir, I expected to have found this inscription not far from Bihâr; but all search in that neighbourhood was in vain. I then directed the attention of my assistant, Mr. Beglar, to Sleemanabad near Jabalpur, which is generally called Salimabad, and near that place he discovered the missing inscription.

No. 10.—At *Bairât*, at the foot of the *Bhim-gupha* hill, forty-one miles nearly due north of Jaypur, and twenty-five miles to the west of Alwar. Bairât is a very old town, which was once famous for its copper mines, and is still widely known by its connection with the wanderings of the Pandus. The inscription was discovered by my assistant, Mr. Carlleyle.

The three copies of this new edict are placed together in Plate XIV.

No 11.—Also at *Bairât*.—This is the well-known inscription which was discovered by Captain Burt, and which has had the good fortune to be translated and annotated by Burnouf and Wilson. As it is engraved on a detached block of granite, the inscription was presented to the Asiatic Society by the Raja of Jaypur, and it now graces their museum, in front of the bust of James Prinsep.

No. 12.—Another rock inscription, of somewhat later date, exists on the Khandagiri hill, near Dhauli in Katak. Its probable date is about B. C. 200. It is a record of an unknown Raja of Kalinga, named *Aira*, or *Vera*, and is generally known as the Khandagiri inscription.

No. 13.—A still later inscription exists on a detached block of stone at *Deotek*, about fifty miles to the south-east of Nagpur. It has been dated, but the year is unfortunately lost, and only the names of the season, the fortnight, and the day now remain. I do not think that it can be earlier than the beginning of the first century B. C.

The *Cave Inscriptions*, which now amount to seventeen, are found at four different places. Nos. 1, 2 and 3 are in the hill of Barâbar, and Nos. 4, 5, and 6, in the hill of Nâgârjuni, both places being about fifteen miles to the north of Gaya in Bihar. Nos. 7 to 15 are in the hill of Khandagiri in Katak, and Nos. 16 and 17 are in Râmgarh in Sirguja.

The three inscriptions at *Barâbar* were discovered by Kittoe after Prinsep's death. They belong to the 12th and 19th years of Asoka, or to 251 and 244 B. C., and have had the advantage of being translated and criticised by Burnouf. The three inscriptions at Nâgârjuni, which belong to the reign of Dasaratha, the grandson of Asoka, were translated by Prinsep himself. Their date is B. C. 218. Of the nine Khandagiri inscriptions, all but the first, which was discovered by Mr. Beglar, were known to James Prinsep. They belong to the reign of Aira, or Vera, Raja of Orissa, and are of a somewhat later date than the Asoka inscriptions, or about B. C. 200. The two inscriptions from the Râmgarh hill in Sirguja were first made known by Colonel Ouseley, but the copies now given are taken from Mr. Beglar's photographs and impressions. One of them has the peculiarity of using the palatal sibilant S in the name of the maker of the cave, a *Sutnuka* named *Devadasi.* The letter *l* also is used for *r* in the word *lupadakhe* for *rupadakha* = sculpsit.

The *Pillars* erected by Asoka would appear to have been very numerous, but only a few of them are now known to exist, besides several fine capitals without their shafts. But only six of these pillars are inscribed, although the Chinese pilgrims make mention of many that bore records of Asoka. One complete pillar with a single lion capital stands at Bakhra in Tirhut, but there is no trace whatever of any ancient inscription upon it. A second pillar, nearly complete, with an eight-lion capital, stands at *Latiya*, fourteen miles to the south of Ghâzipur, but it is also without any inscription. A broken pillar, which once stood at Bakror opposite Bodh-Gaya, and another in the ancient city of Taxila in the Panjáb, are likewise uninscribed. There are also the capitals of six other large pillars still lying at Sankisa, Bhilsa, Sânchi and Udayagiri. All of these I have seen, but as no portions of their shafts could be found, it is impossible to say whether they were inscribed or not.

The sites of the inscribed pillars, which occupy only a limited area in the very heart of Asoka's dominions extending from the Jumna to the Gandak, present a most marked contrast to the scattered positions of the rock inscriptions on the eastern and western frontiers of his kingdom. Six of these inscribed pillars have been found, of which five present, in a slightly variant form, the text of a series of six edicts that were promulgated by Asoka in the 27th year of his reign, or in B. C. 236. These five pillars are now standing at the following places, but it is known that the two Delhi pillars were brought to their present positions by Firoz Tughlak from Siwâlik and Mirat :—

No. 1.—At *Delhi*, now known as Firoz Shah's Lât. This pillar was brought from a place named *Topur Sûk*, in the Siwâlik country. I propose, therefore, to call it the *Delhi-Siwâlik* pillar for the sake of distinction, and to indicate its version of the text by the letters D. S.

No. 2.—At *Delhi.*—This pillar was brought from Mirat by Firoz Shah. I propose, therefore, to call it the *Delhi-Mirat* pillar, and to distinguish its version of the text by the letters D. M.

No. 3.—At *Allahabad*, inside the fort. Its version of the text is distinguished by the letter A.

No. 4.—At *Lauriya*, a small hamlet near the temple of Ararâj Mahadeva, between Kesariya and *Bettia*, and seventy-seven miles nearly due north from Patna. I have already named this as the *Lauriya-Ararâj* pillar, and I propose now to distinguish its version of the text by the letters L. A.

No. 5.—At *Lauriya*, a large village, fifteen miles to the north-north-west of Bettia, and ten miles to the east of the Gandak river. Close beside it there is a lofty ruined fort called Nonadgarh or Navandgarh. I therefore called this the *Lauriya-Navandgarh* pillar, and its version of the text will be distinguished by the letters L. N.

Nos. 6 and 7.—The *Delhi-Siwâlik* pillar has two additional edicts which are not found on any of the other pillars. No. 6 is placed on the east face below the original edicts, and No. 7 encircles the whole shaft.

Nos. 8 and 9.—On the Allahabad pillar there are also two short additional edicts which are peculiar to itself. Of these No. 8 was known to James Prinsep; and as it refers to some queen's gifts, it may be appropriately named the "Queen's edict."

No. 9, which has just been discovered by myself, may be called the Kosâmbi edict, as it is addressed to the rulers of Kosâmbi, a famous ancient city, the ruins of which still exist on the Jumna, thirty miles above Allahabad.

No. 10—Pillar inscription is a short mutilated record on a fragment of a pillar lying beside the great Sânchi Stûpa near Bhilsa. I am afraid that its reading is generally too doubtful to be of any real value.

The sites of all these inscribed rocks and pillars are shown in the accompanying map, with their names printed in red.

Asoka, the generally acknowledged author of these inscriptions, was the third Prince of the Maurya dynasty, and the grandson of Chandra Gupta, who was happily identified by Sir William Jones with Sandrakoptos, the contemporary of Seleukos Nikatar. Chandra Gupta reigned twenty-four years from B. C. 315 to 291. His son Bindusâra reigned twenty-eight years down to B. C. 263, when he was succeeded by Asoka, who reigned thirty-seven years, and died in B. C. 226. I understand that Wilson to the last doubted the identity of Asoka Maurya with the Priyadarsi of these rock and pillar edicts. But as he firmly believed in the identity of Chandra Gupta and Sandrokoptos, his doubts as to the identity of Asoka and Priyadarsi were a manifest inconsistency. For as both Brahmanical and Buddhist accounts agree in stating that Asoka Maurya, the grandson of Chandra Gupta Maurya, was King of Magadha for thirty-seven years, as noted above, it is certain that he was a contemporary of all the five Greek Princes mentioned in the edicts of Priyadarsi.[1] And as Priyadarsi also ruled over Magadha, we thus have two different kings of Magadha at the same time. The simple solution of this difficulty is the fact, mentioned in the Singhalese Dipawanso, that *Asoka* was also

[1] These five Princes are—

Antiochus II—Theos of Syria	B. C.	263	246
Ptolemy II—Philadelphos of Egypt	„	285	246
Antigonus Gonnatas of Macedonia	„	276	243
Magas of Cyrene	„		258
Alexander II. of Epirus	„	272	254

called *Priyadarsi*. The same fact is also stated in the Burmese life of Buddha, where Mahâkâsyapa is made to prophesy that "in after times a young man named *Piadatha* (Piyadasi) shall ascend the throne and become a great and renowned monarch under the name of Asoka."[1] A strong argument in favour of the identity of Priyadarsi Devânampriya with Asoka, is the subsequent use of one of the titles by his grandson Devânampriya Dasaratha in the Nâgârjuni cave inscriptions.

As both the 10th and 12th years of Priydarsi are mentioned in the rock edicts, the dates of their promulgation will be B. C. 253 and 251. Now, as Alexander II of Epirus died in B. C. 254, the mention of his name in the edicts of Priyadarsi which were promulgated just at that time is the most satisfactory proof of the accuracy of the date which has been assigned to Asoka, and most conclusively confirms Sir W. Jones's identification of Sandrakoptos with Chandra Gupta.

That the Antiochus mentioned by Priyadarsi is not Antiochus the Great, as suggested by Wilson, is most fully proved by the omission of the name of Euthydemus of Bactria, the nearest Greek prince on the frontier of India. It is equally disproved by the reference to the governors (*Sâmanta* and *Sâmino*) of Antiochus, which shows that the revolt of the Eastern princes under Diodotus, Pantaleon and Antimachus had not then taken place. These edicts were therefore drawn up during the lifetime of Antiochus Theos, or certainly before B. C. 246.

The following is James Prinsep's summary[2] of the "contents of the edicts":—

"The *first* edict prohibits the sacrifice of animals both for food and in religious assemblies, and enjoins more attention to the practice of this first of Buddhistic virtues than seems to have been paid to it even by the Raja himself, at least prior to the sixteenth year of his reign.

"The *second* edict provides a system of medical aid for men and animals throughout Piyadasi's dominions, and orders trees to be planted and wells to be dug along the sides of the principal public roads.

"The *third* edict enjoins a quinquennial humiliation, or if we read the word, by the alteration of *y* to *s*, as anusasânam, the re-publication every five years of the great moral maxim inculcated in the Buddhist creed, *viz.*, 'Honour to father; charity to kindred and neighbour and to the priesthood (whether Brahmanical or Buddhistical); humanity to animals; to keep the body in temperance, and the tongue "from evil speaking!" And these precepts are to be preached to the flock by their pastors with arguments and examples. This edict is dated after the twelfth year of Piyadasi's inauguration.

"The *fourth* edict draws a comparison between the former state of things, perhaps lawless and uncivilised, and the state of regeneration of the country under the ordinances of the beloved king. The publication of the glad tidings seems to have been made with unexampled pomp and circumstance, and posterity is invoked to uphold the system. This edict is also dated in the twelfth year of Piyadasi.

"The *fifth* edict, after an exordium not very intelligible, proceeds to record the appointments of ministers of religion, or more strictly missionaries; and enumerates many of the countries to which they are to be deputed for the conversion of the young and the old, the rich and the poor, the native and the foreigner. Many highly curious points, especially as to geography, call for notice in this edict, wherein for the first time the name of the celebrated city of *Pátaliputra* is made known to us in the ancient character.

"The *sixth* edict appoints in like manner *pativédakas*, informers, or perhaps more properly *custodes morum*, who are to take cognizance of the conduct of the people in their meals, their

[1] Bishop Bigandet's Legend of the Burmese Buddha, 2nd edit., p. 346.
The Burmese pronounce *s* as a soft English *th*; hence they say Paidatha and Athoka for Pyadasi and Asoka.

[2] Journal, Bengal Asiatic Society, VII, 220.

domestic life, their families, their conversation, their general deportment, and their decease. It also nominates magistrates or officers for punishment, if the word *antiyáyika* (S. *antyayaka*) may be so understood, so that in this edict we have a glimpse of the excellent system of moral administration for which the Greek and Persian historians give credit to our monarch, and we find it actually not very different from that followed twenty centuries later by ourselves; for we too have our judge, and our magistrates, and further, our missionaries are spread abroad among the people to drown them with the overflowing truths of our *dharma*, to release them from the fetters of sin and bring them unto the salvation which 'passeth understanding!'

"The *seventh* edict expresses, not an order, but an earnest desire on the part of the king that all the diversities of religious opinion may be obliterated; that every distinction in rank and in tastes may be harmonised into one system of *bhávasudhi*, that peace of mind, or repose of conscience, which proceeds from knowledge, from faith and entire assent.

"The *eighth* edict contrasts the mere carnal amusements patronised by former Rajas with the more harmless and pious enjoyment prescribed by himself. The dhammayátá, or in Sanskrit dharmayátrá, the festival of religion, is thus set in opposition to the viháráyátra, the festival of amusement; and it is stated to consist in the visits to holy people, in alms-giving, in respect to elders, and similar praiseworthy sources of rational gratification. This edict is dated in (or rather after) the tenth year of Piyadasi's reign.

"The *ninth* edict continues the thread of the same discourse by expatiating on the sources of true happiness, not such as the worlding seeks in marriage, in rearing children, in foreign travel, and such things; but the *dharma mangalam*, the happiness of virtue, which displays itself in benevolence to dependants, reverence to one's pastors, in peace with all men, abundant charity, and so forth, through which alone can the blessings of Heaven be propitiated.

"The *tenth* paragraph comments upon *Yaso vá kíti vá*, the glory of renown, which attend merely the vain and transitory deeds of this world. The Raja is actuated by higher motives, and he looks beyond for the reward for which he strives with heroism (*parákramena*) the most jealous, yet respectful.

"The *eleventh* edict is to be found at Dhauli, but it is well preserved at Girnar, and the meaning is clear throughout. As former paragraphs had vaunted the superiority of every act connected with *dharma*, so this upholds that the imparting of *dharma* itself is the chiefest of charitable donations; and then it points out as usual how the possession of this treasure becomes manifest in good works rewarded with temporary blessings in this world and endless moral merit (as the reward of it) in the next.

"The *twelfth* edict is likewise wanting in the Katak series. It is addressed to all unbelievers, whether domestic or ascetic, with entreaty and with more solid and more persuasive bounty, though direct disavowal that fame is the object. There is some little obscurity in the passages which follow regarding the mode of dealing with the two great divisions of the unbelievers who are distinguished as *áptapásanda* (those fit for conversion or actually converted), and *parapásanda*, ultra heretics, or those upon whom no impression had been made; but the concluding paragraph informs us of the appointment of three grades of ministers, *dharmamahámátrás*, *stairyya-mahámátrás*, and subordinates, in the congregational ceremonies, *karmikás*, thus placing the religion upon a firmer basis, promoting conversion to it, and enhancing its attractiveness among the people.

"The *fourteenth* edict is one of the most interesting of the whole series. It is a kind of summing up of the foregoing, which we have seen are partly laconic and partly diffuse, but the whole is said to be complete itself; and if more were written it would be repetition. We learn from this edict that the whole was engraved at one time from an authentic copy, issued, doubtless, under the royal mandate, by a scribe and pandit of a name not very easily deciphered. It is somewhat curious to find the same words precisely on the rock in Katak. The name of the writer is there erased, but the final letters of *lipikára*, 'scribe,' are quite distinct.

"This may be properly regarded as the last of the peculiar series of edicts to which it alludes."

This account of the general scope of Priyadarsi's edicts was subsequently criticised by Wilson, who objected that "with respect to the supposed main purport of the inscription, ***proselytism to the Buddhist religion***—it may not unreasonably be doubted if they were made public with any such design, and whether they have any connection with Buddhism at all * * *" "The meaning of the language of the inscriptions is, to say the least, equivocal."[1] But notwithstanding these inconclusive evidences of Buddhism, Wilson fully admitted that "Priyadarsi intended to enjoin equal reverence to Brahmans and to Buddhist teachers;" that No. 12 edict "exhibits this intention most unequivocally, and that the prince enjoins in it no attempt at conversion, but universal respect for all forms of religious belief, his own as well as (that of) any other *Páshanda.*" He then explains the true meaning of the term *Páshanda,* as comprising "all who do not regard the authority of the Vedas as infallible and divine, and who draw from them doctrines which tend to set aside the necessity of mere formal ceremonies." "This, in fact, appears to be the main object of all the edicts, whether on the rocks or on the pillars, the exaltation over all ceremonial practices, over a religion of rites, of the observance of moral obligations; the enjoining, in preference to the sacrifice of animals, obedience to parents, affection for children, friends and dependants, reverence for elders, Srâmans and Brahmans, universal benevolence and unreserved toleration." Wilson concludes his arguments with the following words: "The edicts may be taken as historical evidence that Buddhism was not yet fully established, and that Priyadasi was desirous of keeping peace between it and its predecessor by inculcating social duties and universal toleration in place of either ritual or dogma."

The respect paid to Brahmans is satisfactorily accounted for by Burnouf, who remarks that

"in the *early* Buddhist writings very little difference appears between the Buddhists and Brahmans, and Buddha is often described as followed by a crowd of Brahmans as well as Bhikhus and Srâmans."[2]

---

[1] Journal, Royal Asiatic Society, XII, 236.

[2] Journal, Royal Asiatic Society, XII, 242, quoted by Wilson.

I. ROCK INSCRIPTIONS.

1.—Shâhbâz-garhi Rock.

The great inscription of Asoka at Shâhbâz-garhi was first made known by General Court, who described it as being situated *quite close* to Kapurdagarhi, and *almost effaced by time.*[1] But Kapurdagarhi is two miles distant, and the rock is actually within the boundary of the very much larger village of Shâhbâz-garhi, from which it is less than half a mile distant. Court's notice of the inscribed rock stimulated the zeal and curiosity of Masson, who, in October 1838, proceeded to Shâhbâz-garhi,[2] when he succeeded in making a very fair copy of the inscription, which enabled Norris to identify it as another transcript of Asoka's well-known edicts, but engraved in Arian-Pali characters.

Shâhbâz-garhi is a modern name, derived from the *ziârat* or shrine of Shâhbâz-kalandar, a rather notorious saint, who was described to me as a Kâfir, and who is stigmatised by Baber as "an impious unbeliever, who in the course of the last thirty or forty years had perverted the faith of numbers of the Yusufzais and Dilazâks."[3] Baber thus continues: "At the abrupt termination of the hill of Makâm there is a small hillock that overlooks all the plain country; it is extremely beautiful, commanding a prospect as far as the eye can reach, and is conspicuous from the lower grounds. Upon it stood the tomb of Shâhbâz-kalandar. I visited it, and surveyed the whole place. It struck me as improper that so charming and delightful a spot should be occupied by the tomb of an unbeliever. I therefore gave orders that the tomb should be pulled down and levelled with the ground." As this was in A. D. 1519, the death of Shâhbâz must have taken place about A. D. 1490. The old name must, therefore, have been in use down to the time of Baber, but unfortunately he gives only the name of Makâm, which is that of the stream of Shâhbâz-garhi at the present day. Baber also speaks of the hill above the shrine of Shâhbâz as the hill of Makâm; but the name is not that of the town, but of the valley. I accept, therefore, the statement of the people, that the old name of the town was something like Sattâmi or Setrâm, or Sitarâm, which I propose to identify with the city of the famous Buddhist Prince Sudâna.[4]

---

[1] Bengal Asiatic Society's Journal, V, 481.

[2] Royal Asiatic Society's Journal, VIII, 296, where Masson describes Shâhbâz-garhi as the village nearest to the inscribed rock.

[3] Memoirs by Leyden and Erskine, p. 252.

[4] Archæological Survey of India, V, 9

During my stay at Shâhbâz-garhi I made a survey of the neighbourhood, and was surprised to find that the present village was the site of a very old and extensive city, which, according to the people, was once the capital of the country. They pointed to several mounds of ruins as having been inside the city, and to two well-known spots named Khaprai and Khapardarâ, as the sites of the northern and eastern gates of the city. The truth of their statements was confirmed by an examination of the ground within the limits specified, which I found everywhere strewn with broken bricks and pieces of pottery. The old name of the place was not known, but some said it was Sattâmi, and others Setrâm and Sitarâmi, all of which I believe to be simple corruptions of the name of the famous Buddhist Prince Sudâna or Sudatta.

In my account of the ruins at Shâhbâz-garhi I have identified the site with the *Po-lu-sha* of Hwen Thsang, and the *Fo-sha-fu* of Sungyun."[1] The two transcripts are evidently intended for the same name, which M. Julien renders by *Varusha*. The position assigned to it by Hwen Thsang is about forty miles to the north-east of Peshawar, and twenty-seven miles to the north-west of Utakhanda, or Ohind. These bearings and distances fix the site of the city somewhere in the valley of the Makâm Rud, which the subsequent mention of the Dantâlok hill, and of a cave within a few miles of the city, limits to the neighbourhood of Shâhbâz-garhi. That this was one of the chief cities of the country in ancient times, we learn from the traditions of the people, as well as from the extent of the existing ruins, and the presence of the great rock inscription of Asoka. From all these concurring circumstances I feel satisfied that the site of Shâhbâz-garhi represents the ancient city of *Po-lu-sha*, or *Fo-sha*, an identification which will be strongly corroborated by an examination of some of the details furnished by the Chinese pilgrims. As *fu* means "city" I have a suspicion that *Fo-sha* may be identified with *Bazaria*. In this case Hwen Thsang's *Po-lu-sha* might be read as *Po-sha-lu* by merely transposing the last two syllables. In support of this suggestion I may quote Arrian's description of Bazaria, as situated upon an eminence and surroundad by a stout wall,[2] which agrees very closely with the actual position of Shâhbâz-garhi, as well as with the accounts of Sudatta's city given by the Chinese pilgrims.

The great inscription of Asoka is engraved on a large shapeless mass of trap rock, lying about 80 feet up the slope of the hill, with its western face looking downwards towards the village of Shâhbâz-garhi. The greater portion of the inscription is on the eastern face of the rock looking up the hill, but all the latter part, which contains the names of the five Greek kings, is on the western face. The mass of rock is 24 feet long and about 10 feet in height, with a general thickness of about 10 feet.[3] When I first saw the inscription in January 1847 there was a large piece of rock, which had fallen from above, resting against the upper or eastern face of the inscription. At my request this piece of rock had been removed in 1871 by a party of Sappers, and I was thus able to take a complete impression of this side of the inscription. I cleared

---

[1] Archæological Survey of India, Vol. V, p. 15.

[2] Anabasis, IV, 27.

[3] Two views of this rock are given in Plate XXIX. The inscriptions will be found in Plates I and II.

the ground both above and below the rock, and built level terraces in front of both inscriptions so as to be able to examine with tolerable ease any doubtful portions. The eastern face, though not smooth, presents a nearly even surface, the result of a natural fracture; but the western face is rough and uneven, and the letters, though not much worn, do not afford a good impression. I therefore traced them out carefully with ink for the purpose of taking an eye-copy, but the ink was washed out at night by a heavy fall of rain. The same thing happened a second time, but after a third tracing the weather became fair, and I was able to make a complete eye-copy as well as an impression of this important part of Asoka's inscription. Every doubtful letter was examined several times in different lights, and was copied by my native assistants as well as by myself, until by repeated comparisons the true form was generally obtained. Under these circumstances, I believe that I have secured as perfect and as accurate a copy of this famous inscription as it is now possible to make. As no photographs can be taken of either face of the inscription on account of the slope of the hill, an eye-copy, thus checked by an impression, is, I believe, the best possible substitute. The Khalsi and Shâhbâz-garhi texts are nearly perfect in the important 13th tablet which contains the names of the five Greek kings, and of several well-known districts of India. The words of the Shâhbâz-garhi inscription in this part are as follow, from near the beginning of the 9th line :—

ANTIYOKA *nama Yona raja, paran cha tena* ANTIYOKENA *chatura IIII rajani,* TURAMAYE *nama, Antikina nama,* MAKA *nama,* ALIKASANDARE *nama, nicha* CHODA, PANDA, AVAM, TAMBAPANNIYA, hevam mevam hevam mevam raja, vishamtini ? YONA KAMBOYESHU, NABHAKA-NABHAPANTESHU, BHOJA-PITINIKESHU, ANDHRA-PULINDESHU, *savatam,* &c. The name of Alexander is written Alikasandare, which agrees with the *Alikyasadale* of the Khalsi version. Then follow the names of several countries of which not one was recognised by either Norris or Wilson. Of these, *Choda* and *Panda* are the well-known Chola and Pandya of early history. If *Avam* be a proper name, it may be the country of Ptolemy's *Aii*, an identification which is rendered still more probable by the subsequent mention of *Tambapanniya* or Ceylon. Of the last series of names the *Yonas* and *Kambojas* are well known. Of the *Nabhakas* and *Nabhapantis* I cannot offer even a conjecture, but the *Bhojas* are mentioned both in the Mahabhârata and in the Purânas. They are the people of *Vidarbha*, or *Bidar*. The name of the *Pitenikas* occurs also in the 5th edict, and is probably the same as the *Padenekayika* of the Bhilsa Tope inscriptions.[1] The last people are the *Andhras* and *Pulindas*, both well-known names.

This mention is of the highest importance for the ancient history of India, as it proves that the generally accepted chronology which assigns the rise of the Andhras to so late a period as B. C. 21 is undoubtedly erroneous. I had already discovered this error from an examination of the *Kânhari* and *Nâsik* inscriptions of Gotamiputra Sâtakarni and his successor Pudumavi, which clearly belong to the same period as the well-known Gupta inscriptions. After much consideration

[1] Cunningham's Bhilsa Tope, No. 140 inscription. These *Pitenikas* may, perhaps, be identified with Ptolemy's *Belligoi*.

of the career of Gotamiputra Sâtakarni, I ventured to suggest that he might perhaps be identified with the famous Sâlivâhan, or Sâtavâhan, which would place him in A. D. 79 instead of A. D. 320, as generally adopted. That this conclusion as to date was well founded is now proved by the mention of *Andhras* in the edicts of Asoka, which carries back the foundation of the kingdom of Andhra from the latter part of the first century B. C. to the earlier half of the third century B. C. If we adopt the amount of correction which I had already made for Gotamiputra of A. D. 320—78=242 years, then the foundation of the Andhra kingdom will be placed in B. C. 21+242=B. C. 263, or exactly contemporaneous with Asoka.

In the copy of the Shâhbâz-garhi inscription on the back of the rock prepared by Norris and Wilson, the uppermost line is omitted altogether, their first line being my second line. But there must have been at least two other lines above my first, of which some traces yet remain, as only the last four words of the 12th edict now remain at the beginning of the first line. The 13th edict then begins, and continues down to the end, the greater part being distinctly legible.

This Ariano-Pali version of the edict is of special value in determining the true reading of many words in the Indian version, partly from its possession of the three sibilants, and partly from its use of the attached *r*.

The value of the last is best seen in the important name of *Andhra*, which Wilson read as *Andha*,[1] although he had observed that the Shâhbâz-garhi text "departs less from the Sanskrit than the other, retaining some compound consonants as *pr* in *priya* instead of *piya*," to which he might have added *br* in *Bramana*, *sr* in *Sramana*, and other equally distinct examples. The three sibilants are found together in the word *susushu*, which is written simply *sususa* in all the Indian versions excepting some parts of the Khâlsi text, where the *sh* is used of nearly the same form as the Arian letter. The same letter is also found in the word *vasha* year, which replaces *vasa* of the Indian texts, and in the plural forms of *Kamboyeshu* and *Pulindeshu*, which take the place of *Kabojesu* and *Pulindesu* of the other versions.

But the most remarkable departure from the Indian texts is the use of the vernacular word *baraya* for twelfth instead of the Sanskrit *dwâdasa*. This word occurs twice in the inscription, near the beginning of the 3rd and towards the end of the 4th edict. Strange to say, it remained unrecognised by Wilson, who simply remarks, "in place of *dwâdasa*, twelve, and *vasa*, year, the inscription has *baraya vasha*, but the first must be wrong." Of the second example, he says that "there is a blank instead of the number," although Norris's Arian text has the letters for *vara*+*vasha* quite distinct, while his English transliteration gives *va rana vasha*. By thus separating *va* from the following letters, it seems that Norris also failed to recognise the true vernacular *baraya* for "twelfth."

I observe that the word *chatura*, "four," in the 13th edict, is followed by four upright strokes, thus, IIII, in the Shâhbâz-garhi text, and that the corresponding word *chatura*, "four," in the Khâlsi text is followed by a nearly upright cross, thus +, which must therefore be the old Indian cypher for 4. This form was afterwards modified to a St. Andrew's cross, or ×, in which shape it was adopted by all the

---

[1] The suffixed *r* is very distinct on the rock, and was duly inserted by Norris from Masson's hand-copy.

people who used the Arian characters, as may be seen in the different inscriptions of the kings Kanishka, Huvishka, and Gondophares, and of the Satrap Liako-Kujulaka.[1] Previous to the adoption of this Indian symbol, the cyphers of the Western people would seem to have been limited to single strokes, as the words *pancheshu pancheshu*, "every five," are followed by five upright strokes which precede the word *vásheshu*, "years."

2.—Khâlsi Rock.

This inscribed rock is a huge boulder of quartz on the western bank of the Jumna, just above the junction of the Tons river, and about 15 miles to the west of Masûri, or Musooree, as it is spelt in our maps. The rock is situated close to the two little hamlets of Byâs and Haripur, but as the large and well-known village of Khâlsi is not more than a mile and a half to the south, I have ventured to call this inscription by its name.

Between Khálsi and the Jumna the land on the western bank of the river is formed in two successive ledges or level terraces, each about 100 feet in height. Near the foot of the upper terrace stands the large quartz boulder which has preserved the edicts of Asoka for upwards of 2,000 years. The block is 10 feet long and 10 feet high, and about 8 feet thick at bottom. The south-eastern face has been smoothed, but rather unevenly, as it follows the undulations of the original surface. The main inscription is engraved on this smoothed surface, which measures 5 feet in height, with a breadth of 5½ feet at top, which increases towards the bottom to 7 feet 10½ inches.[2] The deeper hollows and cracks have been left uninscribed, and the lines of letters are undulating and uneven. Towards the bottom, beginning with the 10th edict, the letters increase in size until they become about thrice as large as those of the upper part. Owing either to this enlargement of the letters, or, perhaps, to the latter part of the inscription being of later date, the prepared surface was too small for the whole record, which was therefore completed on the left-hand side of the rock.

On the right-hand side an elephant is traced in outline, with the word *Gajatama* inscribed between his legs in the same characters as those of the inscription. The exact meaning of this word I do not know; but as the Junagiri rock inscription closes with a paragraph stating that the place is called *Sweta Hasti*, or 'the white elephant,' I think it probable that *Gajatama* may be the name of the Khâlsi rock itself. Amongst the people, however, the rock is known by the name of *Chhatr Sila*, or 'the canopy stone,' which would seem to show that the inscribed block had formerly been covered over by some kind of canopy, or, perhaps, only by an umbrella, as the name imports. In the present year 1876, a Brahman explained that the true name is *Chitra Sila*, that is, the ornamented or 'inscribed rock.' There are many squared stones lying about close to the rock, as well as several fragments of octagonal pillars and half pillars or pilasters, which are hollowed out or fluted on the shorter faces, after the common fashion of the pillars of Buddhist

[1] See Archæological Survey of India, Vol. III, Plates 13, 14, and 15; and Vol. V, Plate 16, No. 3.

[2] See Plate XXIX for a view of this rock, and Plates III and IV for its inscriptions.

railings. There is also a large carved stone, 7 feet long, 1½ feet broad, and 1 foot in height, which, from its upper mouldings, I judged to have formed the entrance step to some kind of open porch in front of the inscription stone.

When first found by Mr. Forrest early in 1860, the letters of the inscription were hardly visible, the whole surface being encrusted with the dark moss of ages; but on removing this black film, the surface becomes nearly as white as marble. At first sight the inscription looks as if it was imperfect in many places, but this is owing to the engraver having purposely left all the cracked and rougher portions uninscribed. On comparing the different edicts with those of the Shâhbâz-garhi, Girnâr and Dhauli versions, I find the Khâlsi text to be in a more perfect state than any of them, and it is more especially perfect in that part of the 13th edict which contains the names of the five Greek kings—Antiochus, Ptolemy, Antigonus, Magas and Alexander.[1] The Khâlsi text agrees with that of Dhauli in rejecting the use of the letter *r*, for which *l* is everywhere substituted. But the greatest variation is in the use of the palatal sibilant *s*, which has not been found in any other inscription of this early date. This letter occurs in the word *Pasanda*, which curiously enough is spelt sometimes with one *s* and sometime with the other, even in the same edict. As the proper spelling of this word is *Pashanda*, it seems almost certain that the people of India proper did not possess the letter *sh* in the time of Asoka[2].

There are some peculiarities in the Khâlsi alphabet which are not found in any of the pillar inscriptions, or in the rock inscriptions of Girnâr, Dhauli and Jaugada, except, perhaps, in the latter additional edicts. The most remarkable of these peculiarities is the shape of the letter *kh*, which has a large open circle at its foot, instead of the mere dot or knob which is common to all the other great inscriptions. In this, however, it agrees with the mass of the Bharhut inscriptions. The shape of the letter *s* is also modified, the left-hand member being placed below instead of to the side. In this respect, however, the Khâlsi form agrees with that on the coins of Pantaleon and Agathokles, and with the Nâgârjuni cave inscriptions of Raja Dasaratha.

The only compound letters are *ky*, *khy*, and *shm* or *ṣm*. In the upper part of the inscription comprising the first nine edicts the letters are small but well-formed, and the words are generally separated; but in the 12th edict at the bottom of the main face of the inscription the letters become much larger, even twice the size of those at the top, while the words are no longer separated. It is in this edict that the palatal letter *s* appears so frequently in the word *pâṣanda*. It is, however, once used in the earlier part of the inscription, close to the end of the 4th edict, in the name of Piyadasi. The smaller faults in the rock in this latter part, instead of being left blank as in the uppermost edicts, are marked by a straight upright stroke like the letter *r*. At first I thought that this letter had actually been used in the later edicts; but as I examined the words carefully, I soon found that it was a mere conventional mark to denote a blank space.

---

[1] See Plate IV for this portion of the Khâlsi inscription.

[2] See Archæological Survey of India, Vol. I, pp. 246-247.

3.—Girnâr Rock.

The first copy of the Girnâr edicts, so far as I am aware of, is that which was taken by Dr. Wilson of Bombay and forwarded to James Prinsep by Mr. Wathen. A better copy was soon afterwards made by Captains Lang and Postans, which furnished Prinsep with correct readings of some important passages. To Captain Postans also I am indebted for the main points in the following accounts of the inscribed rock.

The Girnâr version of the edicts of Asoka is inscribed on a large rock on the Girnâr hill, half a mile to the east of the city of Junagarh, and forty miles to the north of the famous Pattan Somnâth.[1] Captain Postans describes it as "one of a group of several large granite blocks, and appears to have been chosen for its peculiar form, which approaches to that of a flattened cone. The inscriptions occupy three sides of the rock, that to the east being the most ancient, whilst those on the west and north faces are in a more modern character. The ancient characters recording the edicts of Asoka are deeply cut, and, except where a portion of the stone has been removed by violence, are very perfect." The letters are 1¼ inch in height, uniform in size, and very clearly and deeply cut. On enquiry it was found that the missing portion of the inscription, including part of the 13th edict, which contains the names of the five Greek kings, had been blasted with gunpowder to furnish materials for a neighbouring causeway! By turning up the soil close by, Captain Postans recovered numerous fragments of the rock, amongst which were two pieces bearing Asoka letters, and a third piece with a portion of later date.[2]

The inscription consists of two grand divisions, which are separated by a line drawn from the top of the rock downwards. To the left are engraved the first five edicts, and to the right the next seven edicts from 6 to 12. The 13th edict is placed below, and on its right is the 14th edict. The edicts are separated from one another by horizontal lines drawn right across. Between all is a single imperfect line mentioning that the place was called *Sweṭa Hasti*, or "The White Elephant."

The language of the Girnâr edicts differs from that of the other versions in using some peculiar forms, as the locative singular in *mhi*, in *dhamamhi*, *silamhi*, instead of *si* as in *dhammasi*, *silasi*, &c., and in the compound *samyapatipati*,[3] instead of *sampatipati* of the Shâhbâz-garhi and Khâlsi texts. In this instance, however, the Jaugada text of Ganjam agrees with that of Girnâr.

There are also differences in the forms of some of the letters, and more especially in the *r*, which is a wavy or undulating line, instead of the rigidly straight upright stroke of the Khâlsi and other texts. In this wavy form of the *r*, however, it agrees with the coins of Pantaleon and Agathokles, and with the short inscriptions on the Buddhist railings of Bodh Gaya. The upper stroke of the *p* as well as

---

[1] See Plate XXIX for a view of the rock, and Plates V, VI, and VII for its inscriptions.

[2] Journal of the Bengal Asiatic Society, VII, 1871-72.

[3] In both of the published copies of this edict this word is written *Sammapatipati*, which Burnouf took for an improper abbreviation of *Sumana*. "Le Lotus," p. 736. He suspected, however, that Sammâ might be a special orthography for *Samyak*, "une bienveillance parfaite."

of the *s* is also occasionally bent or waved in a similar manner. The vowels *á* and *e* are attached to the lower member of *m*, and the initial long *a* has the side stroke at the top instead of against the middle of the letter.

4.—DHAULI ROCK.

The Dhauli rock inscription was discovered by Kittoe towards the close of 1837, at the very time when James Prinsep "had just groped his way through the Girnâr text," and was in want of a second text for comparison. To his "surprise and joy," he discovered that the Dhauli inscription was in substance a duplicate of the Girnâr edicts, although the language and alphabet of the two versions had "very notable and characteristic differences."[1]

The actual rock itself is named *Aswastama*, but, from its being situated close to the village of Dhauli, this version of the edicts has always been called the Dhauli inscription. It is thus described by Kittoe[2]:—

"The Aswastama is situated on a rocky eminence forming one of a cluster of hills, three in number, on the south bank of the Dyah river, near to the village of Dhauli, and close to the north-west corner of the famous tank called Konsala-gang, said to have been excavated by Raja Ganges-wara Deva, King of Kalinga, in the 12th century. * * The hills before alluded to rise abruptly from the plains, and occupy a space of about five furlongs by three. They have a singular appearance from their isolated position, no other hills being nearer than eight or ten miles. They are apparently volcanic and composed of unheaved breccia with quartzose rock intermixed. The northernmost hill may be about 250 feet at its highest or eastern end, on which is a ruined temple dedicated to Mahadeva. The other hills, or rather rocks, are less elevated.

"The Aswastama is situated on the northern face of the southernmost rock near its summit; the rock has been hewn and polished for a space of 15 feet long by 10 in height, and the inscription deeply cut thereon being divided into four tablets, the first of which appears to have been executed at a different period from the rest; the letters are much larger and not so well cut. The fourth tablet is encircled by a deep line, and is cut with more care than either of the others.

"Immediately above the inscription is a terrace 16 feet by 14 (A), on the right side of which (as you face the inscription) is the fore-half of an elephant, 4 feet high, of superior workmanship; the whole is hewn out of the solid rock. There is a groove 4 inches wide by 2 in depth round three sides of the terrace, with a space of 3 feet left (a doorway?) immediately in front of the elephant; there are also two grooves, one on either side of the elephant on the floor and in the perpendicular face: these must have been intended probably to fix a wooden canopy.

"There are also many broken caves in the rocks adjoining the Aswastama, and the foundations of many buildings,—one in particular, immediately above the inscription, which may have been one of the *chaityas* or *stûpas* mentioned in the inscription.

"The elephant does not seem to be an object of worship, though I was informed that one day in every year is appointed, when the Brahmins of the temples in the vicinity attend and throw water on it, and besmear it with red lead in honour of Ganesha."[3]

The Asoka inscriptions at Dhauli are arranged in three parallel columns, of which the first eleven of the collected edicts occupy the whole of the middle column

---

[1] Journal, Bengal Asiatic Society, VII, 158.
[2] Journal, Bengal Asiatic Society, VII, 435, 436, 437.
[3] Journal, Bengal Asiatic Society, VII, 437.

and one-half of the right column. Afterwards two local edicts were added, one completing the right-hand column and the other filling the whole of the left-hand column.[1] The latter has been taken by Prinsep as the first of these two separate edicts, although there can be no doubt that the former, from its position *in continuation* of the original edicts, was the first to be engraved, more especially as the duplicate version at Jaugada places it immediately above the other. The matter is not, perhaps, of much consequence, but it is right that it should be brought to notice in case of enquiry hereafter.

The Dhauli edicts are chiefly remarkable for the complete want of the letter *r*, which is always replaced by *l*, even in such a word as *Raja*, for which we have *Lâja*. This peculiarity was overlooked by Prinsep when he proposed to identify the *Tosali* of the two separate edicts with the *Tosali Metropolis* of Ptolemy, which is placed far to the *north* of the Ganges, instead of with his *Dosara* on the *Dosaron* river, which occupies the very position required. This Tosali in Katak agrees also with the position of the *Desarena Regio* of the Periplus, which lies between Masalia, or Masulipatam, and the mouths of the Ganges. These two Greek readings at once suggest the name of the Indian *Dasârnas*, who are several times mentioned in the geographical lists of the Mahâbhârata.[2] Perhaps the old name still remains in Dosa on the Koïl river, in latitude 23° and longitude 84° 50′.

The opening sentence of No. 1 edict at Dhauli is lost, and as it certainly differed from the Shâhbâz-garhi, Khâlsi and Girnâr versions, it is fortunate that the Jaugada text affords the means of restoring the missing words.

Prinsep reads as follows :—

(10 letters) *ghi savata*[3]

which may be compared with the opening of the Jaugada edicts—

Iyam dhammalipi Khepingalasi pavatasi.

Here it will be found that there are exactly ten letters preceding the final syllable of *Khepingalasi*, which Prinsep read as *ghi*, but which is no doubt *si*, as the two letters are easily mistaken in a mutilated inscription. So also are the two letters *s* and *p*, and for Prinsep's *savata*, plus one lost letter, I propose to read *pavatasi*, as in the Jaugada text. Then follow the words *Devânampiyena Piyadasina Lâjina lekhapitâ* in both texts. I therefore read the whole as follows: "This religious edict is promulgated by Raja Priyadarsi, the beloved of the gods, to the people of the *Khepingala* hills." No such name is now known; but as it is common to both inscriptions, I conclude that it was the usual name for the mountain districts of Orissa.

The two separate edicts are local ones addressed to the rulers of Tosali. In the second edict the opening words are—

Devânampiyasa vachanena Tosaliyam Kumâlecha vataviya,

which Prinsep renders—

"By command of Devânampiya! It shall be signified to the Prince and the great officers in the city of Tosali."

---

[1] See Plate XXIX for a view of the rock, and Plates VIII, IX and X for its inscriptions.

[2] See Wilson's Vishnu Purana, pp. 186, 187, 192.

Now, in the first edict there is mention of *Ujeniya Kumâle*, which Prinsep translates as the young "Prince of Ujain," and whom he rightly identified with *Ujjenio*, the son of Asoka. But he erroneously supposed him to be a different person from Mahindo, whereas Ujjeniya was only another name for Mahindo, who was born whilst Asoka was governor of Ujain. By this identification we get a limit to the date of these inscriptions, for Mahindo became a Buddhist priest at twenty years of age,[1] after which he could not have continued in the government of Tosali. Now, Asoka was governor of Ujain for nine years immediately preceding his accession to the throne, from B. C. 272 to 263,[2] and as his marriage with Chetiya Devi only took place on his journey to Ujain, the birth of Mahindo cannot be fixed earlier than B. C. 271. He would, therefore, have been twenty years of age in B. C. 251 when he was ordained a priest, and thirty years of age when he became the head of a fraternity ten years later at the time of the assembly of the Third Buddhist Synod in B. C. 241. But B. C. 251 was the 12th year of Asoka's reign, which is the latest date of some of the edicts in the collected series engraved on the rocks. I conclude, therefore, that Mahindo was governor of Tosali before B. C. 251, and that the two separate edicts at Dhauli and Jaugada must have been put forth towards the end of that year. They are thus only a little later in date than the great body of the rock edicts, but several years earlier than the pillar edicts.

5.—Jaugada Rock.

The Jaugada inscription is engraved on the face of a rock in a large old fort near the bank of the Rishikulya river, about eighteen miles to the west-north-west of the town of Ganjam. The name is pronounced *Jaugoḍo* by the people of the country, and as *Jau* means "lac" in the Uriya language, the place is usually known as the "lac-fort." But my assistant, Mr. J. D. Beglar, who visited the place to make the present copies of the inscriptions, suggests that the original name was *Jagata*, which by both Bengalis and Uriyas would be pronounced *Jogoto*, and from which it would be an easy step to *Jaugoḍo*, or the lac-fort.

When the name had become fixed, the next step was to find a legend to account for it, and so the following story came into being: The fort was made by Raja Kesari, who built the walls of "lac" instead of bricks, in order that an enemy's cannon balls might bury themselves harmlessly inside. Close by on the Rawalpilli hill (about three miles south-west) lived another Raja who quarrelled with Kesari and besieged him for a long time in vain. At last a milkwoman, whose milk had been forcibly taken by one of the besieger's soldiers, being unable to obtain redress, angrily exclaimed, "You fools! you have strength to plunder poor people, but have not the sense to see that the 'lac-fort' can be taken with the greatest ease." On being questioned, she told the besiegers that the walls were composed of "lac," and that they had only to apply fire to them and to increase the flames with bellows, and the walls would come down at once. This was accordingly done and the "lac-fort" was taken. A somewhat different version of the

[1] Mahawanso, p. 36, and Turnour in the Journal of the Bengal Asiatic Society, VII, 931, from the Dipawanso.

[2] Bigandet: "Legend of the Burmese Buddha," p. 376. The Dipamanso, however, says that Mahindo was nine years old at his father's accession to the throne.

legend is given by Mr. Harris. According to him, "the name of lac-fort gave rise to a local tradition that the lofty walls and place were formed by materials impregnable, until the secret was betrayed by a milkmaid, and allowed the besiegers by *the application of water*, taking advantage of floods or freshes down the Rishikulya, to effect an entrance."[1]

It is added that Raja Kesari cursed the woman whose babbling led to the loss of the fort. The curse took immediate effect, and the imprudent milkwoman was at once turned into stone, and to this day her statue is standing outside the walls of the fort. In Mr. Beglar's judgment, however, the petrified milkwoman is only an ordinary Sati-pillar, such as the aboriginal inhabitants of Chutia Nâgpur even now set up over the ashes of the dead. Mr. Beglar is also of opinion that the fort is "clearly of later date than the inscriptions," and is probably of the same age as the coins which are found in the milkwoman's mound. These coins, which are evident imitations of the Indo-Scythian copper money, but without any inscriptions, must therefore belong to the end of the first century A. D., a date which I had already assigned for them from their being found in company with leaden coins of the Andhra kings Gotamiputra and Yâdnya-Sri.

Mr. Beglar describes the groups of rocks inside the fort as picturesque, and such as would at once attract attention. The great inscription is engraved on a large high mass of rock which rises up vertically and faces the south-east, in the direction of people coming from the sea-coast.

Some photographs of these inscriptions were taken in 1859 and forwarded to the Madras Government by Captain Harington, who described them as being "engraved upon a rock near the village of Naugâm in the Pubakonda Tâluk of the Ganjam district, about three miles from the tâluk station of Pursotpur (or Purshottampur) near the Rishikulya river." He calls the place *Joughar*, but as he describes the large square fortification which is plainly shown in the Indian Atlas Sheet of Ganjam, it is certain that the true name is *Jaugada*, or the *Jau-fort*.

Mr. Harington's photographs were sent to the Royal Asiatic Society, and from a memorandum by Mr. Norris I learn that copies of the inscriptions were taken in 1850 by the present Sir Walter Elliot, who was perfectly aware that they contained only another version of Asoka's edicts, which had already been found at Shâhbâz-garhi, Girnâr and Dhauli.

In 1871 an effort was made by the Madras Government to obtain complete copies of these inscriptions both by impressions and by photography. The paper impressions taken by pressure only, without ink, though tolerably legible at first, afterwards almost entirely disappeared, owing to the extreme dampness of the climate. The photographs by Mr. Minchin I have not seen, but I have received from the Madras Government lithographic copies of some hand-tracings by Mr. Harris, which, taken altogether, are very good, but, like all such copies, they are here and there imperfect, and more particularly deficient in the two separate edicts, which it was more important to have minutely copied, as we possess only one other version of their text at Dhauli with which to compare them.

[1] See Mr. Harris's letter dated 26th August 1872, printed in the Proceedings of the Madras Government.

The plates in the present volume have been reduced from Mr. Beglar's paper impressions, one of which had all the fainter letters carefully pencilled over. After reduction they were compared with Mr. Beglar's photographs, which afforded several corrections in vowel marks. Every letter has been twice examined by myself,—*first*, before inking in the pencilled reduction; and *second*, while writing out its text in Roman letters for comparison with the Dhauli versions. I believe, therefore, that my plates present a very faithful copy of these inscriptions.[1] I have done my best to make them so, but I do not expect that they will be found absolutely perfect, as it is quite possible that some errors may have escaped notice.

The Jaugada inscriptions are written on three different tablets on the vertical face of the rock. As at Dhauli, the letters are all of uniform size, and the lines are perfectly straight, and altogether these Orissa and Ganjam inscriptions are the most carefully and neatly engraved of all the rock edicts.

The first tablet contained the first five edicts, but about one-half has been utterly lost by the peeling away of the rock.

The second tablet comprised the next five edicts,—namely, 6 to 10, to which was added the 14th or closing edict of the other versions. About one-third of this tablet has been lost by the peeling away of the rock.

The third tablet contained the two separate or additional edicts which are found at Dhauli. These are less carefully engraved than the other two tablets, and they show, besides, some differences in the shapes of the letters, which certainly indicate a later date, as they are also found in the additional or later edicts of the Delhi pillar. One of these differences is the use of the *kh* with a large open circle at the bottom, instead of the usual dot or knob. In the Jaugada additional edicts both of these forms are used. Another marked difference is the position of the two side strokes which form the medial vowel *o*. In the older edicts the upper stroke is on the right hand; in the later edicts, both on the Delhi pillar and on the Jaugada rock, the upper stroke is on the left hand. There are differences, too, in the forms of *l* and *h*, but I cannot say that they are of later date than those of the earlier edicts.

In this version the opening of the 1st edict, which is injured at Dhauli, is distinctly legible. The two additional words *Khepingalasi pavatasi*, which are inserted after *dhammalipi*, have been already noticed in my account of the Dhauli rock. I presume that these two additional words give the general geographical name of the province, as the "*Khepingala Hills*," in which the two cities of *Tosali* and *Samâpá* were situated. These are the two names which are found in the additional edicts, the former in the Dhauli version, and the latter in the Jaugada version, the edicts themselves being addressed to the respective rulers of those places.

I have just discovered another instance of a local edict on the Allahabad pillar, which was addressed by Asoka to the rulers of Kosâmbi, a very large and famous city on the Jumna,[2] only thirty miles above Allahabad, and which was no doubt the capital of the province in which Allahabad was situated. Of *Samâpá* I can find

---

[1] See Plates XI, XII, and XIII for these inscriptions.

[2] See Archæological Survey of India, I, 301.

no trace in Ptolemy's map, nor in the rambling lists of names preserved by Pliny, but I presume that it may have some reference to the situation of the district on the great Chilka Lake.

6 AND 7.—SEPARATE EDICTS—DHAULI AND JAUGADA ROCKS.

At Jaugada these two additional edicts are enclosed in a frame which separates them from the collected series of Asoka's edicts. At Dhauli only one of these edicts is thus enclosed, the other being engraved to the left hand of the main collection of edicts. I have not thought it worth while to disturb Prinsep's arrangement of these two separate edicts, but there can be no doubt that his No. 2, which is placed above his No. 1 at Jaugada, was the first to be engraved. This conclusion might also have been derived from the relative positions of the two edicts on the Dhauli rock, for there the main series of edicts occupies a column and a half of the whole mass of inscriptions, while the half column is completed by the addition of one of these separate edicts, while the other forms a complete column to the left hand of the main series of edicts. From their relative positions I conclude that the separate edict which follows the main series of edicts and completes the second column was the first to be engraved, and that the other separate edict was then placed by itself on the left. This view is fully corroborated by the relative positions of these two edicts on the Jaugada rock. To prevent confusion, however, I think it best to adhere to Prinsep's numbering.

At Jaugada the separation of these two edicts is more distinctly marked by the accompaniment of the *Swastika* symbol at each of the upper corners of the upper inscription, and of the letter *m* at the upper corners of the lower inscriptions. By reading the latter in combination with the upright line of the surrounding frame which passes through it, we have the mystic word *Aum*. I am, therefore, inclined to look upon the *Swastika* as a propitious invocation, as its meaning imports,[1] while *Aum* is the well-known auspicious opening of all documents even at the present day. Both symbols are found upon many of the old Indian coins.

The geographical names mentioned in these separate edicts have been fully examined in my account of the Dhauli and Jaugada rocks.

8.—SAHASARÂM ROCK.

This new edict of *Devânampiya* is inscribed on the face of the rock near the top of the Chandan Pir hill which forms the extreme northern end of the Kaimur range. The hill takes its name from the shrine of Pir Chandan Shâhid, which is placed on the top. The inscription is found in an artificial cave a short distance below, which is generally known as the Chirâghdân, or "lamp" of the saint. The roof of the cave is formed by a large projecting mass of rock that has most effectually preserved the greater part of the inscription, which is in excellent order, except in three or four places where the rock has peeled off. The entrance, which is only

[1] *Swastika* is the name of the mystic cross, which is a monogram composed of the words *su* × *asti*, "it is well."

4 feet high, is to the west between two built walls. By making an opening in one of these walls, my assistant, Mr. Beglar, obtained a good photograph of the inscription. This photograph compared with our paper impressions has furnished the copy published in the present volume.[1]

The inscription consists of eight lines of well-formed letters, generally about one inch in height. It opens rather curtly with the words

Devânampiye hevam â (hâ)

—"Devânampriya thus declares,"—following which just six letters have been lost. About the same number of letters has been lost in each of the next three lines, after which the inscription is complete to the end. At first sight it would appear as if the letter *r* was frequently used, but on examination it turns out that the single upright stroke, which occurs no less than thirteen times, is only a conventional mark covering a fault in the rock, and intended to point out that the spot was to be passed over in reading the inscription. It is certain that it cannot be the letter *r*, as *l* is used for *r* in the words *alodhe* and *chilathitike*, where the Rûpnâth text uses *arodhe* and *chirathitike;* besides which it is used in positions where it can have no meaning, as between the words *Jambudipasi* and *ammisam*, where no letter is interposed in the two corresponding texts of Rûpnâth and Bairât. A similar device has already been noticed in my account of the latter half of the Khâlsi inscription.

But the most interesting part of this record is the figured date which occurs in the first half of the 7th line. There are three figures which I read as 256. The same date occurs in the Rûpnâth version of this edict, but without the figure for hundreds. As the date of these inscriptions has been fully discussed in the Preface, it need not be examined again. It will be sufficient to state here that as these inscriptions give only the title of Devânampiya, I am disposed to assign them to Dasaratha Devânampiya, the grandson of Asoka, rather than to Devânampiya Priyadarsi, or Asoka himself.

9.—Rupnâth Rock.

The Rûpnâth rock is a single flinty block of dark-red sandstone lying at the foot of the Kaimur range of hills, just below the fertile plateau of Bahuriband. Here a small stream breaks over the crest of the Kaimur range, and, after three low falls, forms a deep secluded pool at the foot of the scarp. Each of these pools is considered holy, the uppermost being named after Râma, the next after Lakshman, and the lowest after Sîtâ. The spot, however, is best known by the name of Rûpnâth, from a lingam of Siva which is placed in a narrow cleft of the rocks on the right. There are similar falls and pools at Râm Tâl, a few miles to the south-west, where the Kair river pours over the crest of the Kaimur range from the plateau of Saleya. This spot is also esteemed holy. An annual fair was formerly held at Rûpnâth on the *Sivarâtri*, in honour of Siva, but this has been discontinued since 1857. The lowermost pool, however, or Sîtâkund, which never dries up, still attracts a few pilgrims.

---

[1] See Plate XIV.

The edict of Asoka is inscribed on the upper surface of the rock, which has been worn quite smooth by people sitting upon it for hundreds of years at the annual fairs. It is now of a very dark dirty-red colour, and the inscription might easily escape observation. The lines follow the undulations of the rock, and are neither straight nor parallel with each other.[1] The inscription is 4½ feet long and 1 foot broad, and consists of six lines, of which the last has only five letters. With the exception of a few letters which are now very faint, the record is complete. It opens with the words

Devânampiye hevam âhâ

—"Devânampiya thus orders," omitting the name of the king, a curt style of announcement which is not found in any of the collected series of edicts. The same form, however, occurs in the later separate edicts at Dhauli and Jaugada, which may, perhaps, indicate that this Rûpnâth inscription belongs to a later date than that of the great collection of edicts. It uses the letter *r*, in common with most of the old inscriptions in Central and Western India, as at Girnâr, Sânchi and Bharhut.

Of the purport of the inscription I am not competent to offer an opinion, but I may point to the occurrence of the words *Sumipâka Sangha*, or *Sumihaka Sangha*, which are found twice in the first line, as indicating that the edict was addressed to the Buddhist Sangha, or assembly of *Sumipâka* or *Sumihâka*. In the second line occurs the well-known name of *Jambudipa;* and the fifth line opens with the words *Sâla-thabhe, Sila-thabha*, which seem to refer to "Sâl-pillars and stone-pillars," on which the edicts were to be inscribed.

The date of 56 occurs at the end of the fifth line. The symbol for 50 is the same as that in the Sahasarâm inscription, but the opening is turned to the left. Both forms are used indifferently in the Hodgson MSS. from Nepâl.[2] The omission of the figure for hundreds is not uncommon in Indian inscriptions.

10.—Bairat Rock.

This inscribed rock lies at the foot of the Hinsagiri hill near Bairât, where the Pândus are said to have lived during the greater part of their twelve years' exile. It is, therefore, more commonly known as the hill of the Pândus, and a cave is still shown as the *Bhîm-guphâ*, or "Cave of Bhîm." In November 1864 I examined all the rocks on the top of this hill very carefully in the hope of finding some inscriptions; but my search was in vain, and I was assured by the people that no inscriptions existed on the hill. My assistant, Mr. Carlleyle, was, however, more fortunate, as he succeeded in discovering an inscription in Asoka characters on a huge isolated block standing at the foot of the hill. The following notice of his discovery is abridged from his own account, which I quote from his report now preparing for publication:—

The Pândus hill is a bare, black-looking, pyramidal-shaped, jagged-edged, peaked hill, composed entirely of enormous blocks of porphyritic and basaltic

[1] See Plate XIV.

[2] See Journal of the Royal Asiatic Society, New Series, VIII, 51, Plate.

rock and hornblende gneiss, as if it had been built up by giants. × . × Some of the huge blocks of which the hill is composed have apparently at some very remote period rolled down on to the slope at the foot of the hill. One of these blocks stands immediately in front of the south side of the hill. In shape it is a great roughly-hewn cube, as big as a house, and some deep water-worn hollows on its perpendicular face, when seen at some distance, look like circular windows. Its actual dimensions are 24 feet in length from east to west, with a thickness of 15 feet and a height of 17 feet. The inscription occupies the lower part of the south face of the rock. It consists of eight lines, and approaches to within one foot of the ground on its left side. The letters average about 2½ inches in height. But the surface of the rock is rough, and has suffered much from the weathering of 2,000 years. A large portion of the middle part of the inscription has altogether gone, and the lesser part on the right is now separated by a blank space of 20 inches from the greater half on the left. This separation led Mr. Carlleyle to believe that there were two separate inscriptions, but a comparison with the more perfect texts at Sahasarâm and Rûpnâth shows most conclusively that these two apparently distinct inscriptions are fragments of a single edict, of which the middle portion has been lost.[1]

At the end of the inscription there are the traces of some large characters or symbols, 4½ inches in height. Mr. Carlleyle read them doubtfully as 315, but I can trace only two definite shapes amongst the confused mass of lines which appear in my own fresh impressions as well as in Mr. Carlleyle's original impressions and hand-copies. At first these did not attract my attention, but, on referring to them lately, I was struck by the very strong resemblance in the forms of these two symbols with those of the two numerical figures in the Rûpnâth text. On comparing all the impressions with Mr. Carlleyle's hand-copy, I am satisfied that these two broken and defaced characters are the same as those of the Rûpnâth inscription, and that they represent the date of 56, or, with the addition of the omitted hundreds, 256.

Mr. Carlleyle made another curious discovery at Bairât, which, though perhaps not connected with this inscription, has certainly some connection with the rock on which it is engraved. Immediately in front of the rock there were two large boulder stones, one of them being 2 feet 6 inches long and 1 foot 6 inches broad. On removing these a layer of smaller boulder stones was found laid upon the earth. Here a fragment of pottery was found, which induced Mr. Carlleyle to dig further, until, at a depth of nearly 3 feet below the surface of the ground, he found four earthen vessels placed in a line on the same level. Two of these vessels were large and wide mouthed, the third was middle sized with a narrow neck, and the fourth was very small and very narrow in the mouth. All of them contained human bones. Mr. Carlleyle remarks that the boulder stones which were lying over these cinerary urns appeared to be *in situ*, and he is, therefore, inclined to believe that they "must have come into the position in which he found them, *jammed* against the rock, by the agency of same powerful flood, and consequently that the cinerary urns and bones may be of very great antiquity."

[1] See Plate XIV.

My own opinion regarding these vessels is that they are most probably of later date than the inscription, as I conclude that the conspicuousness of the inscribed block may have led to the interment.

11.—Second Bairat Rock.

This inscription is engraved on a block of reddish grey granite, which was found by Captain Burt in 1837 on the top of a hill close to the ancient town of Bairât, forty-one miles nearly due north of Jaypur. Vairât, the capital of Matsya, is celebrated in Hindu legends as the abode of Raja Virâta where the five Pândus spent their exile of twelve years from Dilli or Indraprastha. "The residence of Bhîm Pându is still shown on the top of a long, low, rocky hill about one mile to the north of the town. The hill is formed of enormous blocks of coarse gritty quartz, which are much weather-worn and rounded on all the exposed sides. Some of these blocks have a single straight face sloping inwards, the result of a natural split, of which advantage has been taken to form small dwellings by the addition of rough stone walls plastered with mud. Such is the Bhîm-gupha or 'Bhîm's cave,' which is formed by rough walls added to the overhanging face of a huge rock about 60 feet in diameter and 15 feet in height. Similar rooms, but of smaller size, are said to have been the dwellings of Bhîm's brothers. The place is still occupied by a few Brahmans, who profess to derive only a scanty substance from the offerings of pilgrims—a statement which is rather belied by their flourishing appearance. Just below Bhîm's cave a wall has been built across a small hollow to retain the rain water, and the fragments of rock have been removed from a fissure to form a tank about 15 feet long by 5 feet broad and 10 feet deep; but at the time of my visit, on the 10th November, it was quite dry."[1]

The hill on which the inscription was found forms a conspicuous object about one mile to the south-west of the town. It is about 200 feet high, and is still known by the name of Bijak Pahâr, or "inscription hill," and the paved pass immediately beneath it, which leads towards Jaypur, is called Bijak Ghât. The mass of the hill is composed of enormous blocks of grey granite intersected with thick veins and smaller blocks of reddish or salmon-coloured granite. The ruins on the top of the hill consists of two contiguous level platforms, each 160 feet square, which are thickly covered with broken bricks and the remains of brick walls. The bricks are of large size, $10\frac{1}{2}$ inches broad and from $3\frac{1}{2}$ to 4 inches thick. The western or upper platform is 30 feet higher than the eastern or lower one. In the centre of the upper platform there is a large mass of rocks which is said to have been dug into by the Mahârâja of Jaypur without any discovery being made. On examining this mass it appeared to me that it must have been the core around which a brick stûpa had been constructed, and that the relic chamber would have been formed in a crevice or excavation of the rock.

The approach to this platform was on the south side, where I traced the remains of a large entrance with a flight of stone steps. On all four sides there

[1] See Archæological Survey of India, II, 244, 245.

are ruins of brick walls which once formed the chambers of the resident monks of this large monastery.

"In the middle of the lower platform there is a square chamber which was laid open by the Mahârâja's excavations. From its size I judged it to be the interior of a temple. Close beside it, on the east, there is a gigantic mass of rock, 73 feet in length, which is familiary known amongst the people by the name of Tôp, or 'The Cannon,' to which at a distance it bears some resemblance. This rock slopes gently backwards, as the upper end projects considerably beyond the base; its appearance is not unlike that of the muzzle of a great gun, somewhat elevated and thrust forward beyond the wheels of its carriage. Under this part of the rock a small room has been formed by the addition of rough stone walls after the fashion of the chamber on the opposite hill called Bhîm-gupa, or 'Bhîm's cave.' On all four sides of the platform there are the remains of brick walls which once formed the cells of the resident monks.

"These ruins on the Bijak hill I take to be the remains of two of the eight Buddhist monasteries which were still in existence at the time of Hwen Thsang's visit in A. D. 634. Their Buddhist origin is undoubted, as the famous inscription which was found on the lower platform distinctly records the belief of the donor in the ancient Buddhist Triäd of Buddha, Dharma, and Sangha.[1] These two monasteries, therefore, must have been in existence at least as early as the time of Asoka in 250 B. C., when the inscription was engraved. As the proclamation is specially addressed to the Buddhist assembly of Magadha, we must suppose, as Burnauf has suggested, that copies were sent to all the greater Buddhist fraternities for the purpose of recording the enduring firmness of the king's faith in the law of Buddha."

This important inscription is the only one of all Asoka's edicts which mentions the name of Buddha; once alone as *Bhagavata Buddha*, or "the divine Buddha," and in another place in conjunction with *Dharma* and *Sangha*. The bare mention of these names was sufficient to extort from Wilson the reluctant admission that "Priyadarsi, *whoever he may have been*, was a follower of Buddha."

The text has had the good fortune to have been revised and translated by Burnouf as well as by Wilson.[2] Their texts were both derived from the same impressions which were made by the original discoverer, Captain Burt. The block of granite is now deposited in the museum of the Bengal Asiatic Society immediately beneath James Prinsep's bust. From it I have made a fresh impression on which my own reading of the text is founded. The only differences requiring notice are *pâsâde*, "temples," for *pasâde*, "favour;" *chilathitike* for *chilasatitike*; and *bhikhu* and *bhikhuni* for *bhikha* and *bhikhani*. The early transcribers did not recognise the vowel *u*, which is attached to the foot of the *kh* as a prolongation of the upright stroke. But the presence of the vowel is always indicated by a dot or knob which separates it from the stem of the consonant. In later times this vowel was formed by a horizontal stroke at the right foot of the letter. If the new reading of *golane-cha pâsâde-cha* be correct, the translation might be rendered as "circular railings and temples;" but as I do not feel absolutely certain that the first long â of *pasâde* may not be an accidental mark, I do not wish to press its acceptance.

Wilson has noticed the repetition of the word *bhante*, which occurs no less than six times in this short inscription. "Burnouf renders it throughout by

[1] See Plate XXXI for the map of India under Asoka in the position of Bairât. The inscription itself is given in Plate XV.

[2] Journal of the Royal Asiatic Society, XVI, 357; and Le Lotus de la Bonne Loi, p. 725.

seigneurs, 'Sirs,' considering it as the Prâkrit form of the Sanskrit *bhavantah*, the plural of the honorific pronoun *bhavân*, 'your honour, your reverence,' in which Wilson was at first disposed to concur, but afterwards had reason to doubt its accuracy."[1] But in this case Wilson's guess was only a random shot, while Burnouf's explanation was a well-directed aim which hit very near the mark. For the, true original of *bhante* is *bhadantah*, or "Reverend Sirs." This title is said to have been instituted by Buddha himself in his last instructions to the Rahans as to the attention and regard they were to pay each other.

"Let those," said the teacher, "who are more advanced in dignity and years of profession, call those that are their inferiors by their names, that of their family, or some other suitable appellation; let the inferiors give to their superiors the title *Bante*."[2]

Here we see that the term is one of respect addressed to the priesthood; but its actual derivation I owe to Professor Childers,[3] who explains *Bhante* as

"a contracted form of *Bhadante*. It is used as a reverential term of address, 'Lord, Reverend Sir,' and is the proper address of Buddha, of Buddhist priests, of Rishis, Tâpasas, &c."

We now learn from the Bairât inscription that this form of address to the Buddhist priesthood was certainly as old as the reign of Asoka.

At the end of the 5th line are the words *Upatisa pasine echá Lâghulo vâde* which Burnouf renders as—

"la speculation d' *Upatisa* et l' instruction de *Ráhula*,"

conceiving the text to contain the names of Upatissa, one of Sâkya's principal disciples, and of Râhula his son. On this Wilson remarks—

"The reading of the first is doubtful, the initial may be an *u*, but it is indistinct, and the third syllable is more like *tá* than *ti*."

In reply to these doubts I can only say that, after having examined the inscription itself very carefully, I found the initial letter *u* was quite distinct, and that the character *ti* was one of the clearest in the whole inscription. Wilson's remarks on the interpretation of the passage are more to the point:—

"*Pasine* M. Burnouf would connect with *pasya*, 'behold,' as if alluding to the views or doctrines of Upatissa; but, in that case, we should have Upatissa, not Upatisa, and if we could suppose the insertion of an '*s*' after *tá* to be a blunder, it would give us *upatápasine* for *upatapaswinah*, 'inferior or pretended ascetics.' For *e cha lâghulova de* M. Burnouf refers *avâde* to *avaváda*, 'instruction,' but it would rather imply reproof; but, as M. Burnouf indicates there is a *sútra* of the Mahawânso, headed *Ráhulovâda*, or as translated by Turnour, 'admonitory discourse' addressed by Buddha to Râhula, which is no doubt in favour of M. Burnouf's rendering. At the same time it may be allowable to give it a different construction and signification, and to render it *laghu loka váda*, 'the light or censorious language of the world' a sense which would agree with what follows if we explain *musavâcham* as M. Burnouf proposes, 'doctrines fausses.' The next word, *adhigichya*, may be an error for *adhigachya*, the Prâkrit form of *adhigatya*, having gone over, or having overcome, or refuted, *rejeté*.

"The following passage is intelligible enough, and may be connected with the preceding: *Bhagavatá Budhena bhásite etáni, bhante, dhamma paliyayáni ichhâmi*, 'I affirm these things, said by the divine Buddha, and desire (them to be considered) as the precepts of the law.'"

---

[1] Journal of the Royal Asiatic Society, XVI, 361.

[2] Bishop Bigandet's Legend of the Burmese Buddha, 2nd edit., p. 316.

[3] Pâli Dictionary, *in voce*.

Wilson again refers to Burnouf's readings of Upatisa and Râhula, towards the end of his paper in the following words :—

"Although, therefore, unable to offer an entirely satisfactory version of this inscription, and while hesitating to admit it as evidence, as M. Burnouf is disposed to regard it, of the existence at the time of the principal Buddhist authorities, the Vinaya Sútras, Gâthas, and the writings of Upatissa and Râhula, we cannot refuse to accept it as decisive of the encouragement of Buddhism by Priyadarsi; the indications of which are sufficiently positive, setting aside the apocryphal allusions to Upatissa and Râhula."

Long after the preceding notice was written I saw in Mr. Burgess's Indian Antiquary a new version of this important inscription by Professor Kern, in which I am glad to find that this learned scholar upholds the true readings of *Upatisa* and *Laghulo*. His transliteration and version of the edict will be found immediately following those of Wilson and Burnouf.[1]

12.—Khandagiri Rock.

The Khandagiri rock inscription was first published by Stirling, but it remained unread until a more perfect copy was made by Kittoe for James Prinsep. Kittoe thus describes the position of the rock and the places around it[2] :—

"The hillocks of Khandagiri and Udayagiri form part of a belt of sandstone rock, which, skirting the base of the granite hills of Orissa, extends from Autgur and Dekkunâl (in a southerly direction) past Kurda and towards the Chilka Lake, occasionally protruding through the beds of laterite.

"Khandagiri is four miles north-west of Bhubaneswar, and nineteen south-west of Katak. The two rocks are separated by a narrow glen about 100 yards in width.

"Khandagiri has but few caves in the summit. There is a Jain temple of modern construction, it having been built during the Maharatta rule. There are traces of former buildings; I am inclined, therefore, to think that the present temple occupies the site of a Chaitya."

By Stirling it is described as occupying "the overhanging brow of a large cavern."[3]

The very coarse nature of the rock, a coarse sandstone grit, prevented Kittoe from taking an impression of this inscription, and he was obliged to be content with a hand-copy, a work of great labour, which he performed with remarkable success. The present copy has been reduced from a large photograph of a plaster cast taken by Mr. Locke. Many of the letters are very clear, but there are numbers of others that are very indistinct from the abrasion of the rock. Every letter has been carefully compared with two copies of the photographs, as well as with Kittoe's hand-copy, and I believe that the present copy is as perfect a facsimile as can now be made.[4]

Regarding its alphabet, Prinsep remarks :[5]—

"One prominent distinction in the alphabetical character would lead to the supposition of its posteriority to that of the *lats*, but that the same is observable at Girnâr: I allude to the adoption of a separate symbol for the letter *r* instead of confounding it with *l*. Hence also it should be later than the Gaya inscription, which spells *Dasaratha* with an *l* (*dasalathena*). There are a few

[1] See The Indian Antiquary, V, 257, for September 1876.
[2] Researches, Bengal Asiatic Society, XV.
[3] Journal, Bengal Asiatic Society, VI, 1079.
[4] See Plate XVII for the copy of this inscription.
[5] Journal, Bengal Asiatic Society, V, 1080.

minor changes in the shape of the *v, t, p* and *g;* and in the mode of applying the vowel marks centrally on the letters, as in the *m* of *namo;* the letter *gh* is also used; but in other respects the alphabet accords entirely with its prototype, and is decidedly anterior to the Sainhadri cave inscription."

I fully agree with Prinsep that this record must be later than the Asoka edicts, and earlier than the inscriptions in the caves of Western India. I think that it may be placed as early as from B. C. 200 to 175, as there is no appearance of heads, or *mâtras*, to any of the letters. I do not infer, as Prinsep does, that the use of the letter *r* shows it to be of later date than Asoka, as I believe that the want of the letter was a peculiarity of the Magadha dialect, which was copied in the Dhauli and Jaugada versions from the original text supplied from the capital of Pâtaliputra. At the same time the use of the letter *r* throughout this great inscription of Aira Raja, as well as in *all* the cave inscriptions of Khandagiri and Udayagiri, would seem to show that the dialect of Orissa differed from that of Magadha.

All who take an interest in Indian antiquities will agree with James Prinsep as to the great value of this record, which he was disposed to think was "perhaps the most curious that has yet been disclosed to us."[1] He offers a graceful apology for his imperfect translation, but at the same time is satisfied that "there can be little doubt of the main facts, that the caves were executed by a Buddhist Raja of Kalinga (named AIRA ?) who, at the age of twenty-four, after having pursued his studies regularly for nine years, wrested the Government from some usurper, distributed largesses bountifully, repaired the buildings, dug tanks, &c." * * "Each change of inclination is consistently followed by a description of corresponding conduct, and we have throughout a most natural picture of a prince's life, wavering between pleasure and learning, between the Brahmanical and Buddhist faith, then doubtless the subject of constant contention. The history embraces his alliance with the daughter of a hill chieftain, and perchance even his death, though this is very unlikely."

13.—DEOTEK SLAB.

For the knowledge of this inscription I am indebted to Mr. R. Egerton of the Civil Service. The inscribed slab is a solitary block now lying in a field at Deotek, a small village about fifty miles to the south-east of Nâgpur. The spot has been visited by my assistant, Mr. J. D. Beglar, from whose pencilled impressions the accompanying copy of the inscription has been made. There are two distinct inscriptions on the slab, one of which is of a much later date than the other. This is also given in the plate, as it confirms the reading of a geographical name contained in the older record. This name in both inscriptions is *Chikambari.*[2]

The stone slab, which is 4 feet long by 2½ feet broad, has been at some previous period converted into an *argha* or receptacle for a *lingam*. The hollow channel for carrying off the water poured over the lingam has been cut right through the middle of the later inscription.

[1] Journal, Bengal Asiatic Society, VI, 1084-85.

[2] See Plate XV for both of these inscriptions.

The earlier inscription is dated, but the year is unfortunately lost; and I can only fix its date approximately from the style of the characters as about B. C. 100.

In the later inscription there is mention of a king named Rudra Sena, whom I take to be one of the Kailakila Yavanas of Vâkâtaka. The Seoni copper-plate inscription gives a genealogy of the early kings of Vâkâtaka, of whom the 2nd and 4th bear the name of Rudra Sena. There is a date, which I read as 200, or A. D. 278, and as this is said to be the eighteenth year of the reign of King Pravara Sena, son of Rudra Sena 2nd, the father's accession may be placed in A. D. 230, and that of the great-grandfather Rudra Sena 1st in 170 A. D. From the early forms of some of the characters, I prefer the reign of Rudra Sena 1st, or the latter end of the 2nd century A. D., for the date of the Deotek inscription. The interval between the dates of the two inscriptions will thus be upwards of 250 years, which certainly does not appear to be too great for the very wide differences in their alphabetical characters.

If I am right in identifying the Rudra Sena of the second Deotek inscription with one of the Rudra Senas of *Vâkâtaka,* then *Chikambari* must have been in the Vâkâtaka territory, and would have been either the ancient name of the district or that of its principal town. No such name is now known. The chief town in this part of the country at the present day is Pauni, which is an old fortified place with several ancient temples.

CAVE INSCRIPTIONS.

CAVES OF BARÂBAR AND NÂGÂRJUNI IN MAGADHA OR BIHAR.

BARÂBAR CAVES.

THE famous caves of Barâbar and Nâgârjuni are situated sixteen miles due north of Gaya, or nineteen miles by the road, in two separate groups of granite hills on the left or west bank of the Phalgu river. By the people these caves are usually called *Sâtghara*, or "the seven houses," although this name is by some restricted to two of the caves in the Barâbar group. But as there are four caves in the Barâbar hills, and three caves in the Nâgârjuni hills, or altogether "seven caves," I think that the name must belong to the whole number.[1]

The Barâbar caves are named as follows:—1, *Sudâmâ-Gupha*, or "Sudâma's cave," is a large room, 32¾ feet long by 19 feet wide. The roof is vaulted, and the whole of the interior is quite plain, but highly polished. At one end there is an inner room, nearly circular, with a hemispherical domed roof. The walls are 6¾ feet high to the springing of the vault, which has a rise of 5½ feet, making the total height 12¼ feet. The doorway, which is of Egyptian form, is sunk in a recess 6½ feet square and 2 feet deep. On the east wall of this recess there is an inscription of two lines,[2] which records the dedication of the *Nigoha* cave by Raja Piyadasi (or Asoka) in the twelfth year of his reign, or in B. C. 251. An attempt has been made to obliterate the greater part of this inscription with a chisel, but, owing to the great depth of the letters, the work of destruction was not an easy one, and the deeply-cut lines of the original letters, with the exception, perhaps, of one at the end, are still distinctly traceable at the bottom of the holes made by the destroyer's chisel.

2. The *Viswa-jhopri*, or "Viswa's hut," also consists of two rooms, an outer apartment 14 feet long by 8 feet 4 inches broad, which is polished throughout, and an inner room 11 feet in diameter, which is rough and unfinished. On the right-hand wall there is an inscription of four lines, which records the dedication of the cave by Raja Piyadasi in the twelfth year of his reign, or B. C. 251. The last five letters have been purposely mutilated, but are still quite legible.[3]

3. The *Karna Chopâr*, or "Karna's hut," is a single-vaulted room 10¾ feet high and 33½ feet long by 14 feet broad. The whole of the interior is quite plain, but

---

[1] See my detailed account of all these caves in Archæological Survey of India, I, 45. See also Major Kittoe in the Journal of the Bengal Asiatic Society, XVI, 405.

[2] See Plate XVI, No. 1.

[3] See Plate XVI, No. 2.

polished. On the west side of the entrance, in a slightly sunken tablet, there is an inscription of five lines, which records the dedication of the cave by Raja Piyadasi in the nineteenth year of his reign, or 244 B. C. The inscription being fully exposed to the weather has been very much worn, so that it is very difficult to make out the letters satisfactorily.[1]

4. The *Lomás Rishi Gupha*, or "Cave of Lomás Rishi," is the fellow of the Sudáma cave, both as to the size and arrangement of its two chambers. But the whole of the circular room has been left rough, and both the floor and the roof of the outer apartment are unfinished. The straight walls of this room are polished, but the outer wall of the circular room is only smoothed and not polished. The chisel-marks are still visible on the floor, as well as on the vaulted roof which has only been partially hewn. The work would appear to have been abandoned on reaching a deep fissure in the roof, which forms one of the natural cleavage lines of the rock. The entrance to this cave is sculptured, but the existing inscriptions are not older than the Gupta period. I infer, however, from the polished walls that the cave was actually excavated about the Asoka period.

NÂGÂRJUNI CAVES.

5. The *Vapiya* cave is so named in its own inscription. It has a small porch, 6 feet long by 5½ feet broad, from which a doorway, not quite 3 feet wide, leads to the principal room, which is 16¾ feet long by 11¼ feet broad. The roof is vaulted and rises to 10½ feet. The whole of the walls are highly polished. On the left side of the porch there is an inscription of four lines, which records that the cave was given to the Bhadantas as a dwelling-place by Dasaratha, the beloved of the gods, in the beginning of his reign.[2] This prince was the grandson of Asoka, and as his father reigned only eight years, Dasaratha's accession must have taken place in B. C. 218. The characters of this inscription, and of two others about to be described, retain the Asoka forms unchanged, but they are only about half the size of those of Asoka's Barâbar cave inscriptions.

6. The *Gopika* cave is so named in its own inscription, which is engraved on the outside just above the entrance. This is the largest of the Magadha caves, being 46 feet 5 inches long by 19 feet 2 inches broad, with a vaulted roof 10½ feet in height. Both of the ends are semicircular. The whole of the interior is highly polished, but quite plain. The inscription of this cave is word for word the same as the last, with the single exception of the name.[3] It therefore belongs to the same date of 218 B. C.

7. The *Vadathi* cave is so named in its own inscription. It is situated in a cleft of the rock to the west of the Vapiya cave. The entrance to the cave, which lies in this gap, is a mere passage, only 2 feet 10 inches in width, and 6 feet 1½ inches in height, with a mean length of 6½ feet. On the right side of the passage there is an inscription of four lines, which, with the exception of the name, is word

---

[1] See Plate XVI, No. 3. [2] See Plate XVI. [3] See Plate XVI.

for word the same as the two preceding inscriptions of Raja Dasaratha.[1] Its date is therefore 218 B. C.

In two of the Asoka inscriptions the caves are said to be situated in the "*Khalati* or *Khalanti* hills"—*Khalatika pavatasi.* Burnouf has most ingeniously referred the name to the Sanskrit *Skhalatika,* "slippery," which agrees with Kittoe's description of the "steep and *slippery* face" of the rock.[2] My own account of these hills, which was noted on the spot in 1861, makes use of the same terms:—

"The principal entrance to the valley lies over large rounded masses of granite, now worn smooth and *slippery* by the feet of numerous pilgrims.[3]

The slipperiness, indeed, was so great that I found it convenient to take off my shoes. Hence Burnouf's derivation of the name of *Khalatika* from *Skhalatika,* "*slippery,*" is fully borne out by the character of the hills themselves.[4] But without the initial *S* the name might be connected with *Khala,* "low, vile, bad," as an abusive epithet, which the Brahmans were so fond of bestowing on the aboriginal races, and from which the Burmese might have derived their name of *Kalá,* which they apply to all Indians with such contemptuous tones.

As the two groups of the Barâbar and Nâgârjuni hills occupy a very conspicuous position in ancient Magadha, lying, as they do, on the high road from Bodh Gaya to Patna, and in sight of the high road to Nâlanda, it seems possible that they may have given their name to the people who occupied the country round about them. In this case the people of the *Khalatika* and *Khalanti* hills might be identified with the *Kalatii* or *Kalantii* of Herodotus, and the *Kalatiæ* of Hekatæus. [5] The latter simply calls them an Indian nation, but the former describes them as practising the peculiar rite of eating their parents. In another place he speaks of the Æthiopians as eating the same "grain" (*spermati*) as the Kalantii. But as he has not said anything about the kind of grain which the Kalantii ate, various emendations of the text have been proposed, such as *sêmati,* &c. I think, however, that *sômati* is preferable, and that the father of history was guilty of a grim joke in describing the Æthiopians as eating the same "flesh" as the Kalantii. Beyond the Kalantii—that is, further to the eastward—lived the Padæi, who had the strange custom of killing and eating all the old and weakly persons. Perhaps they may be identified, as I have before suggested, with the people living on the *Padda* river, or lower course of the Ganges, and if so, this identification would very much strengthen that of the *Kalantii* with the people of the *Khalatika* or *Khalanti* hills.

KHANDAGIRI CAVES IN KATAK.

The inscriptions in these caves were first made known by Kittoe, who thus describes their position[6]:—

"The hillocks of Khandagiri and Udayagiri form part of a belt of sandstone rock, which, skirting the base of the granite hills of Orissa, extends from Autghar Dekkunal in a southerly

---

[1] See Plate XVI.

[2] Journal of the Bengal Asiatic Society, XVI, 405.

[3] Archæological Survey of India, I, 42.

[4] Le Lotus de la Bonne Loi, Appendices, p. 779.

[5] Herodotus, III, 38 and 97. Hekatæus quoted by Stephanus Byzantinus, *in voce.*

[6] Journal of the Bengal Asiatic Society VI, 1079.

direction past Khurda, and towards the Chilka Lake. * * Khandagiri is four miles north-west of Bhobaneswar, and nineteen miles south-west of Katak. The two rocks are reparated by a narrow glen, about 100 yards in width. * * *Khandagiri* has but few caves on the summit. * * *Udayagiri* is entirely perforated with small caves on its southern brow. The natives have a tradition that there were formerly 752, inclusive of those now called *Lalitindra Kesari naur*. A great many still remain perfect. None are of any size; they are mostly small chambers, about 6 feet by 4 and from 4 to 6 feet high, with verandahs in front and small doorways to them hewn out of the solid rock. Several are cut out of detached blocks in fantastic shapes, such as the 'Snake Cave' and 'Tiger Cave,' &c."

The short inscriptions in these caves are of little interest, except Nos. 6 and 7, which certainly refer to Raja Aira and his family. Prinsep has read the opening of No. 6 as VERASA *Maharájasa Kalingadi patino*, for which I propose to substitute AIRASA *Maharajasa Kalingadi patino*. The short inscription, No. 7, over a small door in the same cave is read by Prinsep as *Kumáro Vattakasa lonam*, but the correct reading seems to be *Kumáro Vaddakasa lenam*—that is, "The cave of Prince *Vaddaka*," or perhaps *Vaduka*. Here, then, we have most probably the name of one of the sons of Raja Aira, who added another small room to his father's original cave. The age of these caves will, therefore, be about B. C. 200.

No. 8 is unfortunately incomplete, otherwise it would most probably have been interesting, as it also refers to the Rajas of Kalinga. For my copy of the text I have had the advantage of a large photograph of a plaster cast taken by Mr. H. H. Locke. There are several important differences between Prinsep's readings and mine.

RAMGARH CAVES IN SIRGUJA.

The two inscribed caves in the Ramgarh hill in Sirguja were first made known by Colonel Ouseley.[1] They have also been described by Colonel Dalton.[2] But the inscriptions themselves were first published by Mr. Ball of the Geological Survey.[3] The copies given in the present volume are taken from photographs and paper impressions made by Mr. Beglar in December 1875.[4] I was especially anxious to obtain good copies of these inscriptions, as the copies made by Mr. Ball gave the name of the "*Thera Devadata*," and I thought it very probable that these few lines might prove to be records of some followers of the heretical school of Devadata, the cousin and opponent of Buddha. This, however, is not the case, for the name is not Devadata, but Devadarșin. But these inscriptions are otherwise interesting from the use of the palatal sibilant ș, which occurs no less than five times in the second inscription. This record was engraved by a sculptor named *Devadina* for a *Srutanuka* named Devadarsin. The letter *l* is used used for *r* in the last word of the inscription *lupa*, which I take to be the well-known *rúpa*. A very full account of the caves is given by Colonel Dalton.

[1] Journal of the Bengal Asiatic Society, XVII, p. 66.
[2] Journal of the Bengal Asiatic Society, XXXIV, Part II, p. 26.
[3] Indian Antiquary, September 1873, p. 243.
[4] See Plate XI for these Inscriptions.

PILLAR INSCRIPTIONS.

1—DELHI PILLAR *from Siwâlik.*

THE inscribed pillars of Asoka have long been known to Europeans owing to the favourable positions which they occupy in the very heart of his empire. Of these the best known, and the earliest to be noticed by Europeans, is the Delhi Pillar, commonly known as Firoz Shah's Lât. According to Shams-i-Sirâj, a contemporary of Firoz, this pillar was brought from a place "on the bank of the Jumna, in the district of Salora, not far from Khizrâbâd, which is at the foot of the mountains ninety kos from Delhi."[1] Owing to the lamentable uncertainty of the Persian character in the expression of proper names, the name of the place from whence the pillar was brought may be variously read as Tobra, Topar, Topera, Toparsuk, Tohera, Tamera, and Nahera.[2]

The distance from Delhi and the position at the foot of the mountains point out the present Khizrâbâd on the Jumna, just below the spot where the river issues from the lower range of hills, as the place indicated by Shams-i-Sirâj. Salora is perhaps Sidhora, a large place only a few miles to the west of Khizrâbâd. From the village where it originally stood, the pillar was conveyed by land on a truck to Khizrâbâd, from whence it was floated down the Jumna to Firozâbâd, or new Delhi. From the above description of the original site of this pillar, I conclude that the village from whence it was brought was perhaps the present Paota, on the western bank of the Jumna, and twelve miles in a direct line to the north-east of Khizrâbâd. Now, in this immediate neighbourhood on the western bank of the Jumna, and at a distance of sixty-six miles from Thanesar, Hwen Thsang places the ancient capital of Srughna, which was even then (A. D. 630—640) in ruins, although the foundations were still in existence. The Chinese pilgrim describes Srughna as possessing a large Vihâr and a grand Stûpa of Asoka's time, containing relics of Buddha, besides many other stûpas of Sâriputra, Maudgalyayana, and other holy Buddhists. The village of Topar, which was the original site of Firoz Shah's pillar, was certainly within the limits of the ancient kingdom of Srughna, and I think it probable that in the word Suk, which is appended to one of the various readings of the name of the village of Topar, we still have a fair approximation to Sughan, the popular form of the Sanskrit Srughna.

---

[1] Journal of the Archæological Society of Delhi, I, 74. Shams-i-Sirâj was twelve years old when these pillars were set up by Firoz.

[2] Journal of the Archæological Society of Delhi, I, pp. 29 and 75. See also H. M. Elliot's Muhammadan Historians, by Dowson, III, p. 350, where the name of the village is given as Tobra.

When the pillar was removed from its original site, a large square stone was found beneath it, which was also transported to Delhi.[1]

This stone was again placed beneath the pillar in its new situation on the top of a three-storied building called Firoz Shah's Kotila, where it may now be seen, as a gallery has been pierced through the solid masonry immediately beneath the base of the pillar. According to Shams-i-Sirâj, the whole length of the shaft was 32 *gaz*, of which 8 *gaz* were sunk in the building. As the pillar at present stands, I found the total height to be 42 feet 7 inches, of which the sunken portion is only 4 feet 1 inch. But the lower portion of the exposed shaft to a height of 5 feet is still rough, and I have little doubt, therefore, that the whole of the rough portion, 9 feet in length, must have been sunk in the ground on its original site. But according to Shams-i-Sirâj, even more than this, or one-fourth of its whole length,—that is, 10 feet 8 inches,—was sunk in the masonry of Firoz Shah's Kotila. This I believe was actually the case, for on the west side of the column there still remain *in situ* the stumps of two short octagonal granite pillars that would appear to have formed part of a cloister or open gallery around a fourth storey, which cannot have been less than 6½ or 7 feet in height. I conclude, therefore, that the statement of Shams-i-Sirâj is quite correct.

When the pillar was at last fixed, the "top was ornamented with black and white stone work surmounted by a gilt pinnacle, from which no doubt it received its name of *Minâr Zarin*, or 'Golden Pillar.' This gilt pinnacle was still in its place in A. D. 1611, when William Finch entered Delhi, as he describes the 'stone pillar of *Bimsa* (or Bhim-sen), which, after passing through three several storeys, rising 24 feet above them all, having on the top a globe surmounted by a crescent.'[2] The 24 feet of this account are probably the same as the 24 *gaz* of the other, the *gaz* being only a fraction less than 16½ inches.

The "Golden Pillar" is a single shaft of pale pinkish sandstone, 42 feet 7 inches in length, of which the upper portion, 35 feet in length, has received a very high polish, while the remainder is left quite rough. Its upper diameter is 25·3 inches, and its lower diameter 38·8 inches, the diminution being ·39 inch per foot. Its weight is rather more than 17 tons. In its dimensions it is more like the Allahabad pillar than any other, but it tapers much more rapidly towards the top, and is therefore less graceful in its outline.

There are two principal inscriptions on Firoz Shah's pillar, besides several minor records of pilgrims and travellers, from the first centuries of the Christian era down to the present time. The oldest inscriptions for which the pillar was originally erected comprise the well-known edicts of Asoka, which were promulgated in the middle of the third century B. C. in the ancient Pâli or spoken language of the day. The alphabetical characters, which are of the oldest form that has yet been found in India, are most

---

[1] A similar large square stone was found under the Pahládpur pillar when it was removed to the grounds of Queen's College at Benâres.

[2] Kerr's Voyages and Travels, IX, 423.

clearly and beautifully cut, and there are only a few letters of the whole record lost by the peeling off of the surface of the stone. The inscription ends with a short sentence, in which King Asoka directs the setting up these monoliths in different parts of India as follows :[1]

"Let this religious edict be engraved on stone pillars (*sila thambha*) and stone tablets (*sila phalaka*) that it may endure for ever."

In this amended passage we have a distinct allusion to the rock inscriptions, as well as to the pillar insciptions. The record consists of four distinct inscriptions on the four sides of the column facing the cardinal points, and of one long inscription immediately below, which goes completely round the pillar. I may mention that the word *Ajakânâni*, at the end of the seventh line south face, was not omitted "accidentally," as James Prinsep supposed, by the original engraver, but has been lost by the peeling away of the stone for about four inches. The vowel *i* of the final letter is still quite distinct. The penultimate word on the eastern face is not *agnim*, as doubtfully read by Prinsep, but *abhyum*, and, as he rightly conjectured, it is the same word that begins the ninth line. The last word in the eleventh line which puzzled Prinsep is not *atikata*, but *atikantam*, the same as occurs near the beginning of the fifteenth line.

The last ten lines of the eastern face, as well as the whole of the continuous inscription round the shaft, are peculiar to this pillar. Their position alone declares them to be an after addition. But there is also a marked difference in the appearance of the letters of this part of the inscription which shows that it must have been engraved at a later date than the preceding edicts. The whole of the additional matter is executed in thinner and less carefully formed letters, many of which have a sloping or cursive form that is not to be found in any one of the five examples or the earlier inscriptions. The vowel marks also are generally sloping instead of being horizontal or perpendicular. Some of them are, besides, either differently formed or differently attached. Thus the *o*, which in the older edicts is formed by two horizontal side strokes, one at top to left, and one lower down to right, has now become either a single continuous stroke across the top of the consonant, or has the positions of the two separate strokes reversed, the upper one being to the right and the lower one to the left. So also the vowel *u*, which in the earlier edicts is a horizontal stroke at the right foot of the letters *ch* and *dh*, has now become a perpendicular stroke attached to the same point. The letter *t* is formed of only two strokes instead of three, the longer one sloping to the left and the shorter one to the right. I observe also that the vowel *u*, in *anu*, has been shifted from the right end of the horizontal stroke of the *n* to a point midway between the end and the junction of the perpendicular stroke. As all these differences in the forms of the letters begin in the middle of the inscription on the east face, it seems absolutely certain that this portion of the edicts, as well as the still lower portion round the shaft, must have been engraved at a later date than the upper half.

[1] See James Prinsep in Bengal Asiatic Society's Journal, 1837, p. 609. He reads *sila dhulakâni* instead of *phalakâni*, which is quite distinct on the pillar. See Plates XVIII, XIX, and XX of this volume.

2.—Delhi Pillar—*from Mirat.*

The second of Asoka's Delhi pillars according to Shams-i-Sirâj was brought from Mirat by Firoz Shah, and set up near the Kushak Shikâr or "Hunting Palace," which we know was situated on the ridge to the north-west of the modern city. According to the popular belief, this pillar was thrown down by an accidental explosion of a powder magazine in the reign of Farokhsir, 1713 to 1719 A. D. Padre Tieffenthaler, who visited Delhi towards the middle of last century, saw this pillar lying in five pieces on the top of the ridge, beside a square pedestal of large stones. He also ascribes its destruction to gunpowder.[1] There the five pieces remained undisturbed for upwards of a century, when the inscribed portion was sent down to Calcutta to the Museum of the Asiatic Society. Within the last few years this piece has been returned to Delhi, and the pillar has again been set up in its old position.

The inscriptions on this pillar are very imperfect, partly owing to its mutilation, and partly to the worn surface of the existing pieces.[2] Impressions of the remaining portions of the edicts were furnished to Prinsep, who published copies of them and compared the text with that of the other pillars.[3] But the impressions must have been imperfect, as the published plates omit the right-hand portion of the north compartment and the bottom line of both. The omitted portions will be seen at once in the accompanying plate. The thin letters in the middle of the west compartment I have added from the other texts so as to show exactly how much is missing in this part. Altogether nearly one-half of the inscription still remains.

3.—Allahabad Pillar.

The well-known Allahabad pillar is a single shaft of polished sandstone 35 feet in length, with a lower diameter of 2 feet 11 inches and an upper diameter of 2 feet 2 inches. The capital of the column was no doubt of the usual bell-shape of Asoka's other pillars, but of this there is now no trace. The circular abacus, however, still remains with its graceful scroll of alternate lotus and honeysuckle, resting on a beaded astragalus of Greek origin. This was once surmounted by the statue of a lion; but the lion must have disappeared many centuries ago, as when the pillar was re-erected by Jahângir in A. D. 1605, it was crowned by a globe, surmounted by a cone, as described and sketched by Padre Tieffenthaler in the middle of the next century.[4] It then stood in the middle of the fort.

The great inscription of Asoka, containing the same series of six edicts which are found on the other four pillars, is engraved in continuous lines around the column.[5] The letters are uniform in size, and are very neatly and deeply engraved. But a great portion of the third and fourth edicts, comprising seven lines, has been

---

[1] Description de l'Inde, par Bernoulli, I, 128—"On a fait santer en l'air ce monument avec de la poudre."
[2] See Plate XXI for the remains of these edicts.
[3] Journal of the Bengal Asiatic Society, VI, 794, and Plate XLII.
[4] Description de l'Inde, par Bernoulli, I, 224, and Plate VI.
[5] See Plate XXII.

ruthlessly destroyed by the cutting of the vain-glorious inscription of Jahângir, recording the names of his ancestors. Two lines of the fifth edict are nearly intact, but nearly the whole of the remainder has been lost by the peeling off of the surface of the stone. The sixth edict is complete with the exception of about half a line.

Immediately below the Asoka edicts comes the long and well-known inscription of Samudra Gupta. The upper portion of this inscription is confined between a crack in the stone on its left, and two short Asoka inscriptions on its right. The lower one of these, consisting of five lines, was translated by Prinsep, and as it refers to Asoka's queens, I propose to name it "the Queen's edict." But the upper inscription, consisting of four lines, was discovered by myself, and as it is addressed to the rulers of Kosâmbi, I propose to name it "the Kosâmbi edict." All that remains of these Asoka edicts is given in Plate XXII of the Pillar Inscriptions.

Of middle age inscriptions there is no trace, but the mass of short records in rudely cut modern Nâgari covers quite as much space as the two inscriptions of Asoka and Samudra. Above the Asoka edicts there is a mass of this modern scribbling equal in size to the Samudra Gupta inscription. But besides this, the whole of the Asoka inscription is interlined with the same rubbish, which is continued below on all sides of the two shorter edicts, one of which has been half obliterated by the modern letters.

Regarding these minor inscriptions, James Prinsep remarks[1] that

"it is a singular fact that the periods at which the pillar has been overthrown can be thus determined with nearly as much certainty from this desultory writing as can the epochs of its being re-erected from the more formal inscriptions recording the latter event. Thus that it was overthrown some time after its first erection by the great Asoka in the middle of the third century before Christ, is proved by the longitudinal or random insertion of several names in a character intermediate between No. 1 and No. 2, in which the *m*, *b*, &c., retain the old form."

Of one of these names he remarks,—

"Now it would have been exceedingly difficult, if not impossible, to have cut the name No. 10 up and down at right angles to the other writing, *while the pillar was erect*, to say nothing of the place being out of reach, unless a scaffold were erected on purpose, which would hardly be the case, since the object of an ambitious visitor would be defeated by placing his name out of sight and in an unreadable position. The pillar was erected as Samudra Gupta's arm, and there it probably remained until overthrown again by the idol-breaking zeal of the Musalmâns; for we find no writings on it of the Pâla or Sârnâth type (*i. e.*, of the tenth century), but a quantity appears with plain legible dates from the Samvat year 1420, or A. D. 1363, down to 1660 odd, and it is remarkable that these occupy one side of the shaft, or that which was uppermost when the pillar was in a prostrate position. A few detached and ill-executed Nâgari names with Samvat dates of 1800 odd show that ever since it was laid on the ground again by General Garstin,[2] the passion for recording visits of piety or curiosity has been at work."

I have gone through the mass of modern scribbling in the hope of finding something that might throw further light on the history of the pillar, and I have not been altogether disappointed. I have found seven dates ranging from Samvat 1297 to 1398, or from A. D. 1240 to 1341; five ranging from Samvat 1464 to 1495, or A. D. 1407 to 1438; twelve ranging from Samvat 1501 to 1584, or A. D. 1444 to

---

[1] Journal of the Bengal Asiatic Society, VI, 967.

[2] According to my information it was General Kyd, whose name is still preserved in Kydganj at Allahabad who threw down the pillar. Kittoe also assigns its overthrow to Kyd.

1527; three ranging from Samvat 1632 to 1640, or A. D. 1575 to 1583; and three of Samvat 1864, or A. D. 1807. These dates, combined with the total absence of any mediæval Nâgari inscriptions, are sufficient to show that the pillar was standing out of the reach of pilgrims' scribbling from the time of the Guptas until that of the early Musalmân kings of Delhi. There are then twelve dated inscriptions coming down to near the death of Muhammad Tughlak. There is not a single record of the time of Firoz Tughlak which leads me to suspect that he may have re-erected this pillar with its globe and cone, like those of the *Zarin-Minar*, or Golden Pillar, at Delhi. But if he did set it up, it must have been thrown down again during the troubled times of his immediate successors, as the dates begin again in A. D. 1407 and 1408. It was *next* set up by Jahângir in A. H. 1014, or A. D. 1605, to be pulled down by General Kyd in A. D. 1798. It was once more scribbled upon in A. D. 1807, and finally in 1838 it was set up as it stands at present.

From the address of Asoka to the rulers of Kosâmbi, in the newly-discovered edict, it seems probable that this pillar may have been originally erected in that city, and afterwards removed to Prayâg or Allahabad. But if so, the removal was not made by Jahângir, as I have found amongst the modern Nâgari records a short inscription of the famous Birbar, the companion and favourite of Akbar. The words of the short record are as follows :—

1.—*Samvat* 1632, *Sâke* 1493, *Mârgabadi panchami.*

2.—*Somwâr Gangâdâs sut Maharaja Birba* (*r*) *Sri.*

3.—*Tîrth Râj Prayâg ke jâtrâ Saphal lekhitam.*

"In the Samvat year 1632, Sâke[1] 1493, in Marga, the 5th of the waning moon, on Monday, Gangâdâs's son Maharaja Birba (r) made the auspicious pilgrimage to Tîrth Râj Prayâg. Saphal scripsit."

The Samvat date is equivalent to A. D. 1575, and as the building of the fort of Allahabad was finished in A. H. 982=A. D. 1572, it is probable that Birbar took advantage during one of his attendances on Akbar to pay a visit to the meeting of the waters of the Gangâ and Yamuna under the holy tree of Prayâga. But whatever may have been the occasion of Birbar's visit, its record is sufficient to prove that the pillar was then *lying* on the ground at Prayâga. If, then, it was originally erected at Kosâmbi, it seems highly probable that it must have been brought to Prayâga by Firoz Tughlak, whose removal of the Siwâlik and Mirat pillars to Delhi gives countenance to this suggestion. The silence of the Chinese pilgrim Hwen Thsang is also in favour of my suggestion that the present Allahabad pillar was originally set up at Kosâmbi.

4.—Lauriya Ararâj Pillar.

This pillar is situated close to the small hamlet of *Lauriya*, between Kesariya and Bettia, at a distance of twenty miles to the north-west of the Kesariya Stûpa, and one mile to the south-west of the much-frequented Hindu temple of Ararâj-Mahâdeo.

---

[1] There is an error of four years in this Sâke date of 1493, which should be 1632—135 = 1497 Sâke. If this was due to Birbar himself, and not to the scribe Saphal, it confirms the account of Badaoni that he was of poor origin. His real name was Mahesh Dâs. See Blochmann's Ain-i-Akbari.

The pillar itself is simply called *Laur*,—that is, "the phallus,"—and the neighbouring village, which lies not more than 100 yards to the westward, is called *Lauriya*. This is the pillar which, on the authority of Mr. Hodgson's Munshi, has been called the Radhia Pillar. Now, as the other pillar to the north of Bettia is also called *Laur*, and the large village close to it Lauriya, while Mr. Hodgson has named it Mathiah, I presume that his Munshi intentionally suppressed the phallic name of Lauriya, and named the two pillars at random after some of the neighbouring villages. Thus *Rahariya* (Rurheea of Indian Atlas Sheet No. 102), which is Mr. Hodgson's Radhia, lies two and a half miles to the west-north-west of the southern pillar, while Mathiah lies three miles due south from the northern pillar. In describing these pillars I have preserved the characteristic name of Lauriya, and for the sake of distinguishing the one from the other, I have added to each the name of the nearest village. Thus the village near the southern pillar I have called "Lauriya Ararâj," and that near the northern pillar "Lauriya Navandgarh."

The Ararâj pillar is a single block of polished sandstone, 36½ feet in height, above the ground, with a base diameter of 41·8 inches, and a top diameter of 37·6 inches. The weight of this portion only is very nearly 23 tons, but as there must be several feet of rough shaft sunk in the earth, the actual weight of the single block must be about 30 tons. This pillar has no capital, although there can be little, if any, doubt that it must once have been crowned with a statue of some animal. The people, however, know nothing of it, and not a fragment of any kind now exists to suggest what it may have been. The site of the village is a very secluded one, and there are no ruins or other remains to attract attention. It has accordingly escaped the notice of travellers and the disfigurement of their names; the only record being that of "Reuben Burrow, 1792," besides a few flourished letters, or marks, of the kind which James Prinsep called "shell-shaped characters."

The edicts of Asoka are most clearly and neatly engraved, and are divided into two distinct portions, that to the north containing eighteen lines, and that to the south twenty-three lines.[1] I made a copy of the inscriptions by the eye, which I then compared with James Prinsep's text, and afterwards I re-examined every letter in which our copies differed. I also made an inked impression of the whole inscription on paper. But though the variations from Prinsep's text are not many, yet, as no facsimile has yet been made public, it is important, for the sake of comparison, to afford access to an authentic copy which has been carefully examined in every letter.

The inscription of Asoka is engraved in two columns, one facing the south comprising the first four edicts, and the other facing the north containing edicts five and six of the Delhi pillar. The characters are neatly and deeply cut, and the words are generally separated. The forms of the letters are the same as those of the Delhi and Allahabad pillars, with the single exception of *j*, which has a decided knob or small circle attached to the middle stroke. There are six compound letters, *kkh*, *ty*, *dhy*, *khy*, *sy*, and *sw*, of which the first three do not occur on the Delhi pillar.

---

[1] See Plates XXIII and XXIV.

5.—Lauriya Navandgarh Pillar.

The graceful lion pillar at Lauriya, near the great ruined fort of Navandgarh, or Nonadgarh, is the only one of Asoka's columns which still retains its original capital.[1] The lion is seated on its haunches with the mouth wide open; but the mouth is partly broken, and the shaft itself bears the round mark of a cannon shot just below the capital, which has been slightly displaced by the shock. One has not far to seek for the name of the probable author of this mischief. By the people the outrage is ascribed to the Musalmâns, and on the pillar itself, in beautifully cut Persian characters, is inscribed the name of *Mahiuddin Muhammad Aurangzib Pádsháh Alamgir Ghâzi, Sanhu* 1071. This date corresponds with A. D. 1660-61, which was the fourth year of the reign of the bigoted Aurangzib, and the record was most probably inscribed by some zealous follower in Mir Jûmla's army, which was then on its return from Bengal, after the death of the emperor's brother Shujâ.

This pillar is much thinner and lighter in appearance than those of Ararâj and Bakhra. The height of the polished shaft is 32 feet 9½ inches, with a base diameter of 2 feet 11½ inches, and a neck diameter of 2 feet 2¼ inches. The capital, which is bell-shaped, has a circular abacus, ornamented with a row of *hansas* (wild geese) pecking their food. The height of the capital, including the lion, is 6 feet 9 inches, which makes the total height of the pillar rather more than 39½ feet.

The edicts of Asoka, which are arranged in two columns, one facing the north and the other the south, are engraved in the same clear and deeply-cut letters as on the Ararâj pillar.[2] The two inscriptions, with only a few trifling variations, correspond with each other, letter for letter, including the use of the six compound letters already noted.

This pillar has been visited by numerous travellers, as it stands in the direct route from Bettia to Nepal. There are a few unimportant inscriptions in modern Nâgari, the oldest being dated in *Samvat* 1566, *Chait badi* 10, equivalent to A. D. 1509. Another inscription, without date, refers to some petty royal family, *Nripa Nárâyana Suta Nripa Amara Singha*,—that is, "King Amara Singha, the son of King Nârâyana." The only English inscription is the name of Rn. Burrow, 1792.

The pillar itself has now become an object of worship as a phallus or lingam. Whilst I was copying the inscription, a man with two women and a child set up a small flag before the pillar, and placed offerings of sweetmeats around it. They then all knelt before it, bowing down their heads to the ground with their hands behind their backs and repeating some prayer. The erection of the pillar is ascribed to Raja Bhim Mâri, one of the five Pândava brothers, to whom most of the pillars in India are now ascribed. I could not learn anything regarding the title of Mâri. There are two fine pipal trees close to the pillar, one to the north and the other to the south; but there are no traces of buildings of any kind near it.

Close to the pillar there are three rows of earthen mounds, of which one line runs from east to west, and the other lines from north to south. The loftiest of

---

[1] See Archæological Survey of India, Vol. I, Plates XXII and XXV.

[2] See Plates XXV and XXVI.

these mounds reach the height of 50 to 55 feet. I believe them to be the tombs of the early inhabitants before the time of Asoka. Indeed, a human skeleton has been found in one of them, which, according to native report, was enclosed in an iron coffin.

6.—Sanchi Pillar.

The inscribed pillar at Sânchi near Bhilsa is only a fragment of a large polished shaft; but near it there still lies a beautiful broken capital crowned by four lions, which, no doubt, once surmounted it.[1] The inscription is unfortunately very much mutilated, as may be seen by the only two copies of it which have yet been published.[2] I have again lately visited Sânchi, and the present copy has been prepared from my recent impressions. It seems scarcely possible that it can be satisfactorily deciphered, but it will still be valuable, as affording, by the characters in which it is written, a direct proof that the pillar was erected in the time of Asoka.[3] And as the pillar was subordinate to the stûpa, it affords also an indirect proof that the stûpa cannot be of a later date.

[1] See Colonel Maisey's drawing in Fergusson's Tree and Serpent Worship, Plate XXXIX, fig. 1.

[2] Prinsep in Journal of Bengal Asiatic Society, VII, Plate 23, and Cunningham's Bhilsa Topes, Plate XIX, No. 177.

[3] See Plate XX for this inscription.

II. LANGUAGE OF THE INSCRIPTIONS.

THE inscriptions of Asoka are quite invaluable for the study of the vernacular languages of India, as they present us with several undoubted and authentic texts of the common language of the people in the third century B. C. As revealed in these engraved records, this spoken language was essentially the same throughout the wide and fertile regions lying between Himalaya and Vindhya from the banks of the Indus to the mouths of the Ganges. There are, however, some marked points of difference which show that there were at least three distinct varieties of Pâli in the time of Asoka. These may be called, according to their geographical distribution, the *Panjâbi* or north-western dialect, the *Ujjeni* or middle dialect, and the *Mágadhi* or eastern dialect.

1. The *Panjâbi*, or dialect of North-Western India, is fully exhibited in the great inscription at Shâhbâz-garhi in the Sudam valley, as well as on the coins of the Greek and Indo-Scythian princes of Ariana and India. Its chief characteristic is the retention of the subjoined *r*, in such words as *Priyadarsi*, *Srâmana*, *Andhra*, and *prati* of the inscriptions, and in *Eukratidasa*, *Strategasa*, *bhrátasa*, and *putrasa* of the coins. It is also distinguishable by its nearer approach to pure Sanskrit forms, shown in the above-quoted *prati*, which becomes *paṭi* in all the other texts, as well as in the Pâli of Ceylon. Another characteristic is the possession of the three distinct sibilants of Sanskrit, which are all blended into one common form of the dental *s* in the other texts as well as in the Pâli of Ceylon. The whole of the three sibilants occur in the word *suṣusha*, which is written simply *sususa* in all the Indian versions, excepting only in a few passages of the Khâlsi text, where the palatal *ṣ* or *sh* is used of nearly the same form as the Arian letter of the Shâhbâz-garhi inscription. The same letter is also found in the word *vasa* or *vasha*, "year" which replaces *vasa* of the Indian texts; and in the plural forms of *Kamboyeshu* and *Pulindeshu*, which take the place of *Kabojesu* and *Pulindesu* of the other versions.

But the most remarkable departure from the Indian texts is the use of the vernacular word *baraya* for twelfth, instead of the Sanskrit *dwádasa*. This word occurs twice in the inscription, near the beginning of the third and towards the end of the fourth edict. Strange to say, it remained unrecognised by Wilson, who simply remarks, "in place of *dwádasa*, 'twelve,' and *vasa*, 'year,' the inscription has *baraya vasha*, but the first must be wrong."[1] Of the second example, he says that "there is a blank instead of the number," although Norris's Arian text has the

[1] Journal of the Royal Asiatic Society, XII, p. 171.

letters for *vara* + *vasha* quite distinct, while his English transliteration gives *va rana vashá*. By thus separating *va* from the following letters, it seems that Norris also failed to recognise the true vernacular *baraya* for "twelfth."

I observe that the word *chatura*, "four," in the thirteenth edict, is followed by four upright strokes, thus, IIII, in the Shâhbâz-garhi text, and that the corresponding word *chatura*, "four," in the Khâlsi text, is followed by an upright cross, thus +, which must, therefore, be the old Indian cypher for 4. This form was afterwards modified to a St. Andrews' cross, or ×, in which shape it was adopted by all the people who used the Arian characters, as may be seen in the different inscriptions of the Kings Kanishka, Huvishka, and Gondophares, and of the Satrap Liako-Kujulaka. Previous to the adoption of this Indian symbol, the cyphers of the Western people would seem to have been limited to single strokes, as the words *pancheshu-pancheshu*, "every five," are followed by five upright strokes, which precede the word *vasheshu*, "years."[1]

2. The *Ujjeni*, or middle Indian dialect, is exhibited in the Girnar version of Asoka's edicts, in the rock edict of Rûpnâth, and in all the numerous donative records of the great stûpas of Bhilsa and Bharhut. Its chief characteristics are the occasional use of the palatal sibilant *s*, as in *páṣaṇḍa*, and its possession of *r* as well as *l*, as shown in the use of *Raja* instead of *Laja*, *guru* instead of *gulu*, *oro* for *olo*, &c.

The few coins that we possess with legends in Asoka characters also use the *r* in its proper place, as in *Purushadatta*, *Bârâniya*; and as none of them have been found to the east of Benares, I conclude that the power of pronouncing the letter *r* was confined to Northern and Central India, and to the people of Orissa and Kalinga.

3. The *Mâgadhi* or eastern dialect is broadly marked by the entire want of the letter *r*, for which *l* is uniformly substituted. Thus we have *Laja* for *Râja*, *lopapita* for *ropapita*, *antalam* for *antaram*, *chalana* for *charana*, *Dasalatha* for *Dasaratha*, &c.,—a peculiarity which would seem to connect the people of Eastern India with the Indo-Chinese, who also want the *r*.[2] There is a curious account in the Lalita-Vistara regarding the teaching of the young Prince Sâkya Sinha in the *lipisâla*, or "Writing School." There the alphabet which he was taught was the common Sanskrit alphabet with the omission of the letters *l*, *ṛi* and *ṛî*.[3] But as no inscriptions with this peculiarity have yet been found, I cannot help suspecting that the author of the Lalita-Vistara has made a mistake, and that the letter actually omitted was *r*, as we find to have been the case in numerous inscriptions, including those of the Lauriya pillars, which stand within 125 miles of Kapilavastu, where Buddha was born.

The affinities of the language of Asoka's inscriptions with Pâli and Sanskrit have been briefly discussed by the competent pen of Professor H. H. Wilson, whose opinion was formed after a very careful and searching examination of the

---

[1] Archæological Survey of India, Vol. V, p. 22, by Cunningham.

[2] It is true that the Burmese have actually got the letter *r*, which they borrowed from India along with their alphabet, but they have not got the pronunciation, as they say *Yangoon* for *Rangoon*, *Yahoo* for *Rahu*, &c.

[3] History of ancient Sanskrit literature by Professor Max-Müller, p. 519.

complete texts of four different versions of the rock edicts. I quote his words as they stand, with the single exception of the substitution of the name of Shâhbâz-garhi for that of Kapurdagiri, as the great inscription of Asoka is actually within the lands of the former place, and more than two miles distant from the smaller village of Kapurdagiri[1]:—

"The language itself is a kind of Pâli, offering for the greater portion of the words forms analogous to those which are modelled by the rules of the Pâli grammar still in use. There are, however, many differences, some of which arise from a closer adherence to Sanskrit, others from possible local peculiarities, indicating a yet unsettled state of the language. It is observed by Mr. Prinsep, when speaking of the Lât inscriptions: 'The language differs from every existing written idiom, and is, as it were, intermediate between the Sanskrit and Pâli. The nouns and particles in general follow the Pâli structure; the verbs are more frequently nearer to the Sanskrit forms; but in neither, any more than in grammatical Pâli, is there any great dissimilarity from Sanskrit. It is curious that the Shâhbâz-garhi inscription departs less from the Sanskrit than the others, retaining some compound consonants, as *pr* in *priya* instead of *piya;* and having the representatives of the three sibilants of the Devanâgari alphabet, while the others, as in Pâli, have but one sibilant. On the other hand, the Shâhbâz-garhi inscription omits the vowels to a much greater extent, and rarely distinguishes between the long and short vowels—peculiarities perhaps not unconnected with the Semitic character of its alphabet.

"The exact determination of the differences and agreements of the inscriptions with Pâli on the one hand and Sanskrit on the other would require a laborious analysis of the whole, and would be scarcely worth the pains, as the differences from either would, no doubt, prove to be comparatively few and unimportant, and we may be content to consider the language as Pâli, not yet perfected in its grammatical structure, and deviating in no important respect from Sanskrit. Pâli is the language of the writings of the Buddhists of Ava, Siam and Ceylon; therefore it is concluded it was the language of the Buddhists of Upper India when the inscriptions were engraved, and consequently they are of Buddhist origin. This, however, admits of question; for, although the Buddhist authorities assert that Sâkya Sinha and his successors taught in Pâli, and that a Pâli grammar was compiled in his day, yet, on the other hand, they affirm that the doctrines of Buddha were long taught orally only, and were not committed to writing for four centuries after his death, or until B. C. 153—a date, no doubt, subsequent to that of the inscriptions. In fact, the principal authorities of the Singalese Buddhists appear to have existed in Singalese, and to have been translated into Pâli only in the fifth century after Christ.

"According to M. Burnouf and Mr. Hodgson, the earliest Buddhist writings were not Pâli, but Sanskrit, and they were translated by the Northern Buddhists into their own languages—Mongol and Tibetan. It does not appear that they have any Pâli books. The Chinese have obtained their writings from both quarters, and they probably have Pâli works brought from Ava or Ceylon. They have also, according to M. Burnouf, translations of the same Sanskrit works that are known in the north. It is by no means established, therefore, that Pâli was the sacred language of the Buddhists at the period of the inscriptions, and its use constitutes no conclusive proof of their Buddhist origin. It seems more likely that it was adopted as being the spoken language of that part of India where Piyadasi resided, and was selected for his edicts, that they might be intelligible to the people. Hence, also, the employment of different alphabets, that of Shâhbâz-garhi being the alphabet current in Afghanistan and Bactria, as we know from the Græco-Bactrian coins. The use of the provincial or local alphabet was evidently designed for the convenience of those to whom it was familiar, while the ancient form of Devanâgari was that employed in Hindustan as being there in general use. The popular currency of the language, admitting that it might have been the spoken dialect of the north-west of India, would be more likely to prevent, than to recommend, its use as a 'sacred'

---

[1] Journal of the Royal Asiatic Society, XII, 236-238.

language, and its being applied to such a purpose by the Southern Buddhists was in some degree probably owing to their being as a people ignorant of it, and it would then assume in their eyes a sanctity which as a spoken dialect it was not likely to possess. At the same time we can scarcely suppose that the language of the inscriptions was understood in all the countries where they have been discovered,—beyond the Indus, at Delhi, in Bihar, in Orissa, and Gujarat, where we know that very different dialects, however largely borrowing from a common source, at present prevail. Neither is it likely that edicts intended to regulate the moral conduct of the people at large should have been intelligible only to Buddhist priests, or should have been perpetuated on pillars and rocks solely for their edification. We may therefore recognise it as an actually existent form of speech in some part of India, and might admit the testimony of its origin given by Buddhists themselves, by whom it is always identified with the language of Magadha or Bihar, the scene of Sâkya Sinha's first teaching; but that there are several differences between it and the Mâgadhi, as laid down in Prâkrit grammars, and as it occurs in Jain writings. It is, as Messrs. Burnouf and Lassen remark, still nearer to Sanskrit, and may have prevailed more to the north than Bihar, or in the upper part of the Doab, and in the Punjâb, being more analogous to the Sauraseni dialect, the language of Mathura and Delhi, although not differing from the dialect of Bihar to such an extent as not to be intelligible, to those to whom Sâkya and his successors addressed themselves. The language of the inscriptions, then, although necessarily that of their date, and probably that in which the first propagators of Buddhism expounded their doctrines, seems to have been rather the spoken language of the people in Upper India than a form of speech peculiar to a class of religionists, or a sacred language, and its use in the edicts of Piyadasi, although not incompatible with their Buddhist origin, cannot be accepted as a conclusive proof that they originated from any peculiar form of religious belief."

James Prinsep had already noticed the "marked difference" between the dialects of the Girnar and Dhauli versions of the edicts.[1] "In the former, he says:—

"We find *bhavati, asti* = 'is'; *anusati* = 'command,' * * following closely upon the Sanskrit etymology; whereas in the latter we have *hoti, athi, anusathi*, as in the modern Pâli.

"The dialect of Girnar, then, is intermediate between Sanskrit and Pâli, or rather the pillar idiom; for Pâli, so called, agrees in some respects better with one, in some with other, and in orthography decidedly with neither! Thus the word *idha*, used at Girnar for *iha*, 'here,' is correctly the Pâli term, as may be seen in the long quotation about the erection of a stûpa in Ceylon inserted in last month's Journal.

"The corresponding word in the eastern dialect is curiously modified to *hida*—a fact I only ascertained by the collation of the two texts, and one which at once opens an important discovery to aid our studies. In several of the Dhauli inscriptions the expressions *hidalokika, paralokika, hidaloka, paraloka*, occur; at Girnar (13th tablet) we have also *ilokiká, paralokiká cha:* all these are evidently *ihalokiká, páralokikácha*—'of this world and of the next world.' Now, the opening of the pillar inscription which so much perplexed us has the same elements *hidata pálata*—*iha para* or *ihatoparatah*, 'here and hereafter' a sense which at once renders the passage intelligible. The same may be said of *hidatakaye pálatakaye* in the north compartment.

"The eastern dialect is remarkable for this species of cockneyism, which, as far as I know, has no parallel in any of the grammatical Prâkrits: thus the *h* is inserted before *evam (hevam), idam* and some other words beginning with vowels.

"On the other hand (but this is also a cockneyism) the semivowel *y* is cut off in many words, such as *athá, adá, ata, am*, which are correctly spelt at Girnar,—*yathá, yadá, yatá*, (S. *yatra*) and *yam*. In these instances the pillar language is remotest from the Sanskrit. There is a singular exception, however, in the feminine pronoun *iyam*, which is preserved throughout at Dhauli and on the pillars;

[1] Journal of the Bengal Asiatic Society, VII, 277, 281.

whereas at Girnar, *ayam* is made both masculine and feminine, as in modern (or rather written) Pâli.

"There cannot be a better test of the gradual change of language than the word *prati*, a prefix in Sanskrit extensively used, implying relation, direction, or return. In the Pâli of Girnar this is merely altered to *pati*, by omission of the *r*. In the language of the pillars the same preposition is always written *paṭi*, with the cerebral *ṭ*. The orthography varies in the written Pâli of books, being in Ceylonese *paṭi*, in Burmese *pati;* while in Prâkrit, the rules of which generally change the hard to soft consonants, *t* to *d*, *ṭ* to *ḍ*, the word is written *padi* as *padihâissati* for *pratikhyâsyati*, &c.; and perhaps we may recognise a final change into *par* in the modern Hindi,—for instance, in *paros* from *prativesa*, vicinity, and other words.

"Substantives suffer modifications not so great in extent, but equally remarkable, and significant of gradual corruption.

"The word *man* may serve as an example:—Sans. *manushyas*; at Girnar *manuso;* at Dhauli and on the pillars *munise;* Pâli *manusso;* Prâkrit—(?Bháka,) *mánus*. Again, the Sanskrit *purushas* is made at Girnar *puruso* (?); at Dhauli, *pulise*; Pâli, *puriso* or *poso;* Prâkrit *puriso*. In modern dialects it is only used as a Sanskrit word.

"Of the changes undergone by the verbs, a good example may be selected in the substantive verbs, *bhu*, *bhavati*, 'be;' which is found unimpaired in several instances at Girnar, though never so on the pillars; *hoti*, the Pâli form, sometimes takes its place in the Girnar tablets,—always on the pillars. The Prâkrit changes this to *hodi*, whence it is further softened to *hai* and *hœ* in the modern dialects.

"*Asti* and *násti* (Sanskrit *asti* and *nasti*) are also retained in the original form at Girnar: at Dhauli they became *athi* and *nathi;* whereas in Pâli they are converted into *auhi* and *nauhi*. The future passive participle terminates as the Sanskrit in *tavya* at Girnar, and *taviya* at Dhauli; while Pâli makes it *tabba*, Prâkrit *dabba;* and the form is altogether lost in the modern *bhâshas*. This gradual transition is well marked in the verb *kri;* 'do':—Sans. *karttavyam;* Girnar *katavyam;* Katak *kataviyam*; Pâli *katavvam;* Prâk. *kadabbam*.

"In writing many Sanskrit words in which the *sth* or *st* dental, or cerebral, are required, a curious rule is adopted at Girnar of representing them by a cerebral *ṭ* with the *s* subjoined, as *tisṭeyâ* for *tishteyât* "may remain" *anusaṭi* for *anusasti*, *adhisṭâna* for *adhisthan*. In all these the lowermost consonant is pronounced first.

"Another similar anomaly is remarked in the mode of writing *vy* in *vyâptâ* (S. *vayâpta*); *katavyam*, *karttavyam*, &c., the *v* being placed below the *y*, whereas on the pillars (where the double consonant is employed at all) it is correctly written *vy*. The word *Bâmhana*, *Brahmana*, is written with the *h* below; it may, therefore, on the above principle, be read with the *h* first, *bahmana* as nearer to the Sanskrit. At Dhauli this word is invariably written *bâbhana*. In modern Pâli it is written *brâhmano* with the dental *n*.

"In the inflexion of the seventh case we have at Girnar often *mhi* (hmi); at Dhauli *msi* or *si*. These correspond, of course, with Sanskrit *smin* in *asmin*, &c., and all forms are allowed in the facile grammar of the written Pâli, along with the regular locative in *e*. It is impossible not to recognise the Hindi postposition *men* in the Girnar form of the locative case.

"The conjunctive *va* seems to be used for 'and' as frequently as *vá* for 'or.' It is the Persian conjunction, and is used in written Hindi, though seldom in the spoken tongue; *aur* the pandit pointed out in one place written *âro*, but I doubt the reading.

"A great many other instances might be cited to prove that the language of Girnar is not precisely either pure Sanskrit or the pure Pâli of books; but as the Buddhist volumes of Ceylon are acknowledged to be posterior by 450 years to the death of Sâkya, his tenets having been first reduced to writing in Ceylon, about ninety years before Christ, some change may be allowed to have taken place in the meantime, and we may presume that the Girnar inscriptions represent the Pâli (or vulgar) tongue, as it was in the time of Asoka on the west of India, as the pillars show it to us as it was pronounced on the east, or in Magâdha proper. Now, it is curious enough that some of the distinguishing traits of the pillar dialect are just such as are pointed out by the grammarians of a later day as constituting the differences between Mâgadhî and Pâli—names, it must be remembered, which are indifferently employed in Ceylon, Ava, Siam, and even China, to express the sacred language of the Buddhists. Thus, quoting from M.M. Lassen and Burnouf's Essai sur le Pâli, p. 156,—'*Ra* devient *la* en Mâgadhî; *poulise*, Pali *pouriso*. Ce changement a quelque fois lieu en Prâkrit jamais en Pâli'—and again in the next paragraph,—'en Mâgadhî le nominatif singulier est en *e* (which takes the place of *visarga*) tandis qu'en Pâli il est terminé en *o*.' The use of *o* in lieu of *e* for the masculine nominative is general, but not universal in the text before us. The conclusion to which the same savans were led at that early period of their studies may now require a slight modification.

"Une comparaison attentive du Prâkrit et du Pâli nous a conduit á cette conclusion :—

"1. Qu il existe, entre ces deux dialectes, une ressemblance telle qu'an peut avancer qu'ils sont presque identiques;

"2. Que le Prâkrit altère plus le Sanskrit que ne le fait le Pâli, et qu'il offre en quelque sorte, le second dégré d'alteration, comme le Pâli en est le premier et le plus immédiat. *Essai sur le Pâli*, 15.

"The second position is quite true, and it has been fully developed in a recent work (Institutiones Prâkriticæ) by Professor Lassen, which should be in the hands of every Indian philologist.

"The position assumed by M. Lassen, that the Pâli of Ceylon was immediately derived from the shores of Kalinga, independently of its being matter of history, is supported by the evidence of the records now discovered in the country. Yet it must be confessed that in some respects there is a nearer connection with the dialect of Gujarât, and it is not unnatural to suppose that a maritime intercourse also prevailed at a very early period between the western emporia of Surashtra and Tambapanni, the island so fruitful in aromatics, which would lead to an intercommunion of those professing the same faith in the two countries.

"The vernacular language of India at that period, then, varied in different provinces it approached more to the Sanskrit in the north-west; diverged from it in Magâdha and Kalinga; but it was in both places essentially what is now called Pâli, a word supposed to be derived from *palli*, a village; as we should now-a-days distinguish *gaonwâri*, villager, boorish, from *ûrdû*, the language of the Court. There is no trace of genuine Prâkrit in either of the dialects, and we may, therefore, agree with Professor Lassen that the *patois* of the dramas was not used until three or four centuries later. The grammarians who subsequently framed the rules of this corrupted idiom cease to mention Pâli at all—a proof that it had already been banished the country along with the Buddhist religion; while the Maâgadhî, by them set down as nearly the lowest of jargons, is evidently quite different from the inferior language of the pillars and the Katak inscriptions."

III. ALPHABETICAL CHARACTERS.

The inscriptions of Asoka are engraved in two distinct characters,—one reading from right to left, which is confined to the Shâhbâz-garhi version, and also found on the coins of the Greek and Indo-Scythian Princes of Ariana; and the other reading from left to right, which is confined to the coins of Pantaleon and Agathokles, who reigned beyond the Indus, but which is the common character of all the other texts of the inscriptions, as well as of all the donative inscriptions of the Sânchi and Bharhut Stûpas. The former has been called *Ariano-Pali*, and the latter *Indo-Pâli*, from the countries in which they were principally used.

The *Ariano-Pâli* alphabet, as seen in the Shâhbâz-garhi inscription as well as on the coins, comprises all the letters of the Indo-Pâli alphabet. But that this was not the case originally is clear from the fact that, while the hard aspirates *kh, chh, th,* and *ph* are distinct characters, independent of the forms of the non-aspirated letters *k, ch, t,* and *p,* the soft aspirates *gh, dh,* and *bh* are simply the letters *g, d,* and *b,* with the aspirate letter *h* attached to the right. The very same peculiarity is noticeable in the Tibetan alphabet, which was also originally wanting in the aspirated tenues. The Tibetan language did not require them, and accordingly, when the Nâgari alphabet of India was adopted by the Tibetans, the soft aspirates were omitted. But afterwards when it was found necessary to express numbers of Sanskrit words and Indian names in which these letters occur, new compound forms were invented by simply adding the aspirate to each of the unaspirated letters.

Similarly, the series of cerebral letters, which was also wanting originally in Tibetan, was afterwards supplied by the invention of new letters, which are simply the five dental letters reversed. This is not exactly the case with the cerebral letters of the Ariano-Pâli alphabet, but their forms differ so slightly from those of the dentals, that it seems highly probable they must have been a late addition to the original alphabetical scheme.

In *Indian-Pâli* such compound forms as *sp, sw, st,* and *sr* were altered either by the suppression of one of the two consonants, or by their separation into two syllables. We thus have *asa* for *aswa, nâthi* for *nâsti,* and *siri* for *sri.* But in *Arian-Pâli,* which abounds with such names as Hystaspes, Zariaspes, Haustanes, Spitamenes, &c., compound letters were invented to represent the *sp* and *st* and *sr,* and thus we find the words *aspa* and *asti* and *sramana* in their regular forms. The *r* was attached to the right foot of each letter, as in *priya,* which occurs so often in the Asoka edicts. But as the same stroke is attached to the right foot of *dh* in *dharma*, and to the right foot of *d* in *darsi*, it seems probable that in the Shâhbâz-garhi text, at least, the compound letters may have possessed the double sounds of *dhra* and *dhar*, *dra* and *dar;* otherwise we must read *dhrama* and *drasi.*

At what time this alphabet was invented, or whence it was derived, nothing certain is known. The subject has been discussed by Mr. Thomas, who concludes that it has no claim whatever to an indigenous origin, "based, as it manifestly is, upon an alphabet cognate with the Phœnician."[1]

Some of the more prominent letters are common to both alphabets. And the differences in others may, he thinks, have been developed by "the insertion of medial vowels in the body of the covering consonant"—a scheme which he justly believes to have been adopted from the Pâli alphabet of India, as it is quite unknown to Western caligraphy.

But the Ariano-Pâli vowel scheme differs from that of India in having only one set of vowels, as no distinction has yet been discovered between the short and long vowels, unless perhaps a dot or short return at the left foot may be taken for the long *ā*. The initial vowels are formed exactly in the same manner as the medial vowels, the same straight strokes being added to the primitive stem, or short *a*, to form the vowels *i*, *u*, *e*, and *o*. The letter *r* and the vowel *n* are also attached to the vowels after the same manner as to the consonants.

The use of this peculiar alphabet would appear to have been originally confined to Ariana, or the countries lying to the west of the Indus between India and Persia. The earliest known specimens of the writing are the edicts of Asoka at Shâhbâz-garhi and the rare coin of Agathokles, of which only three specimens are known to me. The former cannot be older than the 12th year of Asoka, or B. C. 251, and the latter must be of nearly the same date, or about B. C. 240. But as the alphabet is here seen in its full development with all the soft aspirates and cerebral letters complete, it must have been in use for some considerable time previously. The date of this development I would assign to the end of the 4th century B. C., when the provinces to the west of the Indus were ceded to Chandra Gupta by Seleukos Nikator, and thus came directly under the influence of Indian learning, which necessitated the adoption of some additional letters to express new Indian sounds. This alphabet continued in use during the whole period of Greek supremacy, and under the Indo-Scythian princes it was carried to the eastward of the Sutlej, an inscription of Kanishka in this character having been found in a Buddhist Stûpa near Bahâ-walpur. About the end of the first century A. D. it would appear to have fallen into disuse, as all the gold coins which may be assigned to the second century bear Indian letters only. The latest dated record yet made known is my inscription from Panjtâr, which bears the *Samvat* year 122.[2] If this be the so-called Vikramâditya Samvat, as I believe it is, it will refer to the year A. D. 65; but if it be the Saka era, the date will be exactly A. D. 200.

Three different specimens of the Ariano-Pâli alphabet are given in the accompanying plate:[3] *1st*, from Asoka's edicts at Shâhbâz-garhi, which date as early as B. C. 252; *2nd*, from the coins of the Greek princes of Ariana and India, which range

[1] Numismatic Chronicle, New Series, III, 229.
[2] See Archæological Survey of India, Vol. V, p. 61.
[3] See Plate XXVI.

from B. C. 210 to 120; and 3*rd*, from the coins and inscriptions of the Indo-Scythian princes, the Sacæ and Tochari, which range from B. C. 120 down to A. D. 79.

The *Indo-Páli* alphabet differs from that of Ariana in two very important particulars,—1*st*, in being read from left to right; and 2*nd*, in being formed exclusively either of rigid straight lines or of portions of circles. Owing to the latter peculiarity, it has never been found in a cursive form, into which indeed it was hardly possible to force its inflexible elements.

Three specimens of this alphabet are given in the accompanying plate;[1] 1*st*, from the edicts of Asoka and Dasaratha on rocks and pillars, which range from B. C. 252 to 218, and from the few native Hindu coins which belong to the same period; 2*nd*, from the coins of the native princes contemporary with the later Greeks and earlier Indo-Scythians, which may range from B. C. 150 to 57; and 3*rd*, from the Mathura inscriptions of the Indo-Scythian princes, Kanishka, Huvishka Vasu-deva, and others, which range from B. C. 57 to A. D. 79.

The letters of the Indo-Pâli alphabet have become pretty well known through James Prinsep's writings. The whole of the consonants were discovered by him, with the exception of the guttural nasal *ng*, which has not yet been found, and the two sibilants *s* and *sh*. One of these I have since discovered in the Khâlsi version of the edicts, where it is several times correctly used, in the word *pâshanda*, instead of the dental sibilant *s*. Its form is not unlike that of the Ariano-Pâli *sh*, from which it *may* have been derived, although it seems to me equally probable that the Indian letter was the original form.

The vowels also were discovered by Prinsep, excepting only the initial *o*, which he took to be a long *ū*, and for which he proposed a new form derived from the later Gupta alphabet. It is strange that the true value of the letter did not strike him, as it is the only initial which remains absolutely unchanged as a medial. It has two distinct forms, of which the later is only the earlier one reversed, both as an initial and as a medial. The earlier form consists of a perpendicular stroke with a horizontal stroke on each side, one at the top and one at the foot. In the earlier form the upper stroke is on the left hand and the lower stroke on the right. This was the letter which James Prinsep took for the initial long *u*. The latter form is found in the additional edicts of Dhauli and Jaugada, and in the later edicts on the Allahabad pillar. The initial long â is of frequent occurrence, but no other initial long vowel has yet been found in Asoka's inscriptions. The initial diphthong *ai* occurs in *Aira* Raja's inscriptions, unless the name is to be read as *Vera*. The medial long vowels *ā*, *i*, *ū*, are common; but no examples of medial *a* or *au* are at present known. The *anuswára* is frequently used, either for the duplication of *m*, as in *dhamma*, or as a substitute for the guttural nasal *ng*, as in modern Hindi. The question of the probable origin of this Indian alphabet has been very ably discussed by Mr. Thomas, who concludes that it is "an independently devised and locally matured scheme of writing." He adds that the Indian Pâli alphabet possesses

"in an eminent degree the merit of simplicity combined with extended distinctive capabilities and remarkable facility of lection, and that its construction exhibits not only a definite purpose

---

[1] See Plate XXVI.

throughout, but indicates, moreover, a high order of intellectual culture on the part of its designers, who discriminated by appropriate letters gradations of sound, often inappreciable to European ears, and seldom susceptible of correct utterance by European organs of speech." [1]

Mr. Thomas adverts more pointedly to the independent origin of the Indo-Pâli alphabet, because, as he explains,

"a tendency exists in many cultivated minds to depreciate the originality and antiquity of Indian "civilisation."

And he quotes the facts that Professor Max-Müller

"will not admit that the Indians acquired the art of writing till a comparatively late period;"

that Dr. J. Wilson of Bombay

"asserts that Asoka's Buddhists derived their letters from Greek and Phœnician models,"

while Dr. Weber affirms that they

"are emanations from a Phœnician stock."

Upwards of twenty years have now passed since I came to the same conclusion which Mr. Thomas has thus boldly advanced,—namely, that the Indian-Pâli alphabet was a perfectly independent invention of the people of India. My opinion was formed after a careful comparison of all the characters with the pictorial representations of simple objects of which many of the letters represent either the whole name or the first syllable of the name.

The first attempts of mankind at graphic representation must have been confined to pictures, or direct imitations of actual objects. This was the case with the Mexican paintings, which depicted only such material objects as could be seen by the eye. An improvement on direct pictorial representation was made by the ancient Egyptians in the substitution of a part for the whole, as of a human head for a man, a bird's head for a bird, &c. This system was still further extended by giving to certain pictures indirect values or powers, symbolical of the objects represented. Thus a jackal was made the type of cunning, and an ape the type of rage. By a still farther application of this abbreviated symbolism a pair of human arms with spear and shield denoted fighting, a pair of human legs meant walking, while a hoe was the type of digging, an eye of seeing, &c. But even with this poetical addition the means of expressing thoughts and ideas by pictorial representations was still very limited. For, as each picture could convey only one idea, the number of separate pictures requisite to form an intelligible story must have been very great. The difficulty also of remembering the precise application of so many different symbols and of discriminating an actual vulture or other animal from a symbolical one must have been felt very early, as the oldest specimens that we possess of Egyptian writing on the monuments of Sephuris and Soris, of the third and fourth dynasties, are not pictorial, but phonetic. It seems certain, therefore, that at a very early date the practice of pure picture writing must have been found so complicated and inconvenient that the necessity for a simpler mode of expressing their ideas was forced upon the Egyptian priesthood. The plan which they invented was highly ingenious, though somewhat cumbrous; and as it seems probable that the Indians might have gone through a similar process, a brief account of it will not be out of place.

---

[1] Numismatic Chronicle, new series,—"On the Bactrian alphabet."

To the greater number of their pictorial symbols the Egyptians assigned the phonetic values of the particular sounds or names, of which each symbol previously had been only a simple picture. Thus to a mouth, *ru*, they assigned the value of *r*, and to a hand, *tut*, the value of *t*. But as each of the symbols still possessed an inherent vowel sound, the system was one of complete syllables, or a syllabary, and not one of simple letters, or an alphabet. Occasionally the vowels were separated from the consonants, as when *mu*, a hole, was represented by a "boatstand," *m* followed by an outstretched arm, or *u*. Had this plan of separating the vowels been generally adopted, it must soon have led to a complete alphabetical system, but, like the first possessor of the *Koh-i-nûr*, the Egyptian had a treasure within his grasp, without knowing its value.

A similar process would appear to have taken place in India, as I will presently attempt to show by a separate examination of the alphabetical letters of Asoka's age with the pictures of various objects from which I believe them to have been directly descended. I have neither time nor space at present to attempt to complete, nor even to continue, this curious investigation. But, perhaps, a few of the more prominent examples which I will presently bring forward will be sufficient to arrest the attention, even if they do not lead to the conviction, of many of my readers. My own conclusion is that the Indian alphabet is of purely Indian origin, just as much as the Egyptian hieroglyphics were the purely local invention of the people of Egypt. The only alternative that I can see to this conclusion is that the Indians must first have borrowed the plan of their system from the Egyptians, and afterwards have concealed the loan by adapting the different symbols to their own native words. But as this would have entailed a complete change in the values of all the symbols, I must confess that such an alternative seems to me to be very improbable. I admit that several of the letters have almost exactly the same *forms* as those which are found amongst the Egyptian hieroglyphics for the same things, but their *values* are quite different, as they form different syllables in the two languages. Thus a pair of legs separated as in walking was the Egyptian symbol for walking or motion, and the same form, like the two sides of a pair of compasses, is the Indian letter *g*, which as *ga* is the commonest of all the Sanskrit roots for walking, or motion of any kind. But the value of the Egyptian symbol is *s*; and I contend that if the symbol had been *borrowed* by the Indians, it would have retained its original value. This, indeed, is the very thing that happened with the Accadian Cuneiform symbols when they were adopted by the Assyrians. The original symbols retained their *power* as syllables, but lost their *value* as pictorial representations of things on being transferred to a different language.

The present arrangement of the Indian alphabet is the only one known to the grammarians. It was certainly in use before the Christian era, as the Lalita Vistara, in recording that the youthful Buddha was taught the Indian alphabet, arranges the letters in their present order. But this artificial division of the letters into classes of gutturals, palatals, &c., must have been preceded by some much simpler grouping of the letters. Perhaps the simplest arrangement that could be made would have been according to similarity of form. For, if I am right as to the local development of the alphabet from original pictorial representations of things, it would follow as a matter of course that objects of somewhat similar shape would be represented by symbols more or less alike. And if any attempt had been made to classify the different symbols, I think that the most obvious and natural arrangement would have been that of similitude of shape. As any arrangement is better than none at all, I have adopted this grouping of the letters in the accompanying plate. I have also ventured to name each group after that member of the human body which seems to me to have suggested the original picture or ideograph. At first the figures would have been more or less rude representations of the different members. But these would gradually have given way to simpler forms, until each symbol acquired a separate phonetic value, and thus became a distinct syllable. At this point the Chinese have stopped; but in India the syllables must have given way very early to the more convenient system of alphabetic letters that is now in use.

GROUP 1.—*Kh*, *G*.—ARMS AND LEGS.

This group comprises only two lettters, *kh* and *g*, of which the former would seem to represent the action of the human arms, and the latter the action of the legs. Both have concave or hollow forms in the Asoka alphabet, which, as they represented different kinds of action, would necessarily be distinguished by some slight difference of shape. Thus the *g* is either a half circle, or a parabola, or an angle formed by the two sides of an isosceles triangle, while the *kh* has the left limb about one-half the length of the right one.

Kh.—The form of this letter appears to me to have been derived from that of the common Indian *hoe* or *mattock*, which has been used by the people from time immemorial for *digging* their fields. Now, the radical word for this operation is *khan*, " to dig;" and as the original mattock was made of a natural knee-joint of *Khayar* or *Khadir* wood, it would seem that this tree (*Mimosa catechu*) may have been so named from the purpose to which it was applied as the " digging-wood." In some parts where the *Khayar* is easily procurable, the mattock is still made in the ancient fashion of wood alone, but in most places the instrument now in use is an angle joint of *Khayar*, or other strong wood, shod with a small iron blade. One of these is represented in the accompanying plate.[1] The letter is therefore a symbol of the arm's action in the characteristic form of digging.

Now, the Indian letter is only a simplified form of the picture of the mattock, a variety of which is known amongst Egyptologists as the " hand-plough." But as the hieroglyphic value of the symbol is *m*, I infer that the Indian letter *kh* must have been an independent local invention of the Indian people.

There are other objects whose forms seem to point to a close connection with the old shape of the *kh*. These are, *kha*, vacuity, or the sky, that is, the hollow vault of heaven, the Greek *koilos* and the Latin *cœlum;* *kharga*, the rhinoceros,

---

[1] See Plate XXVIII.

from the curved tip of his horn, and also a scymitar with a similar curved point; *khuri*, a hoop, to which may be added *khola*, open, and *khokhra* or *khokhla*, hollow.[1]

G.—The form of this letter would seem to have been derived from a pair of human legs separated as in the action of walking, or simple *motion*, as distinguished from the numerous forms of action displayed by the arms. Now, the radical word for motion is *gam*, to go. Hence *Gangâ*, which designates a river in general, means simply "*go-go*," or the "*goer*;" similarly, *gagan*, "the sky," which appears to turn round both day and night, has precisely the same meaning. Hence, most probably, sprang the legend of the descent of the River Ganga from the sky.

Now, the Indian letter G of Asoka's alphabet is a simpler form of the Egyptian "pair of legs" with feet attached, which, according to Birch, had the value of *t*, and meant "walking or running." A second hieroglyphic, with a flat top and two straight sides, is used to represent the "sky or heavens." But this is only a variety of the other form, and serves all the more forcibly to prove the correctness of the origin which I have suggested for the form of the Indian letter.

Several other names seem to have a direct reference to the shape of this letter; but a single illustration will, perhaps, be sufficient. Thus the words *guha* and *gupha* both signify "a cave," which the Egyptians represented by three sides of a square, open at the bottom. But this hieroglyph had the power of *b*, from *beb*, a "cave." Here, again, we have another illustration of the independent origin of the Indian symbols, as the same forms have different values, although they represent the same things.

GROUP 2.—*Y, J, Ch, Chh*—MONS VENERIS, OR VULVA.

In this group the letters *Y* and *J* have the same forms, the latter being simply turned sideways. The character in the Asoka alphabet is clearly intended for a representation of the *mons veneris*, in proof of which I may cite the similar form of the Egyptian hieroglyph for the same member, as well as its common Indian names *yoni* and *jaghan*.

Y, J.—The Asoka forms of these letters are both open, but there seems reason to suspect that the original symbol may have been a pictorial representation of a grain of barley, *ya* or *yava*, which is divided into two parts by a perpendicular line. But as the two parts form one whole, this symbol was used to denote union, as in the radicals *ya*, union, and *ya*, "*mons veneris*," from which sprang *yuga*, a "yoke or pair," the Latin *jugun*, and Hindi *jora*. The peculiar small circle or dot in the middle of the Asoka J seems to be directly referred to in the term *netra-yoni*, one of the epithets of the moon. This means simply the "eye of the *yoni*," which really is in the symbol, and is supposed to refer to the shape of the spots on the moon, to account for which was invented the legend of Soma attempting to debauch the wife of the sage Gautama. The name of *Juno*, the goddess of the moon, must be con-

[1] I have purposely included several Hindi words, as their use in India is at least as old as that of Sanskrit.

nected with the Indian *jun*, and with *junhaiya*, the "moon or moonlight," as well as with the Latin *jubâr*. I presume also that the Sanskrit terms *yosha* and *josha* for "woman" were derived from the root *ya* or *yoni*, as the symbol of the female sex. The Tibetan *cho-mo* or *cho*, a "woman," is perhaps connected with the same root.

Ch, Chh.—As the two letters *Y* and *J* signified the *union* or *junction* of the two halves of the symbol, so the letters *Ch* and *Chh* would seem to have referred to the *division* or *separation* of the two parts, as the words *chîr* and *chhed* are the roots for "slit, split, divide, &c." From the first of these were derived the terms *chirâ-vali* and *chirâband*, a "maiden;" and from the other several terms connected with the female sex. Such words as *chamas* or *chamcha* a "spoon or ladle," *chhurika*, the "nostrils," *chhatra*, an "umbrella or mushroom," *chappu*, a "paddle or oar," and *châk*, the "potter's wheel," all point to the forms of the Asoka letters *ch* and *chh*, as striking pictorial representations of their particular forms. The resemblance to the *ladle* and *oar* is specially striking in India, where the former is often made of a half gourd or cocoanut with a stick fastened across it, while the latter is formed of a round flat piece of wood with the bambu handle fastened down the middle of it.

Group 3.—*Ṭ, Ṭh, Th—Dh*—Eye.

Th.—The most obvious representation of the eye would be a circle, either with or without a dot in the centre. The former is the cerebral *th*, the latter the dental *th*, of the Asoka alphabet. The symbol, therefore, would represent roundness in general, and accordingly the cerebral *tha*, or simple circle, is a radical name for the disc of the sun, as well as for a circle, while the dental *tha* with a dot in the middle is one of the names for the eye. The similarity between the human eye and the sun in heaven is so striking, that it has been made use of by the poets from the time of the Vedas down to Lord Byron.[1] In the Egyptian hieroglyphs a circle with a dot in the middle represented the sun, according to Clemens of Alexandria.

There is a direct connection between the Asoka forms of the cerebral and dental *th*, and the round flat iron *thâwâ*, or cooking "girdle," and the *thâli*, or "low circular wall," which is built around a young tree. Here the dot in the middle represents the tree, and the pictorial symbol is perfect. I presume that *Thakkur*, a god, was derived from *ṭha*, the "sun."

Ṭ, Dh.—The cerebral *ṭ* in the Asoka alphabet is an open semi-circle, and the dental *dh* a semi-circle closed by the diameter. These I take to be pictorial representations of a *ṭokra*, or "basket," and of a *dhanu*, or "bow." In the Egyptian hieroglyphs the basket is represented by the latter symbol with the value of *n* from *neb*, a basket. Here, again, the pictorial symbol of the object is the same in India as in Egypt, but as the phonetic value is different, the Indian form must have been arrived at by an independent process.

---

[1] Rig-Veda, Vol. IV, p. 138; Wilson's translation, "the eye of all." Compare Byron's "eye of the universe" in *Manfred*.

D.—As the probable origin of the letter *d* was the pictorial representation of a tooth, *danta*, this might have been at first a mere half circle like the *dh*, which was afterwards altered to the Asoka form by pointing the curved line and breaking the diameter or straight line into two short lines attached to the ends of the curve. But this is a mere suggestion which I put forward with much diffidence.

Another illustration of the pictorial form of the Asoka letter *dh* may be seen in the female breast, *dharana*, from the root *dhri*, to "support, hold," &c. From the same root come the terms *dhrá*, *dharani*, and *dhátri* for the "earth;" and as these also signify "mother," they may be compared with the *Demeter* or "mother earth" of the Greeks.

GROUP 4.—*P*, *B*—HAND *and* FOOT.

The characteristic form of this group is a square, the P having the shape of three sides of a square open at the top, while the B is a complete square.

P.—The radical words connected with this letter are *páni* the hand, and *pad*, the foot, with which are naturally connected the number "five" or *pancha*. The original pictorial representation was no doubt a "hand," with the five fingers pointed upwards. In course of time the three middle bars would have been omitted, leaving the symbol in the exact form of the Asoka letter. In its original shape it perhaps also represented the "ribs," *parsu*, which are pictured by a similar symbol in the Egyptian hieroglyphs, but with the totally different value of *sh* In the latter form, with the middle bars omitted, the Asoka letter has a fair pictorial representation of a "pair of wings," *paksha*, as well as of a "flower," *pushpa*, and more especially of the act of "worship or adoration," *pujá*, in holding up the outstretched arms towards heaven. This very form was in fact used by the Egyptians as their hieroglyph for "adoration," with the hands raised in worship. But the value of the Egyptian symbol was *K*, so that the Indian form could not have been borrowed from Egypt, but must have been reached by an independent local process.

B.—The verbal roots connected with this letter are *bás*, a "house," *bári*, a "window," *bári*, a "garden" or courtyard, and *berra*, a "boat," all of which are of a square or oblong shape. The last is a Panjâbi term for a flat-bottomed boat, with square prow and square stern. In the Egyptian hieroglyphs, the square or oblong represents a water tank, with the power of *sh*; or, with a small opening like a door, it represents a house with the power of *e*, both values being totally distinct from that of the Indian letter.

GROUP 5.—*M*—MOUTH.

The characteristic of this letter is a curved oblong form representing the mouth, which is found in exactly the same shape in the Egyptian hieroglyphs. But in Egypt the symbol had the value of *r*, from the term *ru*, a mouth. Perhaps the original Indian form may have had two short diverging lines attached on the top to represent moustaches, so that the symbol would then have been but slightly different from the Asoka shape of the letter. With this addition the suggested old Indian form would have been a very good pictorial representation of a "fish;" *matsya*, of an oblong bead; *mankâ*, of a *mangus* or ichneumon, of a *makara*, or crocodile, as well as of a *músa*, or mouse. Amongst the Egyptian hieroglyphs there is a similar form,—namely, an oblong with a fan-shaped top, but this is a picture of the eye with its upper lid or eyebrow.

Group 6.—*T, V, N, K, R*—Nose.

The grouping together of so many apparently different letters may, perhaps, be thought rather arbitrary. But they appear to me to have the common *tie* of general similitude, as each character consists of an upright straight line, with a swell or extension at bottom, somewhat similar to the expansion of the human nostrils from the upright ridge of the nose. Perhaps the original form of some, if not of all, of these characters was a wedge or acutely-pointed triangle expanding at the base.

T.—The characteristic root of this letter is the word *tan*, to "spread," or "stretch," which is preserved in the Greek *teinô*, *tanumi*, and in the Latin *tendo* and *tenuis*, which last is the same as the Sanskrit *tanu*, "thin." Regarding the origin of the symbol, I can only suggest that it may have been derived from the hand with "outstretched" fingers, representing a "span" or *tâlah*, or from the "spreading" foliage of the *tâla* or "fan-palm." To this three-pointed form I would also refer the word *târa*, a "star," *tarang* a "wave," and *tri*, "three."

V.—The shape of this Asoka letter is an upright stroke with a small circle, at the bottom of which the most characteristic pictorial example is the *vînâ*, or Indian "lute." This instrument was also one of the Egyptian hieroglyphs, but its phonetic value was *n* from the Egyptian *nofre*, a "guitar." Perhaps the Indian symbol included all straight lines with a single knob at the end. If so, it would be connected with *va* and *vahu*, an "arm," *vena* and *vansa*, a "bambu," *vindee*, a drop of water, and *vân*, an "arrow."

N.—In the Asoka alphabet this letter is an upright stroke with a short straight stroke at bottom, of which I take the human nose to have been the original picture. The root *na* means the "nose" as well as the longer words *nak*, *nakat*, *nâsa*, &c., and the Latin *naso*. The common *nemi*, or wooden frame for the well-rope, seems to refer to the shape of the Asoka letter, as it usually consists of an upright timber let into a horizontal one below. Perhaps also *nâku*, a white-ant hill, derived its name from its "nosey" or pyramidal appearance.

K.—This letter in the alphabet of Asoka has no pictorial connection with the other gutturals *kh* and *g*, but seems rather to belong to the group of which I am now treating. Its form is an upright cross with even arms. But the pictorial forms which seem to be best suited to this shape are the "dagger," *ka* and *kattâr*, the "straight sword," *katti*, or the "cutter," *kuta*, a "peak," and *kîla*, a spike, all of which would seem to require the cross stroke nearer to the bottom of the letter. Perhaps *kîla*, flame, or lambent flame, refers to the narrow pyramidal shape of the original letter.

R.—In the Asoka alphabets this letter is either a simple upright straight stroke, or a slightly undulating upright line. But as the radical *ra* means "fire," it seems probable that the original form may have been a very thin wedge. This conjecture seems to be borne out by the word *rasmi*, a "sunbeam or ray of light." Other words, however, would seem to refer to a perfectly straight line, such as *rāji* and *rekhā*, a "line, row, ridge;" *rajju*, a "cord or rope;" *rana*, a "fiddlestick;" and *ratha*, a "cane or ratan." But, perhaps, the Greek *ris*, a "nose," is in favour of the suggestion that the original symbol may have been a simple wedge.

GROUP 7.—*L, H.*—LINGA *or* PHALLUS.

I have placed these two letters together on account of their exact similitude in the Asoka inscriptions. It is true that they face different ways, but they have precisely the same shape, and were most probably connected with each other in their original conception. The former I take to be a simplified pictorial representation of the *linga*, or male member, and the latter of the elephant's trunk. But the exact shape of both the Asoka letters *l* and *h* is that of a sickle, with the handle placed horizontally, and the point of the curved blade upwards. Now, it is a curious corroboration of the suggested original connection between these two letters that the common names for a sickle begin with *l* and *h*. These are *lavāka*, *lavanaka*, and *lavitra* from the Sanskrit *lu*, "to cut," and the Hindi *hansiya* and *hansüa*, which were probably so named from their resemblance to the form of a *hansa*, or goose.

L.—This letter monopolises most of the names in common use for the *phallus* or male member, such as *lar*, *lār*, *laur*, *lul*, *land*, *lāngal*, and *linga*. The names of other objects suggested by the shape of the letter are *langar*, an "anchor," and *lāngal*, a "plough." These words recal the old Sicilian *Dànklon* or *Zanklon*, a "sickle," which gave its name to the island of Zankle. And as all these names represent some *bent* object, it seems probable that the Indian term *ankus* for an "elephant goad" may have been originally *lankus*, as descriptive of its hooked form. Perhaps also the Greek *ankṓn*, *ankulḗ* and *ankura*, and the Latin *angulus*, may each have lost an initial *l* or other letter.

H.—The "hand," *hasta*, in the shape of the elephant's trunk, or *hasti*, is the characteristic form of this letter. The striking handiness of the animal's trunk suggested to Lucretius the well-known epithet of *anguimanus*.[1] I have already noticed that the letters *L* and *H* furnish separate names for the "sickle;" and I may now add for the "plough" also, as the Sanskrit *hala*, a plough, is the exact equivalent of the Hindi *lāngal*. The sickle is also one of the Egyptian hieroglyphs.

GROUP 8.—*S, Sh.*—*The* EAR.

The representatives of this class are the three sibilants, the palatal *s*, the cerebral *sh*, and the dental *s*. Now, the only member of man's body that has not been included in the previous summary is the *ear*. This has several names in Sanskrit, all

[1] De Rerum Natura, II, 538. Anguimanûs elephantos.

beginning with the palatal *s* as *srava*, *sruti*, and *srotra*, from the root *sru*, to "hear." But what is heard is "sound," or *sabda*, and the element that makes the most noise is "water," or *sár*. Hence we have *saras*, a "lake," and "*sarit*," a river, as well as *sarsarána*, to "ripple." I take the palatal *s* of Asoka's time to be a simple form of the original pictorial representation of the human ear. Its shape is that of a parabola with a vertical line, or a dot in the middle, the latter representing the *meatus auditorius*. As the cerebral *sh* is only the last letter reversed, and is not found in any of Asoka's inscriptions, it seems probable that it was the invention of a later date. As such its shape need not be discussed here.

The dental sibilant is formed of two undulations, one up and one down, with a short stroke attached at the top of the rise. The whole represents pictorially both a serpent with a single coil and a complete wave, with its hollow and its crest. Now, the radical word of this letter is *sa* or *sarpa*, a "serpent," which was probably the original picture of the symbol.

In my comparison of the characters of the ancient Indian alphabet with the pictorial forms of different objects, I have not thought it worth while to make any examination of the vowels for two reasons: *first*, because their shapes do not suggest any pictorial representatives; and *second*, because I believe them to be of a comparatively late date, that is, somewhat posterior to the formation of separate syllabic characters in which the vowel formed part of the complete syllable, and, therefore, of exactly the same age as the first alphabetic characters.

In devising the vowel marks I think it probable that an arbitrary system of simple strokes was adopted. At first these would seem to have been independent marks not attached to the consonants, as in the two examples on the black stone seal from Harapa which I have read as *a* and *i*.[1] At the foot of the accompanying plate I have given all these conjectural forms of the archaic vowels side by side with the Asoka vowels for the sake of easy comparison. Some of these forms appear to me to be almost certain, while the remainder are at least highly probable, if a similar system was followed in their formation.

In this brief examination of the letters of the old Indian alphabet, I have compared their forms at the time of Asoka, or B. C. 250, with the pictures of various objects and of the different members of the human frame; and the result of my examination is the conviction that many of the characters still preserved, even in their simpler alphabetical forms, very strong and marked traces of their pictorial origin. My comparison of the symbols with the Egyptian hieroglyphs shows that many of them are almost identical representations of the same objects. But as the Indian symbols have totally different values from those of Egypt, it seems almost certain that the Indians must have worked out their system quite independently, although they followed the same process. They did not, therefore, borrow their alphabet from the Egyptians. It is, of course, quite possible that the hint may have been taken from Egypt; but considering the distance and the difficulty of communication between the two countries in those early times, this does

---

[1] This will shortly be described and examined. See Plate XXVIII.

not seem very probable. Indeed, there is one very strong argument against it, which I think is almost, if not quite conclusive,—namely, that the Indians do not seem to have possessed any extended scheme of numerical notation before the time of Asoka, which they certainly would have had if they had borrowed their alphabet from Egypt, as I contend that they would have taken the Egyptian system of numerals at the same time.

Now, if the Indians did not borrow their alphabet from the Egyptians, it must have been the local invention of the people themselves, for the simple reason that there was no other people from whom they could have obtained it. Their nearest neighbours were the peoples of Ariana and Persia, of whom the former used a Semitic character of Phœnician origin reading from right to left, and the latter a cuneiform character formed of separate detached strokes, which has nothing whatever in common with the compact forms of the Indian alphabet.

But if the Indian alphabet was thus locally elaborated by the people themselves, it may be urged that some traces of its previous existence would ere this have been discovered, if not of its earlier stages of pictures and hieroglyphs, at least of its later stages of syllables and archaic letters. This would be a formidable objection if all our ancient sites had been already thoroughly explored. But as yet, except in a few places, we have but skimmed the surface, and gathered whatever was to be found above ground, while the older remains still lie buried beneath the soil. It is possible, also, that some specimens even of the earlier writings may have been found previously, and have been passed by as rude sculptures of little or no value. I have, however, come across one monument which I believe to be a specimen of the archaic alphabetical writing. Its age is, of course, quite uncertain, but I do not think its date can be later than 500 or 400 B. C. This monument is a seal of smooth black stone, which was found by Major Clark in the ruins of Harapâ in the Panjâb.[1] On it is engraved very deeply the figure of a bull without hump, looking to the right, with a symbol on its shoulder and a second symbol and a star under its neck. Above the bull there is an inscription of six unknown characters, which on first seeing I thought could not be Indian, but which I now think may be archaic Indian letters of as early an age as Buddha himself. Taking the characters from the left, the first may be an ancient form of the letter *l*, as it approaches very close to the shape of the Asoka character. The third seems to be an old form of *chh*, and the fourth a true archaic *m* in the shape of a fish, *matsya*. The fifth must be another vowel, perhaps *i*, and the sixth may be an old form of *y*. The whole would thus read *Lachhmiya*.

The chief difficulty about this reading is the detached position of the two sets of symbols read as vowels. But there does not seem to be any good reason why the vowels should not have been detached letters originally. The two short strokes which I have read as *i* are precisely the two strokes of the long attached *i* in the Asoka inscriptions, and the two long strokes read as *a* may easily have been the archaic form of the initial *â* of Asoka's inscriptions. This reading is, of course, merely tentative, and I only put it forward in the hope that others who are more com-

[1] See Archæological Survey of India, Vol. V, p. 108, and Plate XXX. fig. 1. See also Plate XXVIII of the present volume.

petent may be induced to take up the subject, and carry it through to some conclusive results which may be generally accepted.

In the meantime, I wish to bring to notice the fact that the well-known conventional signs for the five planets may be formed by merely adding a *star* to the radical letter of each of the five classes of the alphabetical letters of Asoka, while the sun and moon are the actual radical letters of the other two classes of the Indian alphabet without any change or other addition. I find it difficult to believe that this can be an accidental coincidence, but as I am not prepared to offer a complete explanation, all that I can do is to add a few notes pointing out the formation of each sign.[1]

1. *The Sun.*—This is represented by the Asoka *dental* aspirate *tha,* which is a circle with a dot in the middle. *Tha* is one of the Sanskrit names of the sun.

2. *The Moon.*—This is represented by the Asoka *palatal* letter *j,* which has the form of the lunar crescent with a small circle inside. This is called *netra yoni* or the "eye of the yoni," and is one of the Sanskrit names of the moon,—*Jun* is also a name of the moon.

3. *Mars.*—The sign of this planet is the Asoka semi-vowel *r,* compounded with a star or upright cross. *Ra* is the radical for *fire,* which is the element presided over by the regent of the planet.

4. *Mercury.*—The sign of this planet is the Asoka *labial* letter *m* with a star or cross attached below. *Marka* and *Marut* are Sanskrit names for the *wind,* the element presided over by the regent of the planet Mercury, whose Latin name seems to be connected with the Sanskrit word *marka.*

5. *Jupiter.*—The sign of this planet is the Asoka letter *kh* with a star added to the right foot—*kha* is the Sanskrit radical for "*ether or sky,*" the element presided over by the regent of the planet Jupiter, the god of the firmament.

6. *Venus.*—The sign of this planet is the Asoka *cerebral* letter *ṭha,* with a star attached below. *Tha* means the "cherisher or nourisher," and is an epithet of the *Earth,* who, as the general nourisher of all, may be identified with *Alma Venus* as well as with *Demeter.*

7. *Saturn.*—The sign of this planet is the Asoka palatal sibilant *S,* with a star added to the left top. *Sani* is the god of the *watery* element, of which the characteristic is "sound," in Sanskrit *sa* and *sabda.*

To those who may wish to pursue this subject further I may add that each of the planets had its appropriate colour, as well as its own particular metal and wood, of which alone the figure of the regent of the planet ought to be made, thus:—

Firstly.—The colour of the Sun was *yellow;* its appropriate metal *gold,* and its precious stone the yellow *diamond.*

Secondly.—The colour of the Moon was *white,* its appropriate metal *silver,* and its precious stone *rock crystal.*

Thirdly.—The colour of Mars was *green,* its appropriate metal *iron* (or cutting bronze) and its precious stones the *emerald* and the *blood-stone.*

---

[1] See Plate XXVIII, where the symbols are given along with the Asoka characters with which they correspond.

Fourthly.—The colour of Mercury was *black*, its appropriate metal was *quick-silver*, and its precious stones the *sparsamani*, or "touch-stone," and the "magnet," both of which are black.[1] It was the difficulty of procuring black wood that gave currency to the saying, *Non ex quovis ligno fiet Mercurius.*

Fifthly.—The colour of Jupiter was *grey*, its appropriate metal was *tin*, and its precious stones were the *opal* and the *chalcedony* or milk-stone.

Sixthly.—The colour of *Venus* was *red*, its appropriate metal was *copper*, and its precious stones were the *red cornelian* and the *amethyst*.

Seventhly.—The colour of *Saturn* was *blue*, its appropriate metal was *lead*, and its precious stone the *sapphire*, which was generally known as *Sani-priya*, or "Saturn's favourite,"—and *nilamani*, "the blue gem."

---

[1] *Sparsa* means the wind, and the "wind-stone" was, of course, dedicated to the regent of the air. It is now called *Páras*.

TEXTS.

ROCK INSCRIPTIONS OF ASOKA

AT

SHÂHBÂZGARHI, KHÂLSI, GIRNÂR, DHAULI, AND JAUGADA.

EDICT I.

S	Ayam	dharmalipi	[	*omitted*	]	Devanampriyasa	* * *
K	Iyam	dhammalipi	[	*do.*	]	Devânampiyena	Piyadasinâ
G	Iyam	dhammalipi	[	*do.*	]	Devânampiyena	Piyadasinâ
D	* *	dha * *	* * * * *si	pavatasi		Devânampiye *	* * *
J	Iyam	dhammalipi	Khepingalasi	pavatasi		Devanampiyena	Piyadasinâ

S	Ranyo	likhapi .	Hidam	lo ke *	jiva.	* * *	* * *
K	* *	lekhapi .	Hida	no kichhi	jive.	âlabhitu	paja
G	Ranyâ	lekhapitâ .	Idha	na kinchi	jîvam	ârabhidâ	paju
D	Lajo	* * *	* *	* * *	* vam	âlabhitu	pajapa
J	Lajina	likhâpitâ .	Hida	no kichhi	jîvam.	âlabhiti	pajâ

S	* * *	cha pi *	sama*	* * *	* * *	* *
K	hitaviye	[2]no pi cha	samâje.	kaṭaviye	bahukam	hi
G	hitavyam	[4]na cha	samâje.	kaṭavyo	bahukam	hi
D	* * *	* * * *	* * *	[2]* * *	bahukam	* *
J	hitaviye	[2]no pi cha	samaje.	kaṭaviye	bahukam	hi

S	* * *	* * *	* * *	* * *	* * *	* * *	* * *
K	dosâ	samejasâ.	———	Devanampiye	Piyadasi	Lâjâ	dakhati
G	dosam	[5]samâjamhi.	pasati	Devanampiyo	Piyadasi	Râjâ	———
D	* * *	* * *	* *	* *nam*	* * *	* * *	* * *
J	dosam	samejasa.	dakhati	Devânampiye	Piyadasi	Lâjâ	———

S	[2]ati pi * *	* katiya	samayasa	samato	Devânampriyasa
K	athi pichâ	ekatiyâ	samâjâ	sâdhumata	Devânampiyasâ
G	[6]asti pitu	ekachâ	samâja	sâdhumatâ	[7]Devânampiyasa
D	* * *	ekachâ	samâjasâ	sâdhumatâ	Devânampiyasa
J	athi pichu	ekatiyâ	samâjâ	sâdhumatâ	Devânampiyasa

S	Priyadasisa	Ranyo	para	mahanasasa	Devânampriyasa	Priyadasisâ
K	Piyadasisâ	Lâjine	[3]palo	mahânasânsi	Devanampiyasâ	Piyadasisâ
G	Piyadasino	Ranyo	pura	mahânasaphi	[8]Devânampiyasa	Piyadasino
D	[3]Piyadasine	Lâjine	* *	mahâ * *	* *nam * *	Piya *
J	[3]Piyadasine	Lâjine	pulavam	mahânapasi	Devânampiyasa	Piyadasine

S	Ranyo	anudivasam	bahuni	pana	taha* asani	* *
K	Lâjine	anudivasam	bahuni	———	satasahasâni	âlambhiyisu
G	Ranyo	anudivasam	[9]bahûni	pâna	satasahasâni	ârabhisu
D	*	* *	bahuni*	pâna*	satasahâsâni	âlabhiyisu
J	Lâjine	anudivasam	bahûni	pâna	satasahâsâni	âlabhiyi

S	●	● ●	●	● ●	[3]dharmalipi	likhita
K	supathâya	se imâni	yadâ	iyam	dhammalipi	lekhita
G	sûpâthâya	[10]sa aja	yadâ	ayam	dhammalipi	likhitâtî
D	susupathâye	[4]se aja	adâ	iyam	dhammalipi	likhitâ
J	susûpathâye	[4]se aja	(*) adâ	iyam	dhammalipi	likhitâ

S	———	anatam	yo va	pranam	ganeti	● ● ●	jata kato
K	tada	taniye	vi	panâni	âlâbhiyanti	———	[3]deva majali
G	———	———	eva	pâṇa	ârabhire	supâthâya	dwanera
D	———	tinni	● ● ●	● ● ●	*labhiya	● ● ●	● ● ●
J	———	tinniye	vam	pânâni	âlabhiyanti	● ● ●	duvema

S	sti	mago	na	so	pi	mago	na	dhava
K	eke	migo	———	se	piye	mige	no	dhavo
G	eko	mago	———	so	pi	mago	na	dhuvo
D	● ● ●	● ● ●	———	● ● ●	● ● ●	● ● ●	● ● ●	● ● ●
J	eke	mige	———	se	pichu	mige	no	dhuvam

S	esa	pe	———	panam	trayi	pacha	———	arabhisanti.
K	esâni	pi	tini	pânâni	———	———	no	âlabhiyisanti.
G	ete	patî	———	pânâ	———	pachhâ	na	ârabhisante.
D	● ● ●	● ● ●	tinni	pânâni	———	panchhâ	nâ	âlabhiyisanti.
J	etâni	pichu	tinni	pânâni	———	pachhâ	no	âlabhiyisanti.

EDICT II.

S	Savatam	vijite	Devânampriyasa	Priyadasisa	Ranyo	● ● ● ●
K	Savata	vijitamsi	Devânampiyasâ	Piyudasisa	Lâjine	yecha antâ
G	Savata	vijitamhi	Devânampiyasa	Piyadasino	Ranyo	[2]vamapipâchantesu
D	[5]Savata	vijitamsi	Devânampiyasa	Piyadusine	Lâ ● ●	● ● ● ●
J	Savatam	vijitasi	Devânampiyasa	Piyadasine	Lâjine	evâpi antâ

S	yi ●	● ● ●	[4]Paṇḍiya	Satiyaputra	cha	Ketalaputra
K	matha	Choḍâ	Paṇḍiyâ	Sâtiyaputo	———	Keṭhalaputo
G	yathâ	Choḍâ	Pâṇḍâ	Satiyaputo	———	Ketalaputo
D	● ● ●	● ● ●	● ● ●	● ● ●	———	———
J	athâ	Choḍâ	Pâṇḍiya	Satiyaput*	———	———

S	———	Tambapani	ANTIYOKENE	———	Yona	Rajayo
K	———	Tambapanni	[5]ANTIYOGE	nâma	Yona	Lâjâno
G	a	*Tambapaṇṇi	ANTIYAKO	———	Yona	Rajayo
D	———	———	ANTIYOKE	nâma	Yona	Lâjâ
J	———	———	ANTIYOKE	nâma	[7]Yona	Lâjâ o—

S	cha	aranya	tasa	ANTIYOKASA	samanta	Ranyaye
K	cha	alanne	tasa	ANTIYOGASA	sâmantâ	Lâjâno
G	vâ pi	● ● ●	tasa	ANTIYAKASÂ	sâminam	[4]Râjâno
D	[6]vâ pi	———	tasa	ANTIYOKASA	sâmantâ	Lâjâno
J	vâpi	———	tasa	ANTIYOKASA	sâmanta	Lâjâno

S	sarvato	Devânampriyasa	Priyadasisa	Ranyo	kisa	kabha
K	savata	Devânampiyasâ	Piyadasisâ	Lâjine	duvo	chikisâchhâ
G	savata	Devânampiyasa	Piyadasino	Rânyo	dwe .	chikichha
D	savata	Devânampiyasa	*Piyadasino	● ● ●	● ● ●	● ● ●
J	savata	Devânampiyena	Piyadasinâ	Lâji	———	———

S	* * *	* * *	* * *	———	* * *	* * *	* * *
K	katâ	manusa	chikisâ	cha	pasu	chikisâ	cha
G	katâ	[5] manusa	chikichhâ	cha	pasu	chikichha	cha
D	* * *	* sa	chikisâ	cha	pasu	chikisâ	cha
J	———	———	chikisâ	cha	[8] pasu	chikisâ	cha

S	* * *	* * *	* [5]eṣa (?)	janasopakani	cha	paṣopakani	cha
K	osadhâni	———	———	manusopagâni	cha	pasopagâni	cha
G	osudhâni (*a*)	cha	yâni	manusopagânî	cha	[6] pasopagâni	cha
D	(osa) dhâni	[7] ———	anni	munisopagâni	———	pasun opagâni	cha
J	osadhâni	———	âni	munisopagâni	———	pasun opagâni	cha

S	yata	yatra	nasti	savatra	harapiti	cha
K	âta	tâ	nâthi	[6] savatâ	hâlâpitâ	châ
G	yata	yata	nâsti	savatâ	hârâpitâni	cha
D	atata		nathi	savatâ	hâlapitâ	cha
J	atata		nathi	sava	* * *	* * *

S	———	———	——— [	*omitted*]	———	———	———	———
K	lopâpitâ	cha	savameva	mulâni	cha	phalâni	cha	kayatâ
G	ropapitâni	cha	7 ———	mûlâni	cha	phalâni	cha	yata
D	lopapita	cha	———	mulâni	———	———	———	———
J	———	———	———	———	———	———	cha	ata

S	———	———	[	*omitted*]	———	———	———
K	———	nâthi	savata	hâlopita	cha	lopâpitâ	cha
G	yata	nâsti	savata	hârâpitani	cha	ropapitâni	cha
D	———	———	vata	hâlopitâ	cha	[8] lopâpitâ	cha
J	ta	nâthi	savata	hâlâpitâ	cha	lopapitâ	cha

S	vata	cha	kupa	cha	khanapita	———	———
K	matesu	———	lukhâ	cha	mâhithâni	udapânâni	———
G	[8] pathesu	———	kûpâ	cha	khânâpitâ	vachhâ	cha
D	matesu	———	udapânâni	———	khânâpitâni	lukhâni	cha
J	matesu	———	udupânâni	———	khânâpitâni	lukhâni	cha

S	———	pratibhogaye	pasu	manusânam.
K	khânâpitâni	patibhogâye	pasu	munisânam.
G	ropâpitâ	patibhogâya	pasu	manusânam.
D	lopapitâni	paṭibhogâye	pa	* nusânam.
J	———	———	———	———

EDICT III.

S	Devanampriye	Priyadasi	Ranya	———	ahati	Baraya	vasha
K	Devânampiye	Piyadasi	Lâjâ	hevam	âhâ	[7] Duvâdasâ	vasâ
G	Devânampiyo	Piyadasi	Râjâ	evàm	âha	Dwâdasa	vasâ
D	Devânampiye	Piyadasi	Lâjâ	hevam	âhâ	Duvâdasa	vasâ
J	Devânampiye	Piyadasi	Lâjâ	hevam	âhâ	Duvâdasa	vasâ

(*a*). The first letter of this word is the initial *o* and not *u*.

S	———	———	———	———	———	vijite	———
K	bhisite	name	iyam	ânapayite	savatâ	vijitasi	mama
G	bhisitena	mayâ	idam	anyapitam	savata	vijite	mama
D	bhisitena	me—	iyam	ânatam	sa * *	vijite	sâ mo
J	bhisite	name	iyam	â * *	* *	* *	* *

S	yota	———	rajaki	———	padeṣi	va	panchasu	panchasu
K	yutâ	———	lajuki	———	pâdesike	———	panchasu	panchasu
G	yutâ	cha	râjuke	cha	padesike	cha	panchasu	panchasu
D	yuta	———	lajuke	cha	* * sike	cha	[10] panchasu	panchasu
J	———	———	———	cha	pâdesike	cha	panchasu	panchasu

S	❘❘❘❘❘	vashesu (*a*)	anusayanam	nikhamatu	eti	sato	kavayo
K	———	vasesu	anusâyânam	nikhamâtu	etâyevâ	athâye	———
G	———	vâsesu	anusayânam	niyâta	etâyevâ	athâya	———
D	———	vasesu	anusayânam	nikhamâvu	———	athâ	annayopi
J	———	vasesu	anusayânam	nikhamâvu	———	athâ	anâye pi

S	*(omitted)*		imisa	dharmanu sanstiye	sa	anayo	pi
K	———	———	imâya	dhammanusathiyâ	yathâ	aunaya	pi
G	———	———	imâya	dhammanusastiya	yathâ	anyaya	pi
D	kammane	hevam	imâye	dhammânusathiya	———	———	———
J	kammane	* *	* *	* * * * *	———	———	———

S	kramaye	sadhu	mata	———	pitushu	———	suṣusha	mitra
K	kammâne	sâdhu	[8] mâta	———	pitasu	———	sususâ	mita
G	kammâya	sâdhu	mâtari	cha	pitari	cha	susûsâ	mitâ
D	———	sâdhu	mâtâ	———	pitâ	———	sususa	———
J	———	———	———	———	———	———	——— sâ	mitâ

S	santuta	* ta *	———	———	———	———	———
K	santhuta	nâtikyanam	cha	Bambhana	samaṇânam	cha	sâdhu
G	santuta	nyâtinam	———	Bâhmaṇa	samaṇânam	———	sâdhu
D	san * *	[11] nâtisu	cha	Bambhana	samanehi	———	sâdhu
J	santhute	[12] sa nâtisu	cha	Bambhana	samanehi	———	sâdhu

S	———	———	———	———	———	[7] apavayata	apabhidata
K	dâne	pânâna	———	ânalambho	sâdhu	apaviyâti	apabhindata
G	dânam	pâṇânam	sâdhu	anârambho	———	apavyayatâ	apabhiṇḍatâ
D	dâne	jivesu	———	anâlambhe	sâdhu	apaviyati	apabhaṇḍatâ
J	dâne	jivesu	———	anâlambhe	sâdhu	* * *	* * *

S	sadhu	parisapa	yutra	ti * * nadanati?	anapisanti	hetu
K	sâdhu	palisâpi	yutâ	gananasâ	anapeyisanti	hetu
G	sâdhu	parisâpi	yuto	anyapayisati	gananâyam	hetu
D	sâdhu	palisâpi	cha	a * tiyatani	ânapeyisita	(he) tu
J	*	* *	* *	* *	* * yi	[13] hetu

S	* tha	cha	vanyana	to	cha.
K	vatâ	châ	viyaujana	te	cha.
G	to	cha	vyanjana	to	cha.
D	te	cha	viyam * *	*	*
J	te	cha	viyanjana	to	cha.

(*a*) The five upright strokes following immediately after the words *panchasu panchasu* are certainly intended for the figure 5, being only a repetition of the number in words.

ROCK EDICT IV.

S	Atikatam	antaram	bahuni	vashaṣatâni	vadhito va	pranarambho
K	[9] Atikatam	antalam	bahûni	vasasatâni	vadhitevâ	pânalambhe
G	Atikâtam	antaram	bahuni	vâsasatâni	vaḍhito eva	pânârambho
D	[12] Atikantam	antalam	bahûni	vasasatâni	vaḍhiteva	pânâlambhe
J	Atikantam	antalam	bahûni	vasasatâni	vaḍhiteva	pânâlambhe

S	vihisa	cha	bhutânam	nyatinu	asapatipati	Sramanam	Bramanam
K	vihinsâ	cha	bhutânam	nâtinâ	asampaṭipati	Samana	Bambhânânam
G	vihinsâ	cha	bhutânam	nyâtisu	asampaṭipatî	Bâhmaṇâ	Samaṇânam
D	vihinsâ	cha	bhutânam	nâtisu	asampaṭipati	Samana	Bâbhanesu
J	* *	* *	* *	* *	* *	* *	* *

S	sapaṭipati	tu aja	Devânam	priya *	* * * *	* * *
K	asampaṭipati	sâ aja	Devânam	piyasâ	Piyadasino	Lâjane
G	asampatipati	ta aja	Devânam	piyasa	Piyadasino	Rañyo
D	asampaṭipate	[13] se aja	Devânam	piyasa	Piyadasine	Lâjine
J	* * * *	se aja	Devânam	piyasa	Piyadasine	Lajine

S	[2] dharmacharane	bherigosha	aha	dharmagosha	vimanena	daṣanena
K	dhammâchalanenâ	bhelighose	aho	dhammaghose	vimâna	dasanam
G	[3] dhammacharaṇena	bherighoso	aho	dhammaghoso	vimâna	dasaṇâ
D	dhammachalanena	bhelighosam	aho	dhammaghosam	vimâna	dasanam
J	dhammachalanena	bhel * *	* *	* * *	* * *	* *

S	——	——	ne	——	natikadhani	——	anyani
K	——	[10] hathini	——	——	agikandâni	——	annâni
G	cha	hasti	dasanâ	cha	[4] agikhandâni	cha	anyâni
D	* *	hathîni	* *	* *	agakhandâni	* *	annâni
J	* *	* *	* *	* *	* * * *	* *	* *

S	cha	divani	rupani	dusayitu	janasa	yadisam	bahu
K	châ	divyâni	lupâni	dasayitu	janasa	âdisam	bahu
G	cha	divyâni	rupâni	dasayi	pujanam	yârise	bahu
D	cha	diviyâni	[14] lupânam	dasayitu	munisânam	âdise	bahu
J	* *	diviyâni	lupâni	dusayita	munisânam	âdise	bahu

S	hi	vrasha	satehi	na	bhuta	purve	tadiṣe
K	hi	vasa	satehi	nâ	huta	puluve	tâdise
G	hi	vasa	satehi	[5] na	bhûta	puve	târise
D	hi	vasa	satehi	no	hûta	puluve	tâdise
J	hi	vasa	sate	*	* *	* * *	* *

S	aja	vadhite	Devânampriyasa	Priyadarṣisa	Ranyo	dharmanuṣanstaya
K	aja	vaḍhite	Devânampiyasâ	Piyadasino	Lâjine	dhammanusathiye
G	aja	vadhite	Devânampiyasa	Piyadasino	Ranyo	dhammânusastiya
D	aja	vadhi (te)	Devânampiyasa	Piyadasine	Lâjine	dhammânusathiyâ
J	* *	* *	* * *	* * *	* *	[17] dhammânusathiyâ

S	anaram *	* nanam	avihisa	bhutana	nyatasa	* * *	* * *
K	analambhe	pânânam	avihinsâ	bhutânam	nâtisam	[11] sampatipati	Bambhana
G	[6] anârambho	pânânam	avihinsâ	bhutânam	nyâtinam	sampaṭipati	Bahmaṇa
D	[15] analambhe	pânânam	avihinsâ	bhûtânam	nâtisu	sampaṭipati	Samana
J	anâlambhe	pâṇânam	avihinsa	bhutânam	nâtisunam	* * *	* * *

S	[9] Ṣramananam	sampaṭipati	mata	pitashu	tu ara suṣusha esam	inya
K	Samanânâm	sampaṭipati	mâta	pitisu	sususå khûså cha	anno
G	Samaṇânam	sampatipati	mâtari	pitari	[7] susûsâ thairi susûsâ esa	anye
D	Bâbhanesu	sampaṭipati	matu	pitu	susùsâm va susûsâ esa	anno
J	* *	* *	* *	* *	* * * [15] esa	anno

S	cha	bahuvadham	dharmacharanam	vaḍhitam	vaḍhiṣati	chayo	Devânampriyasa
K	cha	bahûvidhe	dhammachalane	vaḍhite	vadhiyisati	chevâ	Devânampiye
G	cha	bahuvidhe	dhammacharaṇe	vaḍhite	vadhayisati	chova	Devânampiyo
D	cha	bahuvidhe	[16] dhammachalane	vaḍhite	vaḍhayisati	chova	Devânâmpiyo
J	cha	bahûvidhe	dhammachalane	vaḍhite	vadhayi	* *	* * *

S	Priyadarsisa	Ranyo	——— dharmacharanam ime	putra pi cha kunatavocha
K	Piyadasi	Lâja	imam dhammachalanam	putâ cha kunatâla châ
G	[8] Piyadasi	Râjâ	dhammacharanam idam	putâ cha potâ cha
D	Piya * *	Lâja	dhammachalanam imam	putapi cha nati *
J	* *	* *	* * * * *	* * * * *

S	pranatika	cha	Devanampriyasa	Priyadarsisa	Ranya	vadhisanti	* *
K	panâtikya	cha	Devanampiyasâ	Piyadasine	Lâjine	[11] vadhâyisanti	yeva
G	papotâ	cha	Devânampiyasa	Piyadasino	Rânyo	[9] vadhayisanti	idam
D	pa	cha	Devânampiyasa	Piyadasine	Lâjine	[17] pavaḍhayisanti	yeva
J	* *	cha	* *	[19] Piyadasino	Lâjine	pavadhayisanti	yeva

S	* * * *	icha	pavata	kupa	dharmaṣila	* * *
K	dhammachalanam	ima	âva	kupam	dhammasi	silasi vâ
G	dhammacharaṇam	â va	savata (a)	kapâ	dhammamhi	sîlamhi
D	dhammachalanam	imam	———	akepam	dhammasi	sîlasi cha
J	dhammachal *	* *	* *	* *	* *	* *

S	ti mato	dharma	anuṣaṣisanti	eva	esa	* *	yuta
K	tithâto	dhammam	anusâsisanti	ese	hi sothe	kamme	am
G	tistanto	dhammam	anusâsisanti	[10] esa	hise ste	kamme	yâ
D	vithitu	* *	anusâsisanti	esa	hise	* me	yâ
J	* *	* *	* *	* *	* *	* *	* *

S	* nusasanam	dharmacharanam	pi cha	na bhoti	aṣilasa se	imasu
K	dhammânusâsanam	dhammachalana	pi châ	no hoti	asilasâ se	imisa
G	dhammânusâsanam	dhammacharaṇe	pi na	bhavati	asila sava	imamhi
D	dhammânusâsanam	dhammachalana	pi chu	[18] no hoti	asilasa se	imasa
J	* * *	[20] dhammachalane	pichu	no ho *	* *	* *

S	yaṭasa	vadhi	ahini	cha	sadhu	etaye	athaye	ima
K	athasa	vadhi	ahini	cha	sâdhu	etaye	athâye	ima
G	athamhi	[11] dhi cha	ahîni	cha	sâdhu	etâya	athâya	ida
D	athasa	vaḍhi *	ahîni	cha	sâdhu	etâye	athayo	iyam
J	* *	* *	* *	* *	* *	* *	* *	* *

S	lipitham	imisa	athasa	vadhiya	nyantu	hini	mahiga
K	likhite	[13] imasa	athasa	vadhiyu	jantu	hini	cha mâ alochayisu
G	lekhâpitam	imasa	athasa	vadhiya	jantu	hîni	cha [12] lochetivya
D	likhite	imasa	athasa	vadhiyu	jantu	hîni	cha mâ alochayisâ
J	* *	* *	* *	* *	* *	hini	cha mâ alochayi

(a) Prinsep's first reading of this word was *pavata*, and the totally different form of the Ariano Pali *p* in the Shahbazgarhi text shows that the first reading of *pavata* may be correct, although the first letter is clearly *s* in the Girnar text.

S	barata	varshabhisitena	Devânampriyasa	Priyadarşisa	Ranya	idam	lipikhatam.(a)
K	duvâdasâ	vaşâbhisitene	Devânampiyena	Piyadasine	Lâjino	———	lekhitâ.
G	dwâdasa	vasâbhisitena	Devânampiyena	Piyadasino	Rânyo	idam	lekhâpitam.
D	19 duvâdasa	vasâniabhisitasa	Devânampiyasa	Piyadasine	Lâjine	ya *	likhite.
J	* *	* * *	* * *	* *	* *		* * *

ROCK EDICT V.

S	11 Devânampriya	Priyadarşi	Rayo	evam	ahatine	kayana	dukara
K	Devânampiyo	Piyadasi	Laja	(omitted)	âhâ	kayâne	dukale
G	Devânampiyo	Piyadasi	Râjâ	evam	âhâ	kalâna	dukaranye
D	20 (De)vânampiya	Piyadasi	Lâja	hevam	âhâ	kayâne	dukale
J	Devânampiye	Piyada	* *	* *	* *	* *	* *

S	va lapachha	so	daşaram	karoti	i	maya	bahu
K	e adikale kayânâ	sâ	dukalam	kaleti	se	mayâ	bahu
G	a ——— kalâṇe	saso	dukaram	karoti	2 ta	mayâ	bahu
D	——— kayânâ	saso	dukalam	kaleti	se	me	bahuke
J	———	* ———	———	———	———	———	———

S	karana	kata	———	maha	putra	cha	nataro cha
K	kayâne	kaṭe	* *	mama	puta	cha	nâta cha
G	kalâṇam	kata	ta	mama	putâ	cha	potâ cha
D	kayâne	kaṭe	tam	ye me	putâ	va	21 nâta cha (b)
J	———	———	———	———	———	———	23 nanti cha

S	paran	cha	tanaya	me apacham	ammanti	ava	———
K	14 palan	cha	tenlya	apatine me	———	âva	———
G	paran	cha	tenaya	me apâcham	———	âva	samvanta
D	palan	cha	tenaye	apatiye me	———	âva	———
J	palan	cha	te * *	———	———	———	———

S	kapam	tatha ye anuvaṭi şanti	te	sakita	kusati	yo cha
K	kapam	athâ anuvatisanti	se	sukatam	kachhânti	tha evu
G	kapâ	anuvatisare tathâ	3 so	sukatam	kâsati	yo tu
D	kapam	tathâ anuvatisanta	sa	sukaṭam	kachhati	* ehe
J	* *	* *	* *	* *	* *	* *

S	ati (c)	deşam	prihapişata	sa	dakatam	kushauti	papamha
K	heti	desam	pihâpayisati	so	dukatam	kâchhati	pîpâ hi
G	ota	desam	pihâpesati	so	dukatam	kâsati	* *
D	ta	desam	pihâpayisati	so	dukatam	kâchhati	pâpehi
J	———	———	———	———	———	———	———

S	sahane	Atikatam	antaram	na	bhuta	puva
K	nâma su padâlayese	Atikatam	antalam	no	huta	puluvâ
G	Sukaramhi pâpam	Atikâtam	antaram	4 na	bhuta	puvam
D	22 supudâlayesu	Atikantam	antalam	no	hûtâ	puluvâ
J	———	———	———	———	———	———

(a). The two letters *p* and *kh* seem to have been transposed in this word, which should be read *likhapitam*.

(b). As the two letters *g* and *t* are easily mistaken, this word should no doubt be *nata* as in the two northern texts, and not *Naga*. Mr. Beglar's impression gives *nata*, and so does his photograph.

(c). The initial letter might perhaps be *â* instead of *a*, as these two characters in Ariano Pali are very much alike.

S	dharmamahamatam	nama	sa	ti	* * varshabhisitena *
K	dhammamahâmâtâ	nâmâ	so	—	dasavasâbhisitenâ mamova
G	dhammamahâmâtâ	nâma	ta mayâ	to	dasavasâbhisi (tena)
D	dhammamahâmâtâ	nâma	se	te	dasavasâbhisitena me
J	—	—	—	—	—

S	[13] deya dharmamahamatra	kiṭa	te	save	pashanḍeshu
K	dhammamahâmâtâ	—	—	sava	pâsaṇḍesu
G	dhammamahâmâta	katâ	te	sava	pâsaṇḍesu
D	dhammamahâmâtâ nâma	kaṭâ	te	sava	pâsaṇḍesu
J	—	—	—	—	—

S	—	dharmadhrithayo	cha	dharmavadhiya	hita	sukhaya
K	viyapaji	[15] dhammadhitanâye	—	dhammavadhiye	hita	sukhâye
G	vyapatâ	dhammadhistânâya	—	—	—	—
D	[23] viyapatha	dhammâdhithânîye	—	dhammavaḍhiye	hita	sukhâye
J	—	—	—	—	—	—

S	dharma yuthasa	—	*Yo (a)*	*Kambayo*	*Gandharanam,*	*Rastikanam*
K	vi dhammâyutaso	tam	*Yonam,*	*Kambojam,*	*Gandhâlânam,*	—
G	dhammayûtasa	cha	*Yonam,*	*Kâmbo(cham),*	*Gandhârânam,* (b)	*Râstika*
D	cha dhammayuta	sâ	*Yona,*	*Kambocha,*	*Gandhâlesu,*	*Lathika,*
J	—	—	—	—	—	—

S	*Pitinikanam,* ta	vapi	—	*Aparanta*	bhaṭamayeshu	—
K	— e	vâpi	anne	*Apalantâ*	bhaṭamayesu	—
G	*Petenikâṇam* ye	vâpi	anna	*Aparâtâ*	bhatamayesu	va
D	*Pitenikesu* e	vâpi	anne	*Apalantâ*	bhaṭi	—
J	—	—	—	—	—	—

S	Bramanibbeshu	—	anatheshu	vathashu	—	hita	sukhaye
K	Bambhanithisu	—	annathesu	vathesu	—	hida	sukhâye
G	—	—	—	—	—	[6] —	sukhâye
D	[24] Bâbhani	bhisâsu	anathesu	mahalokesu	cha	hita	sukhâye
J	—	—	—	—	—	—	—

S	dharmayutasa	aparigodhra	vapata te [13] bandhanam	badhasa	paṭividhanaye
K	dhammayutâye	apalibodhâye	viyapatâ : se bandhanam	badhasa	paṭividhanâya
G	dhammayutânam	aparâgodhâya	vyâpatâ ; te bandhana	badhasa	paṭividhânâya
D	dhammayutâye	apalibodhâya	viyapaṭâ · se bandhanam	badhasa	pativi * * ya
J	—	—	—	—	—

S	aparibodhaye	moohavanavaye	—	—	pajati	kita
K	apalibodhaye	mokhâye cha	eyam	anubandha	pajâvativi	[16] katâ
G	—	—	—	—	pajâ	katâ
D	apalibodhaye	mokhâye cha	[25] iyam	anubandha	pajâti	kaṭâ
J	—	[27] mokhâye	—	—	—	—

S	bhikati	va	mahalaka	va viyapata	ti eha	—	bahireshu
K	bhikaleti	vâ	mahâlâketi	vâ viyapatâ	te hidâ	—	bâhilesu
G	bhikaresu	vâ	thairesu	vâ vyâpatâ	te *Pâṭaliputo*	cha	bâhiresu
D	bhikaleti	va	mahâlaketi	vâ viyâpaṭâ :	se hida	cha	bâhilesu
J	—	—	—	—	—	—	—

(a) The letter *n* is here omitted in the Shahbazgarhi text.

(b). Prinsep here read *Gandhara, Naristika,* but the true reading is that given in the text. Similarly in the Dhauli text the *su* of his *Sulathika* belongs to the previous name *Gandhalesu*—leaving *Lathika* as the corresponding equivalent of *Rastika* in the Shahbazgarhi and Girnar texts.

S	cha	nagareshu	sarveshu	orodhaneshu	——	bhratuna	cha
K	cha	nagalesu	savesu	holodhanesu	——	bhâtâna	cha na
G	cha	——	——	——	eva	——	——
D	cha	nagalesu	savesu (a)	olodhanesu	evâhi	bhâtânam	va
J	——	——	——	——	——	——	——

S	mekasuna cha yevapi anye	nyatika	savatam	viyapata	ya	ayam
K	bhaginiya evâpi anna	nâtikya	savatâ	viyapatâ	e ——	iyam
G	—— [8] ne vâpi mo anye	nyatika	savatâ	vyapatâ	te yo	ayam
D	bhaginînam va [26] annesu	va natita	savata	viyapaṭâ	cha :	iyam
J	——	——	——	——	——	——

S	dharma	nistiṣita tivara dharmaḍhriṭane	tiva	danasayutra	va	——
K	dhamma	nisitetivâ dânasayute	tivâ	savatâ majata	chha	mama
D	dhamma	nistito tiva ——	——	——	——	——
G	dhamma	nisitativam dhammâdhithâne,	tiva	dânasayute	va sava	paṭhaviyam
J	——	——	——	——	——	——

S	asti anati mata	dharmayutasa vana	viyapala	e	dharmamahamatra	etaye
K	——	dhammayutasi	viyâpaṭâlo	——	dhammamahâmâtâ	etâye
G	——	——	——	——	dhammamahâmâtâ	etâya
D	——	dhammayutasi	viyapaṭâ	ime	dhammamahâmâtâ	imâye
J	——	——	——	——	——	——

S	athaya	ayo	dharmalipi	lipi *	* * thiti	va tinika bhota panja	anuvatantu.
K	athâye	[17] iyam	dhammalipi	likhitâ	chilathitikyâ	hotu tathâ che me paja	anuvatantu.
G	athâya	ayam	dhammalipi	likhitâ	——	——	——
D	athâye	[27] iyam	dhammalipi	likhitam	chilathiti	hotu cha me paja *	anuvatatu.
J		——	——	——	——	——	——

EDICT VI.

S	[14] Devanampriyo	Priyadarṣi	Raya	evam	ahati	atikatam	antalam
K	Devânampiye	Piyadasi	Lâjâ	hevam	âhâ	atikatam	antalam
G	——	—— si	Râja	evam	âha	atikâtam	antaram
D	Devânampiye	Piyadasi	Lâja	hevam	âhâ	atikantam	antalam
J	[1] Devânampiye	Piyadasi	Lâjâ	hevam	âhâ	atikantam	antalam

S	na	bhuta	puva	sava	la (b)	——	——
K	no	hûta	puluve	savam	kâlam	atha	kammevâ
G	na	bhûta	puva	sa ——	—— la	atha	kamme va
D	no	hûta	pulûve	savam	kâlam	atha	kamme va
J	no	huta	puluve	savam	kâlam	atha	kamme va

S	patimadhra	ṭa	——	maya	eva	kiṭa	savam
K	paṭivedânâ	vâ sa	ma	mayâ	hevam	kaṭo	savam
G	paṭivedanâ	vâ ta	——	mayâ	evam	katam	save
D	paṭivedanâ	va se	ma	mayâ	——	kaṭo	sava
J	paṭivedana	va se	ma	mayâ	——	kaṭe	savam

(a) This word (savesu) is here repeated in the Dhauli text.
(b) Omitted in original text.

S	kalam	esimana	same	———	orodhanasi	gabhagarasi	vachasi
K	kâlam	adamâna	sâ ———	———	[18] holodhanasi (*a*)	gabhâgâlasi	vachasi
G	kâle	bhungamâna	same	———	orodhanambhi	gabhagâramhi	vachamhi
D	* *	* * na	same	[20] ante	olodhanasi	gabhâgâlasi	vachasi
J	kâlam	[1] * * *	same	ante	olodhanasi	gabhâgâlasi	vachasi

S	———	vinitasi	———	uyanasi	———	savatra	praṭivedaka
K	va	vinitasi	———	uyanâsi	———	savata	paṭivedakâ
G	va	vinîtamhi	cha	uyânesu	cha	savata	paṭivedakâ
D	* *	vinîtasi	———	uyânasi	cha	savata	paṭivedakâ
J	———	vinîtasi	———	uyânasi	cha	savata	paṭivedakâ

S	———	atha	janasa	praṭivedaka	me	———	savatra
K	———	aṭha	janasâ	* ṭivedetu	me	———	savata
G	sṭita	athe me	janasa	paṭivedetha	———	iti	savata
D	———	janasa	aṭham	paṭiveda yantu	me	ti	savata
J	———	janasa	atham	paṭivedayantu	me	ti	savata

S	cha	janasa	atha	karomi	ya pirokika	———	makhata
K	———	janasâ	aṭham	kachhâmi	ha peyam pi châ	———	mukhata
G	cha	janasa	athe	karomê	ya cha	kinchi	mukhatâ
D	cha	janasa	aṭham	kalâmi	[21] ha ampi cha	kinchhi	mukhate
J	cha	janasa	[2] ———	———	am pi cha	kinchhi	mukhate

S	anapayami	———	pika	va	———	———	eva
K	ânapayâmi	sakam	dipakam	vâ	savakâm	vâ	yevâ
G	ânapayâmi	swayam	dâpakam	vâ	sâvâpakam	vâ	yavâ
D	ânapayâmi	———	dâpakam	vâ	sâvâkam	vâ	evâ
J	ânapayâmi	———	dâpakam	vâ	sâvakam	vâ	evâ

S	dhayaka pi nama tadhana	achayika	nya * nasa	bhoti	traya	athaye
K	punâ ——— mahâmatohi [19]	achâyika	———	———	taya	aṭhâye
G	puna ——— mahâthatesu	âchâyika	aropitam	bhavati	tâya	athâya
D	——— mahâmâtehi	atiyâyike	alopite	hoti	tasi	athasi
J	mahâmâtahi	atiyâyike	alopite	hoti	tasi	aṭhasi

S	viyo pa na	———	* * ma	parivayesha	nantariyena	paṭivedetasa
K	vivido ni	kiti	vasantam	palisâyam	anantaliyenâ	* * *
G	vivado ni	kiti	vasanto	parisâyam	ânantaram	paṭivedetayam
D	vivâdeva ni	kîti	vâsantam	palisayâ	[21] anantaliyam	paṭivadeta
J	vivâdeva	[4] ———	———	lisaya	anantaliyam	paṭivedeta

S	———	me	———	savatra	cha (*b*)	a * *	* janasa
K	viye	me	———	savatâ	savam	kâlam	hevam
G	———	me	———	savatâ	save	kâle	evam
D	viye	me	ti	savata	savam	kâlam	hevam
J	viye	me	ti	savata	savam	kâlam	hevam

S	karomi atrayutisa (*c*)		———	——— doka	anapi che	aha
K	ânapanite mamayâ		nathi	hi me doso	uṭhânasi	atha
G	mayâ	anapitam	nâsti	he me to so	uṭṭhânamhi	atha
D	ma	anusathe	nathî	pi me to se	uṭhânasi	aṭha
J	me	anusatha	nathi	pi me to se	uṭhânasi	aṭha

N. B.—The four following lines are found only in the Shâhbâzgarhi text.

( ) As the vowel *o* in the first syllable of this word is attached to the aspirate, the value of the initial letter in the other text is determined to be *o* also, although this was already sufficiently clear from the initial *o* of the Shahbazgarhi text.

(*b*) Norris reads *atrayautaka.*

(*c*) Omitted in original text.

S	dapaka	va	ṣravaka	va	yata	pana	mahamata	na
S	achayiti	me	sava	bhoti	taya	athaya	vividesa	vatijati
S	ra	patishaye	anantariya	na	pativi	detaro	me	savatra
S	savam	kalam	evam	anyapitam	maya * *	sti hi me	tatanya	atha

S	santiranaya	pi	katava	manatrahi	me	sava	loka	hitam
K	santilanâye	cha	kaṭaviya	mutchi	me	sava	loka	hita
G	santiranâya	va	katavya	matchi	me	save	loke	hitam
D	santîlanâya	cha	kaṭaviya	matchi	me	sava	loka	hite
J	santîlanâyam	cha	[5] ——	——	me	sava	loka	hite

S	tasa	cha	——	mulam	etra	aṭanam	atha	santirasa
K	——	——	puna	esi	mule	uthâne ——	[20]atha	santilanâ
G	tase	cha	puna	esa	mûle	ustina cha	atha	santiranâ
D	tasa	cha	puna	iyam	mûle	uthâne ——	——	santilanâ
J	tasa	cha	pana	iyam	mule	uthâne cha	atha	santîlanâ

S	cha	na	i	kammatara	sava	loka	hitî ti + yam	cha	kichi
K	châ	nathi	hi	kammatalâm	sava	loka	hitayam yam	cha	kichhi
G	cha	nâsti	hi	kammataram	sava	loka	hitattaya	cha	kinchi
D	cha	nathi	hi	kammatalam	sava	loka	hitena am	cha	kichhi
J	cha	nathi	hi	kammatalâ	sava	loka	hitene am	cha	kichhi

S	parakamama	——	kiti	——tanam	enâni desa	va cha yam	iha	chashu
K	palakamâmi	hakam	kiti	bhutânam	annaniyam	ye ha — hida	cha	kâni
G	parakamâmi	aham	kinti	bhutânam	anannam	gachheyam idha	cha	nâni (*a*)
D	palakamâmi	hakam	kinti	bhutânam	annaniyam	ye hanti hida	cha	kâni
J	pâlakamâmi	hakam	——	——	——niyam	ye hanti[33] hida	cha	kâni

S	sukhayami	paratam	cha	saga	aradhatu	——	etaye athaye	ayi
K	sukhâyâmi	palatam	cha	swagam	âlâdhayantu	sa	etâyethâye	iyam
G	sukhâpayâmi	paratâ	cha	swagam	arâdhayantu	ta	etâya athâya	ayam
D	sukhayâmi	palatam	cha	swagam	âlâdhayantu	ti	etâye athaye	iyam
J	sukhayâmi	palata	cha	swagam	âladhayantu	ti	etâye athâye	iyam

S	dharmalipi	tha	——	chiranthitika	bhotu	tatha	cha
K	dhammalipi	likhitâ	——	chilathitikyâ	hotu	tathâ	cha
G	dhammalipi	lekhâpitâ	kinti	chirantisteya	iti	tathâ	cha
D	dhammalipi	likhita	——	chîlathîtika	hotu	tathâ	cha
J	dhammalipî	likhita	——	chilanthitikâ	hotu	[7] ——	——

S	me	putranantaro	——	——	parakrama	tasa sa
K	me	puta dale	——	——	palakamâtu	savaloka
G	me	puta pota cha	papota	——	——	savaloka
D	——	puta —— ——	papota	me	palakamâtu	savaloka
J	——	—— pota ——	——	me	palakamantu	savaloka

S	hi athaya	ma bhata ta yasa	ama ya	anyata	age	parakameua
K	hitâ	[22] dukale cha	iyam	annata	agenâ	palakamenâni
G	hitâya	dukarantu ——	idam	annata	agena	parakamena
D	hitâye	dukale chu	iyam	annata	agena	palakamena
J	hitâye	dukale chu	iyam	annata	agena	palakamena

(*a*) From the great similarity of the two letters *n* and *k*, they are frequently mistaken. The true reading in this text is most probably kâni.

EDICT VII.

S	[1] Devânampriyo	Priyasi (*a*)	Râja	savvatra	ichhati	savvam	pâshan
K	Devânampiye	Piyadasi	Lâjâ	* vatâ	ichhati	sava	pâsaṇḍâ
G	[1] Devânampiyo	Piyadasi	Rajâ	savata	ichhati	save	pâsaṇḍâ
D	Devânampiye	Piyadasi	Lâjâ	savata	ichhati	sava	pâsaṇḍâ (*b*)
J	[8] ——	Piyadasi	Lâjâ	savata	ichhati	sava	pâsaṇḍâ

S	vaseyu	save ite	sayaman	bhavaṣudhi	cha	ichhanti [2]	jano
K	vase va	save hite	sayaman	bhâvasudhi	cha	ichhanti	mune
G	vaseyu	save te	sayaman cha	[2] bhâvasudhin	cha	ichhati	jano tu
D	vasevû *	ti save	hota sayaman	bhâvasudhî	cha	ichhanti	munisâ
J	vase *	* save	hite saya am	bhâvasudhî	cha	ichhanti	munisâ

S	cha	uchavacha	chhando	uchavacha	rago	te
K	va	uchâvachâ	chhandâ	uchâvacha	lâga	te
G		uchâvacha	chhando	uchâvacha	râgo	te
D	cha	[2] uchâvacha	chhandâ	uchâvacha	lâgâ	te
J	cha	uchâvachâ	chhandâ	uchâvacha	lâgâ	te [9]

S	savam	vâ	(*a*)	ekadeṣaam va [4] pi	kâshanti	vipule
K	savam	——	(*b*)	ekadesam pi	kachhanti	vipule
G	savam	va	kâsanti	ekadesam va	kâsanti	[3] vipule
D	savam	va	(*c*)	ekadesa *	kachhati	vipulâ
J	——	——	——	ekadesam va	kachhanti	vipule

S	pi cha	dâne	yasa	nâsti	sayaman	[5] bhâvaṣudhi	——
K	pi cha	dâne	tasâ	nathi	[13] sayame	bhâvasudhi	——
G	tu pi	dâne	yasa	nasti	sayame	bhâvasuddhitâ	va
D	pi cha	dâne	asa	nathi	sayame	bhâvasudhî	cha
J	pi cha	dâne	——	——	——	——	——

S	kiṭanyata	——	dridhâbhatita (*d*)	——	niche	pâdham.
K	kiṭanâtu	——	dâḍhibhatitâ	châ	nicha	pâdham.
G	katamnyatâ	va	dadhabhatîtâ	va	nichâ	bâḍham.
D	——	——	——	——	niche	bâḍham.
J	——	——	îla	——	nîche	bâḍham.

EDICT VIII.

S	[17] Atikatam	antaram	ne Raya	viharayatam name	nikhamisham	gamagaye
K	Atikantam	antalam	Devânampiyâ	* * * dhiya * * *	nikhamisuhidâ	migaviyâ
G	Atikâtam	antaram	Râjano	vihârayâtâm nyayâsu	eta	magavyâ
D	[3] * * kantam	antalam	Lâjâno	vâhalayâtam nâma	* khamisâ	* * viya
J	[10] t*kantam	antalam	Lâja	——	——	——

S	anyane	cha	edisani	atasamana	abhavasu	so	Devanampriyo
K	anyâni	cha	hedisâni (*e*)	abhila mâni	hunsam	——	Devânampiye
G	anyâni	cha	etârisâni	[2] abhira makâni	ahumsu	so	Devânampiyo
D	annâni	cha	edisâni	abhilâ mâni	puvam tinam	se	Devânampiye
J	annâni	cha	e ——	a * ila mâni	puvam tinam	se	Devânampiye

(*a*) *Priyasi* in original, the *d* having been omitted by the engraver.

(*b*) *Ilânanda* is read by Wilson, and it is so lithographed; but as *pâsa* might easily be mistaken for *hâsa*, the word has certainly been misread.

(*c*) Omitted in original texts.

(*d*) This reading of the Shahbazgarhi text confirms Westergaard's emendation of *drirha bhaktita* in the Girnar text.

(*e*). This is another instance of the cockney aspirate in the Khâlsi text.

S	Priyadarsi	Ranya	daṣavashabhisito	santu	nikamisaye	* dhitena
K	Piyadasi	Lâjâ	dasavasâbhisite	santu	nikhami thâm sam	[23] bodhinitena
G	Piyadasi	Râja	dasavasâbhisito	santo	ayâyasam	bodhimitena
D	[4] Piyadasi	Lâja	dasavasâbhisite	——	nikhamisam	bodhi * — tena
J	[11] Piyadasi	Lâja	dasa ——	——	——	——

S	sa	dharmayatra	etaya iyam	hoti	Sramaṇam Bramaṇanam	daṣane	na	dava
K	tâ	dhammâyâtâ	etâyam	hoti	Samana Bambhanânam	dasane	châ	dâne
G	sâ	dhammayâtâ	etayam	hoti	Bâhmana Samanânam	dasane	cha	dâne
D	tâ	dhammayâtâ	tesa	hoti	Samana Bâbhanânam	dasana	cha	dâne
J	——	——	tesa	hoti	Sa * * *	* *	cha	dâne

S	anu	* *	* *	* *	hiranya	paṭividhane	cha
K	cha	vidhânam	dasane	cha	hilanna	paṭividhâne	cha
G	cha	thairânam	dasane	cha	hiranna	paṭividhâno	cha
D	cha	vadhânam	dasane	cha	[5] hîlanna	pativídhane	cha
J	cha	vaḍhânam	dasane	cha	[12] hîlanna	pativídhâne	cha

S	pajanasa		janasa	daṣana	——	dharmanuṣati	——
K	janapadasa		janasa	dasanam	——	dhammanusathi	cha
G	jânapadasa	cha	janasa	dasanam	——	dhammânusasti	cha
D	janapadasa	——	janasa	dasane	cha	dhammânusathî	* *
J	——	——	——	——	——	——	——

S	dharma pari	puvachu	——	tadopayam	ete	bhayerati	bhoti
K	dhamma pali	puchhâ	cha	tatâpayo	esa	bhayalâti	hoti
G	dhamma pari	puchhâ	cha	tadopayâ	esa	bhâyarati	bhavati
D	* * *	* chhâ	——	tâdâpayâ	* sa	abhilâme	hotî
J	——	——	——	——	——	* lâme	hoti

S	Devânampriyasa	Priyadarṣisa	Ranye	bhago	anye.
K	Devânampiyasa	Piyadasisa	Lâjine	bhâge	anne.
G	Devânampiyasa	Piyadasino	Ranyo	bhâge	anne.
D	Devânampiyasa	Piyadasine	Lâjine	bhage	anne.
J	Devânampiyasa	[13] Piyadasine	Lâjine	bâhge	a * *

EDICT IX.

S	[18] Devânampriyo	Priyadarṣi	Raya	evam	ahati	——
K	[24] Devânampiye	Piyadasi	Lâja	——	âhâ	——
G	[1] Devânampiyo	Piyadasi	Râjâ	eva	âha	asti
D	[6] Devânampiye	Piyadasi	Lâja	hevam	âhâ	athi
J	[14] Devânampiye	Piyadasi	Lâja	——	——	——

S	jani	ucham vacham	mangalam	karoti	abadhasa	va ativaha
K	jano	uchâvacham	mangalam	ka * *	âbâdhesi	—— avâha
G	jano	uchâvacham	mangalam	karote	âbâdhesu	va [2] avâha
D	jano	uchâvacham	mangalam	kaloti	abâdhesu	——
J	——	——	——	——	——	——

S	——	——	paja patu di	——	pavasa	——
K	vivâhesi	——	pajupadâye	——	pavasasi	——
G	vivâhesu	vâ	putalâbhesu	vâ	pavâsammhi	vâ
D	vî * * *	——	* jupadâye	——	pavâsasi	——
J	——	——	pajupadâye	——	pavâsasi	——

S	ataya		anyaye	va	hadeṣi	* * na datu	mangalam
K	etâye		annaye	cha	edisâye	jane —— bahu	mangalam
G	etamhi	cha	anyamhi		cha	jano uchâvacham	mangalam
D	[7] etâye		annaye	cha	hediṣâye	jine bahukam	mangalam
J	etâye	cha [15]			hedisaye	jane bahukam	——

S	karoti	ata	tu	striyaka	bahu	cha	bahuvidham
K	kâloti	heta	vu	âbakejanibhu	bahu	cha	bahuvidham
G	karote	eta	tu	mahâḍâyo	bahukam	cha	bavuvidham
D	ka	——	——	——	——	——	iṭhibidham
J	——	——	——	——	——	——	——

S	cha	putika	cha	nirastiyam	cha	mangala	karoti	so
K	cha	khudâvi		nilathiyam	vâ	mangalam	kaloti	[25] se
G	cha	chhadam	va	niratham	cha	mangalam	karote	ta
D	cha	puti *	cha	nilathiyam	cha	mangalam	kaloti	[8] so
J	——	——	——	——	——	mangalam	kaloti	so

S	kataviya		mangala	apaphalam	tukho	etadi
K	katavi cheva	kho	mangale	apaphale	(chu) kho (*a*)	* sâ iyam
G	katavyameva	tu	mangalam	apaphalam	tukho	etarisam
D	kaṭiviye	le (dhe) no	* mangale	apapale	chakho	esahedisam
J	kaṭiviye	chevakho	mangale	[16] apaphale	chakho	esaha * *

S	matakho	——		mahaphalam	yema
K	chukho	——		mahâphale	——
G	mangalam	ayam	.. tu	mahâphale	——
D	mangalam	[1] ayam	——	mahâphale	——
J	——	——	——	——	——

S	mangala	[19] ṭi	asa ima	——	dasa	bhatakasa
K	——	ye	dhammamangale	* * *	dâsa	bhaṭakasi
G	mangale	ya	dhammamangale	tateta	dâsa	bhatakamhi
D	——	e	dhammamangale	tatesa	dâsa	bhaṭakasi
J	——	——	——	——	——	bhaṭakasi

S	samapaṭipati	va garanam	apa * ti	pasadhu	sayama	
K	samapaṭipati	gulunam	apâchiti	—— pân * *	sayamme	
G	samyapaṭipati	gujunam	apachiti	sâdhu pâṇesu	sayame	sâdhu
D	sammâpaṭipati	[9] gulunam	apachi *	——	——	——
J	samyâpaṭipati	gulunam	apachiti	pânesu	sayame	

S	Sramaṇa	Bramaṇa	——	dane	eta		anya
K	Sâmana	Bambhanânam	——	dâne	ese		anno
G	Bahmaṇa	Samanânam	sâdhu	dânam	eta	cha	anno
D	Samana	Bâbhanânam	——	dâne	esa		anno
J	[17] Samana	Bambhanâ *	*	——	——	——	

S	cha	——	dharmasa	*	*	*	savo
K	châ	heḍisatam	dhamma	mangale	nâmâ	pe	vataviye
G	cha	etarisam	dhamma	mangalam	nâma	ta	vatavyam
D	cha	——	dhamma	gala (*b*)	nâma	ta	vataviye
J	——	——	——	——	——	——	——

(*a*) Perhaps intended for *Chukha*, or even *tukha*.

(*b*) The *m* of *mangala* is omitted on the rock by a mistake of the engraver or writer.

S	pitana	sava	putena	sa	bhata	*	* * kena	pi'
K	pitinâ	pi	putena	pi	bhâtinâ	pi	suvâmikena	pi
G	pitâ	va	putena	va	bhâtâ	va	swâmikena	va
D	pitina	pi	putena	pi	bhatina	pi	[10] suvâmike	
J	* tina	pi	putena	pi	bhâtina	pi	suvâmikena	pi

S	mâta	sastatena	ava	prativatiyena	imasa	alatha	*saka* (*a*)
K	mâta	santhatena	ava	paṭivesiyenapi	iyam	sâdhu	iyam
G	(	*omitted*		)	idam	sâdhu	idam
D	(	*do.*		)	* *	* *	* *
J	(	*do.*		)	iyam	sâdhu	iyam

S	nasti	mangalam	ya	tasa	atasa cha	taviye	dita	tadika
K	kaṭaviye	mangale	âva	tasâ	athasa	nidhatiya		
G	katavya	mangalam	âva	tasâ	athasâ	nistanaya		
D	* * *	* * lam	ava	tasa	athasa	nidhatiya		
J	kaṭaviye	[10] * *	* . *	* *	* *	* * * *		

At this point of Edict IX the text of the two northern versions differs from that of Girnar, Dhauli, and Jaugada. The remainder of the Edict is therefore given in two separate parts.

Continuation of the SHAHBAZGARHI *and* KHALSI *versions.*

S	[20] ima	kusaye	eva	take	mangalam	sansaye	kitam
K	iyam	kusi *	va	cha la	mangale	sansayi	kyase

S	siyato	tatha	nivakayati	sayapanena	iha
K	sayavatam	atham	nivateyâ	sâyâpanenâ	hida

S	lobha cha	ava	dharma	anuna	* *	*	*
K	lochavase	iyamjanâ	dhammamangale		akâlikyo	ham	che

S	* *	ya	dharma	anutam	atham	na	divati	ita
K	pitam	atham	noniteti	hida	atham	palata	anantam	

S	* *	* *	ha	aprataranam	va panyaprasata
K	punâ	pavasati	panchesu kâtam		

S	thani	tathati	varo	abhi	asaladham	bhoti	orochase
K	atham	nivatati	hida	tatâ	ubhiyetam	[27] adhehoti	hida châ

S	asti pabhata	dhata	panyapasa	ka	pha	dina	ṭa
K	se athe helatâ	châ	anantam	pana		pasâvati	

S	mangale * * *
K	tena dharmapaga.

Continuation of the GIRNAR, DHAULI, *and* JAUGADA *versions.*

G	asti cha	pâvutam	sâdhu	dâna	iti	na	tu	etarisam
D	athi	pavutam	vate	dâne	sathiti			hedisam
J	* *	* *	* *	* *	* *			* *

G	asti dâna	va	anagâho	va	yârisam	dhammadânam	va
D	(athi dâne)	——	anugahe	va	[11] adi va	dhammadâne	——
J	* so dâne	——	anugahe	adi	ve	dhammadâne	——

(*a*) Or perhaps *anetha* or *anyetha*.

G	dhammanugaho	vâ	ta	tukho	mitena	va	suhadayena
D	dhammanuga (he)	———	———	———	———	———	———
J	dhammânugahe	cha	se	chukho •	mitena	———	———

G	va	[8] nyatikena	va	sahayena	va	ovâditavyam
D	———	——— tikena	———	sapâyena	tivi	yovadita
J	———	———	———	———	———	•———

G	tamhi	tamhi	pakaraṇe	idam	kacha	idam
D	tasi	———	pakalanasi	i •	———	———
J	———	———	———	———	———	yam

G	sâdhu	iti	imini	saka	• •	swagam	ârâdhetu iti
D	———	———	[12] imena	——— ka	———	———	alâdhayitave
J	sadhu	———	imena	sakiye	• •	swage	aladhayitave

G	kâcha	• • •	iminâ	katavyataram	yata	swagâradhi.
D	———	———	———	———	tasa	alabhi.
J	kinhi	———	imena	kaṭaviyatala	———	———

EDICT X.

S	[21] Devanampriyo	Priyadarṣi	Raya	yaso	va	kirti	va
K	Devânampiye	Piyadasi	Lâja	yaso	vâ	kiti	vâ
G	Devânampiyo	Piyadasi	Râjâ	yaso	va	kiti	va
D	[13] ——— piye	Piyadasi	Lâja	yaso	vâ	kiti	vâ
J	———	———	———	[21] yaso	va	kiti	vâ

S	na	mahatha	va	ha	manyati	anyata	yo
K	———	mahâthâ	vâ	———	manati	anatâ	yam
G	na	mahâthâ	va	hâ	manyate	anyata	———
D	na	———	va	na	mannati	vakitivâ	
J	(———	———	———	*omitted*		———	———)

S	pi	yaso	sriti	va	imati	tena tasa	ayatiya cha
K	pi	yasa	va kiti	va	ichhati	tadatwaye	ayatiyo cha
G	———	———	———	———	———	tadâdwano	dighaya cha
D	———	———	———	———	ichhati	ta datwaye	anuati
J	———	———	———	———	ichhati	tâ datwâye	anyatiyo cha

S	tada	dharmasuṣusha	suṣusha	a	meti
K	jane	dhammasususâ	sususâ	ta	mati
G	me janâ	dhammasusunsâ	sususa	tam	
D	jane	[14] dhammasususâ	sususa	tam	me
J	jane	dhammasusûsam	sususa	tam	me

S	dharmavatam	cha	annvidhayatam.
K	dhammavatam	vâ	• nuvidhiyâtati.
G	dhammavatam	cha	anuvidhiyatam.
D	dhamma • •	• •	• • • •
J	• • •	• •	• • • •

S	eta	kaye	Devânampriya	Priyadarṣi	Raya	yaso
K	eta	kaye	Devânampiye	Piyadasi	[20] Lâjâ	yaso
G	eta	kâya	Devânampiyo	Piyadasi	Râja	yaso
D	eta	kâye	———	———	———	yaso
J	———	———	———	———	———	———

S	kiti	—	va	ichhati	ya tu	kichi
K	vâ	kiti	vâ	ichha	am châ	kichi
G	va	kiti	va	ichhati	ya tu	kichi
D	va	kiti	va	i —	—	— chi
J	—	—	— —	—	—	—

S	parakramate	Devânampriyo	Priyadarṣi	Raya	ta	savam
K	lakamati (a)	Devânampiye	Piyadasi	Lâja	ta	savam
G	parâkamate	Devânam (b)	Piyadasi	Râja	ta	savam
D	palâkammati	Devânampiye	* *	* *	* *	* *
J	—	Devânampiye	—	—	—	—

S	paratikaye	va sati	sukali	aparisave	siyati eshe	tu parasraveyam apunyam
K	pâlatikyâye	va kinti	sukale	apapalâsava	siyatiti ese	chu palisakha e apunne
G	paratikâya	va kinti	sakale	apaparisave	asa esa	tu parisaveya apunyam
D	pâlatikâye	va [15] kinti	sakale	apapalâsave	puveyati	palisa * * * *
J	pâlatikaye	vâ kinti	sakale	apapalisave	puveyati	[22] —

S	dukarata kho	eshe	va dakena	va	gena	usadhinya	
K	dukalo chukho	ese	khudakena	vâ	vatenâ	usuṭena	vâ
G	[4] dukarantâ kho	etâm	chhudakena	va	janena	usaṭena	cha
D	* * kaje		va	—	—	—	—
J	—	—	—	—	—	—	—

S	tava * gena	parakamena	savam	pari	cha	ji	eta
K	anata agena	palakamenâ	savam	paliti	—	disa	peta
G	anyata agena	parâkamena	savam	pari	cha	jipta	eta
D	(anna) ta agena	* * * na	savam	—	cha	paliti	ti (?)
J	— —	—	—	—	—	jita	* *

S	(	*omitted*	)	cha	usa *	* *	* *
K	chukho	dikena	latasate *		[29] usaṭena	vâ	dukale.
G	takho	—	—	—	usaṭena		dukaram. (c)
D	[16] khu	dakena	vâ usaṭhena	vâ	usaṭena	cha	dukalata.
J	khu	dukena	vâ usaṭena	va	usaṭena	chu	dukalatale.

N. B.—In the Dhauli and Jaugada texts of Asoka's Series of Rock Inscriptions, the 11th, 12th, and 13th Edicts are omitted, but both texts close with a copy of the 14th edict.

EDICT XI.

S	[23] Devânampriyo	Priyadarṣi	Raya	evam ahati ; nasti	edisam	dânam	yarisam
K	Devânampiye	Piyadasi	Lâja	hevam (d) hâ nâthi	hedisam	dânam	yâlisam
G	Devânampiyo	Piyadasi	Râja	evam âha nâsti	etârisam	dânam	yârisam

S	dharmadanam	dharmasanstavo	—	dharmasamvibhago	—	dharmasambandho	va
K	dhammadâne	(*omitted*)	—	dhammasamvibhâgo	—	dhammasambandha	—
G	dhammadânam	dhammasanstavo	vâ	dhammasamvibhâgo	vâ	dhammasambandho	va

(a) The letter *p* is omitted in the original text.

(b) *piye* is omitted in the original.

(c) Burnouf (Le Lotus, p. 659) has given his reading of the text of this Edict, with a translation, which differ from those of Prinsep and Wilson.

(d) The initial letter *â* of *âhâ* is omitted in the original text.

S	* ta	idam	——	datam bhatakanam	samapaṭipati	matapitushu	——
K	tata	ese	——	dâsa bhaṭakasi	samyâpaṭipati	mâtapitisu	——
G	[3] tata	idam	bhavati	dâsa bhatakamhi	samapatipati	mâtari pitari	sâdhu

S	suṣushu	mitasastuta	nyatakanam	Sramaṇa	Bramaṇa	sa * *	[24] danam
K	sususâ	mitasathuti	nâtikyânam	Samana	Bambhanâ	nâ	dâne
G	sususâ	mitasastuta	nyâtikânam	Bâhmaṇa	Samaṇa	sâdhu	dânam

S	prananam	anarambho	——	etam	vatavo	pitrena	pi	putrena
K	[30] pânânam	anâlambho	——ese	——	vataviye	pitina	pi	puto
G	[3] pânânam	anârambho	sâdhu	etam	vatavyam	pitâ	va	putena

S	pi	va	bhatena	pi	va	mitrena	pi	mitra
K	pi	——	bhâtinâ	pi	sava	mikyena	pi	mita
G	——	va	bhâtâ	——	va	——	——	mita

S	sastutana	——	——	ava	pativeṣiyena	——	sadhu	ido
K	ṣanthutâna	——	——	avâ	paṭivesiyenâ	iyam	sâdhu	iyam
G	sastutana	nyâtikena	va	âva	pativesiyehi	idam	sâdhu	idam

S	katavo	so	tatha	karatam	iha	loka cha	aradheti	——
K	kaṭaviye	ṣo	tathâ	kalanta	hida	lokikye dhikam	aladhe	hoti
G	katavyam	[4] so	tathâ	karu	i(ha)	lokachasa	ârâdho	hoti

S	parata	cha	anantam	punyam krasava (*a*)	[25] bho	tena	dharmadanena.
K	palata	cha	anantam	punâ paṣavate	——	tena	dhammadanenâ.
G	parata	cha	anantam	punyam ——	bhavati	tena	dhammadânena.

EDICT XII.

S	——	——	——	——	——	——	——
K	Devânampiye	Piyadasi	[31] Lâjâ	savâ	pâsanḍâni	——	pavajitâni
G	Devânampiye	Piyadasi	Râja	sava	pâsanḍâni	cha	pavajitâni

S	——	——	——	——	——	——	——	——
K	——	gahathâni	vâ	pujati	dânena	——	vividheya	cha
G	cha	gharistâni	cha	pujayati	dânena	cha	vividhâya	cha

S	——	——	——	——	——	——	——	——
K	pujayene	——	——	cha	tathâ	dâne	vâ	pujâ
G	pujâyene	pûjayati	[2] nena	tu	tathâ	dânam	va	pujo

S	——	——	——	——	——	——	——	——
K	va	Devânampiye	manati	athâ	kinti	ṣâlâ	vaḍhiṣiyâti	ṣava
G	va	Devânampiyo	manyate	yathâ	kiti	sâra	vaḍhî asa	sava

S	——	——	——	——	——	——	——	——
K	pâṣanḍânam	ṣâlâ	vaḍhinâ	bahuvidhâ	taṣa	——	cha	iyam
G	pâsanḍânam	sâra	vaḍhitu	bahuvidhâ	tasa	tasa	tu	idam

(*a*). In Arian-Pâli the two letters *k* and *p* may easily be mistaken; but as the dental sibilant of Shâhbazgarhi differs from the palatal sibilant of Khâlsi, it is possible that the words may be different.

S	—	—	—	—	—	—	—
K	mule	ava	chatuti	kinti	• ta ata pâṣandâ	va pujâ	va palapaṣaṇḍâ
G	mûlam ya	va	viguti	kinti	âtta paṣanḍa	pûjâ	parâpâsanḍa

S	—	—	—	—
K	galaha nam	tana apa ṣaka kate vam noṣayâ		
G	garahâ		va no bhave	

S	—	—	—	—	—	—	—
K	32 apakalanaṣi	lahakâ	vâ	ṣiyâ	taṃṣi	taṃṣi	pakalanaṣi
G	apakaranamhi	lahakâ	va	asa	tamhi	tamhi	pakaranye

S	—	—	—	—	—	—	—	—
K	pujeta	viya	chu	—	palapâṣanḍâ	tena	tena	akâlana
G	pûjeta	yâ	tu	eva	parâpâsanḍâ	tena	tena	pakaranyena

S	—	—	—	—	—	—	—
K	hevam	kalata	atapaṣanḍâ	badha	vadhiyeti	palapâṣanḍâ	pi vâ
G	evam	katam	âttapâsanḍa	cha	vadhayati	parâpâsanḍasa	cha

S	—	—	—	—	—	—	—
K	upakaloti	tadâ anatha	kaloti	atapâṣanda	cha	chhanoti	palapâṣanḍa
G	upakaroti	tadantetha	karoti	âttapâsanḍam	cha	chhanoti	parâpâsandasa

S	—	—	—	—	—	—	—	—
K	pi	va	apakaloti	ye	hi	kacha	atapâṣanda	puyâti
G	va	pi	apakaroti	yo	hi	kâchi	âttapâsanḍa	pujayati

S	—	—	—	—	—	—	—
K	33 palapâsanḍa (*a*)	vâ	galahati	save	atapâsanḍa	bhatiyâ	vâ kinti
G	parâpâsanḍam	va	garahati	sava	âttapâsanḍâ	bhatiya	kinti

S	—	—	—	—	—	—	—	—
K	atapâsanḍa	dipaye	ma	so	cha	punâ	tathâ	kâlota
G	âttapâsanḍam	dipayo	ma iti	so	cha	puna	tatha	karoti

S	—	—	—	—	—	—	—
K	—	bâdhatale	upâhanti	atapâsanḍa pi sama	viyeva	sâdhu	kinti
G	âttapâsanḍam	bâḍhataram	upahanâti	tasa ma	vâyo eva	sâdhâ	kinti

S	—	—	—	—	—	—	—	—
K	manuamanusâ	dhammam	suneyu	châ	sususâyu	vâ ti	hevam	pi
G	manyamanyasa	dhammam	sunâja	cha	susunsera	cha	evam	hi

S	—	—	—	—	—	—	—	—
K	Devânampiyasa	ichhâ	kinti	34 savapâsanḍa	bahu	putâ (*b*)	châ	—
G	Devânampiyasa	ichhâ	kinti	savapâsanḍâ	bahu	sutâ (*b*)	cha	asu

S	—	—	—	—	—	—	—	—
K	kalânâgâ	cha hâ	ve yati eva	tatâ	tatâ	pasannâte	hi	vataviye
G	kalânyâgama	cha	asu ye cha	tata	tata	pasannâte	hi	vatavya

(*a*). Here *pâsanda* is spelt with the dental *s* instead of the palatal *ṣ*, as in other places of this latter part of the Khalsi text.

(*b*). Here it is difficult to say whether the engraver has changed the letters *p* and *s*, which are very much alike, as the two words *puta* and *suta* have the same meaning.

S	——	——	——	——	——	——	——	——	——
K	Devânampiye	no	tathâ	dânam	vâ	pujâ	vâ	mannato	athâ
G	Devânampiyo	no	tathâ	dânam	va	pûjâ	va	manyato	yathâ

S	——	——	——	——	——	——	——	——	——
K	kinti	sâlâ	vaḍhi	ṣiyâ	sava	pâsanḍa ti	bahukâ	cha	etâyâ
G	kinti	sâra	vâḍhi	asa	sava	pâsandânam	bahukâ	va	etâya

S	——	——	——	——	——	——	——	——
K	thâye	viyâpatâ	dhammamahâmâtâ	——	ithidhiya	kha	mahâmâtâ	vacha
G	athâ	vyâpatâ	dhammamahâmâtâ	cha	itthijha	kha	mahâmâtâ	cha vacha

S	——	——	——	——	——	——	——	——	——
K	bhumikyâ	— ane	vâyâ	nikâye	[35] iyam	cha	etasâ	phaleyam	atapâsanḍâ
G	bhûmikâ	cha anya	cha	nikâye	ayan	cha	etasa	phaluya	âttapâsanḍa

S	——	——	——	[1] dipana (a)	——	chha vepa	pitasa.
K	vadhi	cha	hoti dhammasa	cha dipanâ	athâ	vepâbhi	pitasâ.
G	vadhi	cha	hoti dhammasa	cha dîpanâ	——	——	——

EDICT XIII.

S	Devânampriyasa	Priyardasisa	Raye	kali *	vi * ta	* *
K	Devânampiyasa	Piyadasine	Lâjine	kalikhyam	vijitâ	diyâḍha
G	——	——	——	——	——	——

S	ma	apana	ṣata	asra ṣata	* * *	aha	vudhi
K	mâ	apâna	satâ		sahaṣeye tuphâ	ahâ	vudhena
G	——	——	——	——	——	——	——

S	patesa	——	etahatam	bahu	ti * *	ka * *
K	ṣatesa	pasamâtam	tatahate	bahu	tivate	kevâ miṭe
G	patasa	pasamâtam	etâhatam	bahu	tîvatâ	kammatu

S	[2] tari nata cha santa	ladheshu	Kali (ngeshu)		——	dhar
K	tatâ tha vâ sâdhuna	ladhesu	Kalingesu	ti	vo	dhammavaye
G	tatâ pachhâ adhûnâ	ladhesu	Kalingesu	ti	ve	dhammavâyo

S	ma mata	dhamanusathi	cha	——	* * * *
K	[36] dhammakammatâ	dhammânusathi	châ	Devânam piyasâ	je athi anusaye
G	* * *	* * *	——	——	——

S	Devânampriyasa	vijitaviya	kayi (?)	[3] avijitamhiti	jina	mano	yota
K	Devânampiyasâ	vijitavi	kalikhyâni	avijitamhi	jine	mane	etu
G	——	——	——	——	——	——	——

S	ta	vata	ti	maranam	sta	apada	——
K	tâ	vadha	vâ	maline	vâ	apavâho	vâ
G	——	vadho	va	maranyam	va	apavâho	va

(a). Here begins the legible portion of the inscription on the back of the Shâhbâzgarhî rock.

S	janasa	———	ye taram radhi lipa	badham	shana	deya	matu
K	janasâ	che	———	bâdhi	vedana	ya	mate (*a*)
G	janasata	———	———	bâdham	védana	———	mata

S	garamata	cha	ma	Devanam priyasa * * ta cha	sa cha
K	galamate (*b*)	ba	va	Devânam piyasa iyampichu tato	galu
G	gannamata	ba	va	De ——— ———	———

S	sacha	matura	Devanampriyasa	savata ba	* vasasti	Bramaṇa
K	mata	—— tâle	Devânampiyasa	[27] savatâ	vasati	Bambhanâ
G	———	———	———	———	———	———

S	Sramaṇa	———	pâshanda	gatethi	vayesa	hatha	jasha
K	va Sama (*c*) vâ	anavâ	pâṣanda	gihithâ	vayeṣu	vihitâ	* thasa
G	———	———	———	———	———	———	- ——

S	etam	bhoti	suṣusha	mata	pitri	suṣusha	shusuri	tana
K	agine	* *	sususâ	mâta	pita	sususâ	gulu	———
G	———	———	* * sa	mâta	pitari	susunsâ	guru	———

S	sususha	mitasantala	sahaya	[5] nyatike	shunasa	bhotikanam	sa * *
K	susa (*c*)	mitasanthata	sahâya	nâtike	susuṣa	bhatikâ	sagâ ma
G	susunsâ	mitasanstata	sahâya	nyâtike	sadâsa	———	———

	pratipapati	tanam sharatam	———	bhoti	apragatho	va	vadham
K	paṭipati	dandḥaliti tâle	santetâ	hoti	pasaghâte	vâ	'vadhe
G	———	———	———	———	———	———	———

S	va	vadho cha anya natarika	manampasharam pi sati	hitanam	sava
K	vâ	abhilâtânam vikhini khamane	[28] yesamvâ pi vavi	hitanam	sine
G	———	———	———	———	———

S	avi pra	adi	atrasha	tara	sastata	sa	aya	nyâti
K	pe avipa	hine	etânam	mita	ṣanthutâ	ṣa	pâ	natikye
G	———	———	———	———	———	———	ya	nyâtika

S	bhavasada	[6] prapunati	tatam	tam	pitesha	vo	upaghato
K	viyâsanam	pâpunâta	tatâ	so	pitanâme	vâ	upâghâtâ
G	vyasanam	papunoti	vata	so	pi tesa	——	upaghâto

S	bhoti panti	bhagam	cha atam sante maneyanam gatamanam	cha	Devânampriyasa
K	pati pati	bhâgam	cha esa sava manayanam gula	vate mâ	Devânampiyasâ
G	patipaṭi	bhago	vâsâ sava ———	——	———yato

S	———	nasti	cha	ekatarehi	pasandehi	(
K	nâthi cha sejana padeyâ tâ	nâthi	———	imenikaya	ânatâyenesa	[29] Bambhane
G	———	nâsti	manusânam	ekataramhi	pâsandamhi	(

S	(*omitted.*)
K	châ samane châ nathi châ ku vâpi janapadasi yatha nathi munisânam eka tala sâ pi pasanisino
G	(*omitted*

(*a*) These two words may be read as *muti* and *galamute*.
(*b*) The *na* of *samana* is omitted in the original.
(*c*) The second *su* of this word is omitted in the original.

S	na nama	prasade	sayame	tre	jatuna	taraka
K	nâma	pasâde	se avata	ke	jane	tada
G	na nâma	pâsâde	yavata	ko	janapada	* *

S	nalagehata	cha	metam	cha	apara	a	cha
K	Kalingesu pinete	cha	maṭa	cha	papavudha	*	ba
G	—— [6] nayasaka *	va	mitaneya	vapi	ataviyo		

S	a cha	tarata	[7] sata	Bhagava	sahasra	Bhagava
K	——	tatâ	puto	Bhâgava	sahasâ	Bhâgavâ
G	——	——	——	——	——	——

S	ajagatra	matra	rava	Devânampiyasa	yo pibho
K	ajagalu	mateva	——	Devânampiyasû	——
G	——	——	——	——	——

S	aprakati	yati	chha	mitratiya	matera		Devânampriyasa
K	——	——	——	——	——	——	——
G	——	——	——	——	——	——	Devânampiyasi

S	yam sako chha manayaya pihi athâbi Devanampriyasa a * * tam bhoti rati anadeti
K	—— —— —— —— —— ——
G	sâpi jite sati —— —— —— —— ——

S	anatija	piti	anatrape	pricha	pabhatre	[8] Devanam	——
K	——	——	——	——	——		
G	——	——	——	——	——		

S	priya	sava	bhutânam	achhati		sayamam	
K	(a)	[3] sava	* * *	——	——	* yama	——
G	——	[7] sava	bhutânam	achhatim	cha	sayamam	cha

S	samam	vatiya	rabhasi	aye	cha	mati	masajuya	Devanampriyasa
K	samam	valiya	madavati	iya	vu	ma	* * *	[3] Devânampiyasâ
G	samam	(5 letters) cherâm			cha	mâdana	cha	——

S	yo	dharma	vijayo	sanam	ḍanaladha	Devanam priyasa	i a
K	ye	dhamma	vijaye	se cha	punaladhe	Devânam pi	* *
G	——	——	——	——	——	——	——

S	cha	save shu	chham	anteshu	[9] ashâsu	piyo jana	sacho	. shasantam
K	cha	[4] save	sacha	atesu	asasu	pichhâ jano	* *	satosa ato
G	——	——	——	——	——	——	——	——

S	ANTIYOKE	nâma	Yona	Râja	paran	cha	tena
K	ANTIYOGE	nâma	Yona	* *	palan	cha	tenâ
G	* * * *	*	* Yona	Râja	paran	cha	tena

S	ANTIYOKENA	chatura	IIII	rajane	TURAMAYE	nama,
K	[5] ANTIYOGENA	chatuli	+	lâjane	TULAMAYE	nâma,
G		chaṭuro		râjâno *	TURAMAYO	cha,

(a) The Khalsi text here begins again with the 2nd line on the S face of the rock.

S	ANTIKINI	nama,	MAKA	nâma,	ALIKASANDARE	nâma
K	ANTEKINA	nâma,	MAKA	nâ [6] ma,	ALIKYASADALE	nâma
G	ANTAKANA	cha,	MAGA	cha	———	———

S	niche	*Choḍa,*	*Panda*	avam	*Tambapaniya*	hevam	mevam
K	nicham	*Choḍa,*	*Pandiyâ*	avam	*Tambapanniyâ*	heva	meva
G	———	———	———	———	———	———	———

S	———	———	hena	raja	visha tini	*Yona-kamboyeshu,*
K	heva	meva	[7] pâdâ (*a*)	lâjâ	vishamvasi	*Yona-kabojesu,*
G	—— ——	———	———	———	———	———

S	*Nabhaka Nabhamateshu*	[10] *Bhoja-Piṭinikeshu,*	*Andhra-Pulindeshu*	savatam:
K	*Nâbhaka-Nâbha-pantisu*	*Bhoja-Pitinikyesu,*	[8] *Andha-Palandesu,* (*b*)	savatâ:
G	———	* * * *	[9] * *dha-Pirindesu,*	savata:

S	Devânampriyasa	dhamanuṣasti	———	———	Devânampriyasa
K	Devânampiyasa	dhammânusathi	anuvatantiyâta	pidutâ	[9] Devânampiyasâ
D	Devânampiyasa	dhammânusastim	anuvatareyata	pidûti	* * * *

S	detanavam chantiti	piṣutu	Devânampriyasa	dhamavutam tivena	dhamanusasti
K	neyantito	pisutu	Devânam pinniya (*c*)	lamavutam vadhanam	[10] dhammânusathi
G	———	———	———	———	———

S	dhamanuvidhiyanti	anuvadhiyesam	* cha sa * ludha	neta	kena	bhoti
K	dhamma anuvidhiyama	anuvidhiyisam	achâyo se * ladhe	[11] eta	kenâ	hoti
G	———	———	———	———	[10] vija	yo

S	savatam		vijaye		vijaye [11]	piti rasa seludha	bhoti
K	savata	vijaye (*c*)	tâ	pitilase	gadhâ sâ hoti	piti	hoti
G	savatha	puna	vijayo	piti raso	ladhâ sâ ——	piti	hoti

S	priti	dhamavijaya	nivam akatutisam	priti	parantika	mevam
K		dhammavijayam	[12] sila hakâ ve kho	sâpiti	pâlantikya	meve
G		dhammavijayamhi	———	———	———	———

S	mahavila	menyati	Devânampriyo	etati	cha	athaye	ayo
K	mahâpha * li	maṇnanti	Devânampiye	[13] etâye	châ	athâye	iyam
G		———	———	———	—— ——	———	———

S	dhamalipi	likhita	kiti	putra	prapotra	me	asam	chanam
K	dhammalipi	likhita	kiti	putâ	papota	me	anam	[14] navam
G	———	———	———	———	———	———	———	———

S	vijaya	ma	vijasavam	amanye	shakhuda	yo	tijasajati
K	vijayam	ma	vijayantaviya	manisu	sayakasi	no	vijayasikhanti
G	vijayam	ma	vijetavyam	mam	nyasarasake	eva	vijâyechhâti

S	chala va	daṇḍa	ta	ha	ronche	tutam rana	vija	manyanye
K	* châ la-va	[15] daṇḍa	tâ	vâ	loche	tutameva chu	vijayam	manataye
G	* *	———	———	———	———	———	———	———

(*a*) This word is not very clear:—it may be *pada* or *panda*.
(*b*) The text is here very indistinct.
(*c*) The word *vijaye* is inserted in small letters above the line, having been originally omitted by the engraver.

S	[13] dhamavijaya	———	———	paralokike	sava	cha
K	dhammavijayese	pida	lokikya	pala [16] lokiye	savâ	cha
G	———	———	———	———	———	———

S	titati bhotu ya numa tata saï	hidelokika		paranlokika,	
K	kanilati ho * uga mala ti sâpi	hidâlokika		palalokikyâ.	
G	———	* i * lokikâ	cha	paralokikâ	cha.

EDICT XIV.

S	[13] Aya	dhamalipi	Devânampriyena	Piṣina (a)	Ranyina	likhapita	———
K	[17] Iyam	dhammalipi	Devânampiyenâ	Piyadasinâ	Lâjinâ	likhâpitâ	athi yevâ
G	Ayam	dhammalipi	Devânampiyena	Piyadasino	Ranyâ	lekhâpitâ	asti evâ
D	[17] Iyam	dhammalipi	Devânampiyena	Piyadasina	Lâjina	likhi * *	———
J	———	———	———	———	———	———	———

S	———	asti	tesam nyitena	asti yo	vistitena	—— hi	savatam sa	savvo
K	[18] sukhitena	athi	majhimenâ	athi	vithaṭenâ	no hi	savatâ	savo
G	sankhitena	asti	majhamena	asti	vistaṭena	nacha	savam (b)	pavata
D	sankhitena	athi	majhamena	——	———	nâpi	save	savata
J	———	——	[24] * jhimena	athi	vithaṭena	nâpi	save	savata

S	gantite	ma olake	hi	vijite	: bahu	cha	likhite	likhipaṣa
K	ghanṭite	mahâlake	hi	[19] vijite	: bahu	va	likhite	lekhapeṣâ
G	ghaṭitam	mahâlake	——	pivijitam	: bahu	cha	likhitam	likhapayisam
D	ghantiṭe	[18] mahantehi	——	vijaye	: bahu	ke cha	likhite	likhi yisa
J	ghaṭite	mahantehi	——	vijaye	——	——	——	——

S	mi cheva	amicha atra	punapane	pa * shanata	tasa tasa	———
K	mi cheva	nikyam athi mi hetâ	punapuna	[20] ladhita	tasa tasâ	athasâ
G	chema	asti cha etakam	punapuna	vutam	tasa tasa	athasa
D	———	athi pa cha	———	———	———	———
J	———	———	———	———	———	[25] * * sa

S	———	———	———	[14] ta *	praṭipajayati	sosiyaya atam kiche
K	madhuliyâye	yena	jane :	tathâ	paṭipajeyâse	sâyâ ata kichhi
G	mâdhuritaya	kiti	jano :	tathâ	paṭipajetha	* tata ekadâ
D	——— taya	[19] kinticha	jane :	tathâ	paṭipajeyâti	epi cha hetam
J	mâdhuliyâye	kinticha	jane	tathâ	paṭipajeyâti	epi cha hetam

S	asamatam	likhitam	desam	va	sankhaye	kâranam	va
K	[21] asamati	likhite	disâ	vâ	sankhaye	kâlanam	vâ
G	asamâtam	likhitam	asadesam	va	sachhâya	kâraṇam	va
D	asamati	likhitesam	* * * sam	——	———	———	——
J	———	———	———	——	———	———	——

(a). Sic in original.

(b). It is clear from the agreement of the other four texts that the initial *p* of this word should be *s*. A single stroke omitted by the engraver on the left hand of the letter has left the unfinished *s* a simple *p*.

S	alochanti	lipikara	sava aparadhena
K	alochayita	lipikala	palâdhena vâ.
G	[6] alovettâ	lipikarâ	paradhena va.
D	* * ti	lipikala	* * * ti.
J	———	———	———

The Girnar text originally concluded with a single isolated line of which only the latter portion now remains. It reads as follows :—

* * * * * *   va   sweto   hasti   savaloka   sukhaharo   nama.

No. 6.

First separate Edict at Dhauli and Jaugada.

See Prinsep, Journal Bengal Asiatic Society, VII, 441, and Burnouf, Le Lotus de la Bonne Loi, pp. 671—693.

D	[1] Devânampiyasa	vachanena	Tosaliyam	mahâmâta	nagala	viyopâlaka (*a*)
J	[1] Devânampiye	hevam âhâ	Samâpâyam	mâhâmâta	nagale	viyopalakahe

D	vataviyam.	Am	kichhi	dakhâmi	hakam	tam	ichhâmi	kinti
J	vataviyi.	Am	kichhi	dâkhâmi	hannam	tam	ichhâmi	kinti

D	———	e *	paṭivedayeham	[2] duvâlate	cha	âlabhe	ham,	esa cha
J	anam	ena	paṭivedayeham	[2] duvâlate	cha	âlabhe	ham,	esa cha

D	me	mokhyamata	duvâle :	etasi	athasi	am	tuphe	si
J	me	mokhiyamate	duvâle :	———	———	am	tuphe	su

D	[4] anusathi	tu	phe	hi	bahûsu	pânasahasesu	âyata	pana me
J	anusathi		phe (*b*)	hi	bahusu	panasahasesu	a *	* * *

D	ga ve ma	sumunisânam	save [5] munise	pajâ mamâ	atha	pajâye	ichhâmi
J	ga vo ma	* munisânam	sava munise	[3] paja ——	atha	pajiye	ichhâmi

D	hakam	sa	vena	hitasukhenam	———	hida lokika	[6] pâlalokikâya
J	* *		vena	hita sukhenam	yujeyuti	hida logika	palalokikayam

D	yujevû ti (he me hasa) (*c*) sûpi	ichhâmi	dukam	no cha	pâphunâtha	âvâ
J	——— he meva me iya sava	munisa	su *	ta he	* * * notha	ava

D	[7] gamake	iyam	atha	kecha va	eka	pulise	manâti
J	gamake	[4] iyam	atha	kecha	eka	pulase	* *

(*a*) Prinsep reads *vihâlaka* omitting the second syllable *yo*, which is distinct in both texts. Burnouf reads the word correctly as *viyopâlaka*. The letter *y* is indistinct in the Dhauli text, but the vowel *o* is quite clear.

(*b*) The syllable *tu* is here omitted in the original text.

(*c*) The four syllables within brackets are taken from Prinsep. The space now blank is sufficient for about eight letters; but the whole may not have been engraved; and the letters given by Prinsep were copied by Kittoe, although they have since been lost.

D etam sepi desam no savam dekhatehi tuphe etam [8] su vihitâ
J * tam sepi desam no savam dekhathahi cha me pi su vitâ

D pi niti yam eka pulise athaya bandhanm va
J pi bahuka athiya eti eka munise ——— bandhanam

D palikilesam vâ pâpunâti tata hota [9] akasmâ tena
J paliki * * ——— papunâti * * * ta * [5] * smagâ tena

D bandhanâtâ ka: anne cha * * bahu janodaviye dukhiyati: tata
J bandha cha yuve daya cha vata bahûke ——— vedayanti: tata

D ichhitaviye tuphe hi: ——— kinti majham paṭipâdaye mâti
J ——— tuphe hi: * * taye kinti majha paṭipâtaye ma *

D Imehi cha jatehi no sampaṭi pajati: isâya, âsulopena,
J Imehi ——— jatehî no sampaṭipajati: isâ * asulopena,

D [11] nithuliyena, tûlanâya, anâvûtiya, âlasiyena, kâlammathena, se ichhitaviye
J nithuliyena, [6] tuliye, anâvûtiye, * * yena, kalamathanam, hevam ichhitaviye

D kinti ——— ete [12] jatânihu mamâti: eta sa
J kinti me eteni jatâm veva mohveyûti: ——— ———

D cha savasa ——— mûle anâsulope ——— atulana cha niti chham
J savasa cha iyam mula anasulope cha * tu * * cha ni * *

D ekilante siyâ · [13] nate uga cha samchalita viyentu va hitaviya ———
J iyam nijat [7] samchalitu uthâya * * tavyatâ va ṭitaviya pi

D etaviye vâ hevam mevam edam * * tuphâ katena vataviye [14] aganam ne dekhata
J etaviye piniti yam eka deveni annâne nijha masaviye ———

D hevam cha hevam cha Devânampiyasa anusathi se mahâ * * sa tasa
J hevam ——— Devânampi * * * sa * * * * * [8] tam

D sampatipâda [15] mahâ apâye asampaṭipati va paṭipâdayamî nehi etannanthi
J ma phalehati ——— ——— asampaṭipati ——— mahâpâye hoti vi paṭipatâyam tanno

D swagasa (*a*) âlâdhino lâja ladhi [16] duâhalehi ima sakam meva
J swaga âladhâno laja dhi du âhale etasa masa

D makate manam: atileke sampaṭi pajamino cha etam ——— swagam ———
J samo * * va * * * * [9] cha ananeyam esatha swagam cha

(*a*) Here Burnouf with his usual sagacity suggested the true reading of *swagasa*, "du ciel." See Le lotus, p. 681.

D	[17] âlâdhayisathîti	tam apaniniyam ehatha.	Iyam	cha	lipi	
J	âlâ (dha) yasathâ	———	Iyam	cha	lipi	anu

D	Tisa	Nakhatena	sotaviyam [18]	antalâpi	cha tise * *	na	sikhanâm ni (a) ekanâpi
J	Tisam	———	sotaviyam	alâpi	va———	na	sata tila e ka * pi

D	sotaviya: hevam cha kâlantam	tuphe [19] cha ghatha	sampaṭipâdayitave	etâye	———
J	* * * *	* * *	* * [10] tave	etâye	cha

D	athâye	iyam	lipi	likhitâ hida	ena	———	[20] nagala
J	athâye	iyam		vata lipî	ena	mahâmâtâ	nagala

D	viyopâlakâ	sâsatam	samayam	yujavû nagala:	janasa (b)	akasmâ · pali	bodha va [21]	akasmâ pali
J	———	———		———	———	———	———	———

D	ki sâne	vano siyâti.	Etâye cha athâye hakam	dhamma te (c)	panchasu	panchasu
J	———	———	———	———	[11] panchasu	panchasu

D	vasesu [22]	———	nikhimayisami	e akha khase	a chanḍa	sa khi nâlambhe
J	vasesu	anusayânam	nikhâmayisami	mahâmâtam	a chanḍa	phela hata * nele

D	hosati: etam atham	jânita	* * *	thâ [23] kalati atha mama anusathîti.	Ujenite (d)
J	———	———	———	——— ———	Ujeni

D	picha	kumâle	etâyevam	athâye	nikhamayisati	hedisammeva vagam,
J	———	kumâle	vi * tasa	te	———	———

D	no cha	atikâmayisati tinivasâni he meva	Takhasilate pi (e)	adâ am *	* [25] te	mahâmâta
J	———	———	———	va chanika	a	ma

D	nikhamisanti	anusayânam,	tada ahâpayita	atane	kammam	etam pi
J	anusâyanam	nikhamisanti;	———	atina	kammam	———

D	jânisanti	[26] tam pitithâ kalanti athâ lâjine anusathîti.
J	——— sa ———	——— ——— ———

(a) This letter is doubtful, it may be *si*.

(b) Burnouf reads *yavaju-kasa*, instead of *nagala janasa*, after which he allows a space for five letters.

(c) Here both Prinsep and Burnouf read *mate*, but the text does not repeat *ma* after *dhamma*.

(d) *Ujeniya* is the reading of both Prinsep and Burnouf, but the letter *te* is quite clear both in the photograph and in Mr. Beglar's impressed copy. Prinsep identifies *Ujenite* with *Ujeniya*, a younger brother of Mahindo (Bengal Asist. Soc. Jour. VII, 454), but Burnouf has rightly pointed out that *Ujeniya* was only a title of Prince Mahindo, who was born at Ujain see:—Le Lotus, p. 688.

(e) Here Burnouf reads *stasi*, supposing that the left limb of the letter *s* had been omitted by Kittoe; but the letter is most distinctly *pi* and not *si*.

No. 7.

Second Separate Edict at Dhauli and Jaugada.

D	Devânampiyasa vachanena: TOSALIYAM *kumâle* —— mahâmâtâ cha vataviya: am
J	Devânampiye hevam âhâ: SAMAPAYAM mahâmâta *Lâja* va cha nika vataviyâ, am
D	kichhi dakhâmi (*a*) hakam tam —— ——
J	kichhi dakhâmi hakam tam ichhâmi hakam kinti * ka mana [2] paṭipâtayeham
D	[2] duvâlate cha âlabheham; esa cha me mokhyamata duvâlâ.
J	duvâlate cha âlabheham; esa cha me mokhiyamato duvâla.
D	Etasi athasi am tuphe (*b*) hi anusathi tuphe hi bahûsu pâna sahasesu âyata jana me gachha cha
J	Etasa athasa am tuphe * anusathi (*c*) (omitted)
D	sumunisânam; save sumunise paja mama [3] atha (*c*) pajâye ichhâmi hakam niti,
J	(omitted) sava manisâ [3] me paja atha pajâye ichhâmi kinti me
D	savena hita sukhena hidalokika pâlalokikâye yujevûti hevam ——
J	savene hita sukhena yu(je) yûti hidalogika pâlalokike na hevam mevam me
D	[4] —— siyâ antânam avijitânam kichham vasu Lâja ——
J	ichhe sava manisâ su sayâ anta kuthâ vijitânam kinchham desu Lâja apho suti eta kâvû
D	meva ichhâmi ma antesu pâpunevute: iti Devânampiye —— vâgûna
J	me ichha —— antesu pâpuneyu: —— Lâja ichhati ame vigina
D	—— mamâye [5] huve vûti, Aswasevu cha —— sukhameva lahevu mama teno
J	heya [6] mamiyaye ——. Aswasepu cha me sukhameva laseya mama teno
D	dukha hevam * nava iti khami tine: Devânampiya ahâ: kâti echa
J	—— hevam la sâha ne yukhamisa tie: Lâja —— [7] echha
D	kiye : khamitave mama nimitam cha dhammam cha levû
J	kiye : khamitave mama nimetam cha dhamma cha lenya
D	—— [6] hidaloka —— palalokam cha âlâdhayevû Etasi ——
J	ti hidalogam cha palalogam cha âladhayeyam etâye [8] cha
D	athasi hakam anusâsâmi tuphe anena (*d*) etakena hakam —— anusâsitam
J	athâye hakam tuphe vi anusâsâmi anena etakena hakam tuphe ni anusâsitu
D	chhandam cha veditam (âhayâmi) (*e*) paṭinyo cha mama [7] ajalâsâ hevam
J	chhandam cha su â mama chiti pâṭinâ cha —— [7] achalasa hevam

(*a*). Burnouf reads *dakhamiham* followed by a gap as far as *duvalecha:* but both the Jaugada and Dhauli texts support Prinsep's reading. (See Le Lotus, p. 692).

(*b*). After *tuphe* Burnouf omits all down to *athapajâya;* but Prinsep's reading is supported by the Jaugada text as far as it extends. This portion has peeled off since Kittoe's time, with the exception of the last two letters *mama*.

(*c*). In the Jaugada text the words from *atha pajaye* down to *yujeyuti* are repeated, and the words following *anusathi* down to *savamanise* are altogether omitted.

(*d*). From this word down to *ajalasa* Burnouf supplied the gap left by Prinsep, and his reading is generally confirmed by that of the Jaugada text, as well as by Mr. Beglar's photographs of the Dhauli inscription itself.

(*e*). I had already supplied *âhayâmi* from Burnouf's reading, which is now fully confirmed by Mr. Beglar's photographs.

D	kaṭukam me chalitaviye aswa * * i cha tâni ena—pâpunevâ				iti.	Athâ pitâ tathâ		Devânampiye
J	kaṭukam me chalitaviye aswasa kiyi cha ta ena te pâpune				—. 10 —Athâ pita hevam ne Lâja			

D	aphâka :	athâ	cha	atâ	nam (*a*) hevam	Devânampiye	anusampati	aphe ——
J	ti ——	athâ	——	atâ	———— nâ	————	anusampatâ	hetam a

D	——	————	* athâ	cha	pajâ	hevam	maye	Devânampiyasa	—— se
J	hevam	anusampati	attâ	——	pajâ	hevam	maye	Lâjine	tuphe ni

D	hakam	anusâ-ita	chhandam	cha	——	phâka—	———— desâ
J	hakam	anusâsita	chhandam	cha	veda	taka pisi	chiti patinâchâ ati lapa 12 desa

D	vutike	hosâmi	Etâye	athâye	paṭibalâhi (*b*)	tuphe	aswâsanâye	hitasukhâye
J	ayutike	hosâmi	Etasi	athasi	————	tuphe	aswâsanâye	hitasukhâye

D	cha	tase	* hidalokika	pâlalokikâye	hevam	cha
J	——	tasam	hitalogika	pâlalokikâya	hevam	cha

D	kalantam	tuphe	swagam	âlâdayisatha	(*c*) mama	cha	ânaniyam	ehatha.
J	kalantam	——	swaga	aladhayisatam	mama	cha	ânaneyam	esatha.

D	Etâye	cha	athâye	iyam	lipi	likhitâ :	hida	ena	mahâmâtâ	swasatam
J 14	Etâye	cha	athâye	iyam	lipi	likhitâ :	hida	ena	mahâmâtâ	saswatam (*d*)

D	* samam	10 yajisanti	Asâsanâye	dhamma	chalanâye	cha tesu	antânam :
J	samam	yajesam	Asâsanâye	16 dhamma	chalena *	————	gatam :

D	iyam	cha	lipi	anachâtun (*e*)	masam Tisena	nakhatena	sotaviyâ
J	iyam	cha	lipi	(ana) châtun	mâsamsotatiyâ	Tisena	antalâpi

D	kâmam cha khano khanasi antalâpi tisena	ekena	11 sotaviyâ :	hevam	kalantam tuphe,
J	cha sotaviyâ 16 khanesantam	ekena	si * * viyâ :	hevam	cha kalantam

D	chaghatha	sampaṭi pâdayitave.
J	sanghatha	sampaṭi pâtayitâve.

(*a*) This word was omitted by the original engraver, and afterwards inserted above the line.

(*b*) In the Jaugada text the word preceding *tuphe* would appear to have contained only three letters, of which the last is *hi* preceded by an anuswâra, thus making the final syllable *mhi*. The word seems to me very like *balamhi*. Both Prinsep and Burnouf read *Dubalahi*, which is certainly incorrect.

(*c*) *tata* is here inserted by Prinsep; but there is no space for the letters.

(*d*) Sic in original.

(*e*) Here Burnouf divined the true reading of *anachâtun* mâsam, which agrees also with that of the Jaugada text.

No. 8.

ROCK INSCRIPTION AT SAHASARAM.

Transcript by Dr. G. Bühler.

1 Devânâṁ piye hevaṁ â [hâ sâtilekâni adhit]i yâni saṁvachhalâni aṁ upâsake sumi, na cha bâdhaṁ palakaṁte

2 Saviṁchhale sâdhike aṁ [sumi bâdhaṁ palakaṁ] te. Etena cha aṁtalena Jaṁbudîpasi aṁmisaṁ devâ [hu] saṁ ta.

3 munisâ misaṁ deva kaṭâ pa la[kamasi hi] iyaṁ phale [n]o [cha i]yaṁ mahatatâ vachakiye pâvatave. Khudakena hi pala—

4 Kamamînenâ vipule suag[e sa]kiye âlâ[dhayita]ve. Se etâye aṭhaye iyaṁ sâvâne: khudakâ cha uḍâlâ cha pa—

5 lakamaṁtu, aṁtâ pi chaṁ jânaṁtu, chilathitîke cha palakame hotu. Iyaṁ cha aṭhe vaḍhisati, vipulaṁ pi vaḍhisati

6 diyâḍhiyaṁ avaladhiyenâ diyaḍhiyaṁ vaḍhisati iyaṁ cha savane vivuthena; duve sapaṁnâlâti

7 satâ vivuthâ ti, [sû ñ phra] 256 Ima cha aṭhaṁ. pavatesu likhâpayâ thâya; [yata] vâ; a—

8 thi hete silâthaṁbhâ tata pi likhâpaya thayi.

Notes by Dr. Bühler.—Materials used: Pl. xiv of General Cunningham's *Corp. Inscr. Ind.*, Vol. I; and a photograph supplied by General Cunningham.

Line 1.—The facsimile and photograph show that seven or eight syllables have been lost. The restoration of the first six is absolutely certain on account of the identical readings of *R.* and *B.*—[*aḍhit*]*iyâni* is less certain. I take it for a representative of *aḍhitisâni*, caused by the change of *s* to *h*, and its subsequent loss, just as in Panjâbi *tih*, thirty, and *ikatti*, thirty-one.

Line 2.—Read *saṁvachhale*, R. Six or seven letters have been lost—*R.* and *B.* have two sentences corresponding to this *lacuna*, containing sixteen letters. *S.* can have had one sentence only. The sense requires the sentence given above. Read *amisaṁ* according to *R.* Read *devâ-husaṁ*, as *R.* has *devâ-husu*, and a verb is required. The vertical stroke in the facsimile is the left hand part of the letter *h*. This emendation I owe to Paṇḍit Bhagvânlâl Indraji. Read *te* for *ta*, according to *R.*

Line 3.—Read *devâ*. The *pala* before the lacuna is probable from the photograph. The restoration is certain on account of the corresponding passage in *R.*, which here, as everywhere, substitutes the root *pakam* for *palakam*. The second and third lacunas have been filled in according to *R.*

Line 4.—Restorations according to *R.* and *B.*—Read *sâvane*.

Line 5.—Read *cha janaṁtu*.

Line 6.—Read *sâvane*; the facsimile has *dute*, but according to the photograph *duve*, which the sense requires, is at least probable, if not certain.

Line 7.—Restoration suggested by the fact that two syllables have been lost, and a relative pronoun is desirable, though not absolutely necessary.

No. 9.

ROCK INSCRIPTION AT RUPNATH.

Transcript by Dr. G. Bühler.

1 Devânâṁ piye hevaṁ âhâ: sâtirakekâni aḍhitisâni va[sâ], ya sumi
pâkâ sa [va] ki no cha bâḍhi pakate. Sâtileke chu chhavachhare,
ya sumi haka saṁgha-pâpite

2 bâḍhi cha pakate. Yi imâya kâlâya Jaṁbudipasi amisâ
devâ-husu, to dâni masâ kaṭâ. Pakamasi hi esa phale,
no cha esâ mahatatâpâ-potave: Khudakenâ hi ka.

3 pi parumaminenâ sakiye pipule svage ârodhave. Etiya aṭhâya
cha sâvane kaṭe: khudakâ cha uḍâlâ cha pakamaṁtu ti, atâ pi cha
jânaṁtu; Iyaṁ pakâre cha

4 kiti? chiraṭhitike siyâ. Iya hi aṭhe vaḍhi vaḍhisiti, vipula
cha vaḍhisiti, apaladhiyenâ diyaḍhiyaṁ vaḍhisati. Iya cha
aṭhe pavatisu lekhâpeta vâlata hadha cha; aṭhi

5 silaṭhubhe silâṭhaṁbhasi lâkhâpeta vayata. Etina cha vayajanenâ
yâvatakatu paka ahâle, savara-vivase tavâyati. Vyuṭhenâ sâvane
kaṭe [sû ā phu] 256 sa—

6 ta-vivâsâ ta.

Notes by Dr. Bühler.—Materials used: Two rubbings forwarded by General Cunningham.

Line 1.—Read *sâtilekâni*, the letter [Brahmi letter] looks blurred, and is a mistake for [Brahmi letter]. For *pâkâ* read *hakâ*. There is a faint mark between *sa* and *ki* which may be *va*;—*sâvaki* is required as synonym for *upâsake*;—*saṁgha ushite* is a possible reading, as the letters appear to be half effaced. The reading given above is supported by *B*.

Line 2.—Under the *vâ* of *devâ-husa* there is a vertical stroke resembling an *u*. Probably it is intended to indicate the absorption of the initial *a* of *ahusu*, and is the oldest form of the *avagraha* S. Read *esa* for *esâ*. A letter may have stood between *khudakenâ hi* and *ka*. But I rather think the marks in the impression are accidental scratches.

Line 3.—Read *pakamaminenâ*; *vipule*; *ârâdhave*;—the long *â* in *pakâre* is not quite certain.

No. 10.

ROCK INSCRIPTION AT BAIRAT.

Transcript by Dr. G. Bühler.

1 Devânaṁ piye âhâ: sâti [lekâni * * *i e sa

2 vasâ naṁ ya haka upâsake n[o cha] bâḍhaṁ

3 * * * aṁ mamayâ saṁghe papayite [bâ]dhaṁ cha *

4 Jambudipasi amisâ- naṁ devahi * * vi * * * [pa la] kamasi esa [pha] le

5 [n]o hi esa mahatane vachakaye * * *[pala] rumaminenâ ya * * * pa

6 vipule pi ṣvaṁge [sa]kye âlâdhetave * * [khuda] kâ cha uḍâlâ châ palakamatu ti

7 aṁte pi janaṁtu , ti chilathiti [ke] * * [vi]pulaṁ pi vadhisati

8 diyaḍhiyaṁ vaḍhisati [ŏ phu] 56

Notes by Dr. Bühler.—Materials used: Cunningham, *Corp. Inscr.*, Vol. I, Pl. xiv—and a cloth copy made by Paṇḍit Bhagvânlâl Indraji.

Line 1.—Cloth copy: *devânâṁ*. The remnants of three letters towards the end of the line are also from the latter.

Line 2.—*Corp. Inscr.*—*paka*. Cloth copy shows lower part of *n[o]*—*Corp. Inscr.*—*bâdhi*. Cloth copy has remnants of these letters towards the end of the line.

Line 3.—*C.I.*—*payaye ate* and *bâdhi*. In the cloth copy the top of *dhâ* is wanting.

Line 4.—Cloth copy: *amisâ-na deve pi* and omits *vi*. I conjecture *amisânaṁ devani[su te dâ] ni*. Portions of the letters *laka* appear on the cloth copy.—*C.I.*—*masi*.

Line 5.—*C.I.* begins the line *ha hi:* the cloth copy shows *o* clearly.—*C.I. mapâtane*. I think *mahatana* should be read, as the word forms a compound with *vachakaye*. Read [*pala*] *kumamimenâ*. The cloth copy omits *ya . . . . pa*, which are not easily explained.

Line 6.—Cloth copy: *vipule him svage takye*—*C.I.*—*vipule pi svamge kiye*. The above reading is conjectural, but supported by the analogy of *S.* and *R.* Possibly *sakiye* may be the right form. Towards the end *C.I.* reads [*khuda*] *kâ che*, which is incorrect.

Line 7.—Cloth copy omits *aṁ*[*te*], shows half a *ta* instead of *ti* in *chilathiti*[*ke*], and omits *pu* in [*vi*] *pulaṁ*.

Line 8.—Cloth copy: *diyadhiya vadhasai*, and omits the numeral signs. I must confess that I doubt the correctness of the latter, on account of their position.

Note by General Cunningham.—These numeral signs were brought to my notice by my Assistant, Mr. Carlleyle, the discoverer of the inscription. I have since had fresh impressions made of the whole inscription, from which the dotted numerals given in the plate were taken. Mr. Carlleyle thought that he could trace three numeral figures. That there are marks on the rock at the end of the inscription is quite certain, but as I have not examined the rock myself, I am unable to affirm positively that they are numerals.—A. C.

No. 11.

SECOND BAIRÂT ROCK.

Bur	Piyadaso	LÂja	mÂgadhe	Saugham	abhivÂdemÂnam	ÂhÂ	apÂbÂdhatam
Wil	Piyadasi	LÂja	mÂgadhe	Saugham	abhivâdemânam	âhâ	apâbÂdhatam
A. C.	Piyadaso	LÂja	Mâgadhe	Saugham	abhivÂdemÂnam	âhâ	apâbÂdhatam

Bur	cha	phÂsuvihÂlatam	cha	[2] viditevÂ,	bhante, Âvatake	hÂ	mÂ	budhasi
Wil	cha	pisu vihÂlatam	cha	viditeva,	bhante, Âvatake	ha	mÂ	budhasi
A. C.	cha	phisu vihÂlatam	cha	viditeve,	bhante, âvatake	ha	mâ	Budhasi

Bur	dhammasi	sanghasiti	galavenchÂm	pasade	cha	ekechi,	bhante,
Wil	dhammasi	sanghasiti	golave cham (?)	pasÂde	cha	ekechi,	bhante,
A. C.	Dhammasi	sanghasiti	golave cha	pâsÂde	cha	ekechi,	bhante,

Bur	[3] bhagavatÂ	budhena	bhâsite	save	se	subhâsiteva	echukho,
Wil	BhagavatÂ	Budhena	bhÂsite	save	se	subhÂsite vÂ	echu kho,
A. C.	BhagavatÂ	Budhena	bhÂsite	save	se	subhasite vÂ	echu kho,

Bur	bhante,	pamiyaye	disiya	hevam	sadhamme	[4] chilasatiti ke	hosatiti
Wil	bhante,	pÂmiyÂye	diseyÂ	hevam	sadhamme	chila (va) ti ke	hosatiti
A. C.	bhante,	pâmiyâye	diseyÂ	hevam	sadhamme	chilathiti ke	hosatiti

Bur	alahÂmi	hakÂm	tÂva	tavÂ	imÂni,	bhante,	dhammapayÂyani (a)
Wil	alahÂmi	hÂ (ki)	tavÂ	tÂve	imÂni,	bhante,	(dham) mapaliyÂyÂni
A. C.	alahÂmi	hakam	tavi	tave	imÂni,	bhante,	dhammapaliyÂyÂni

Bur	vinayasa	makase	[5] aliyavasÂni	anÂgata bhayÂni	munigÂthÂ	moneyasûte
Wil	vinayasa	makase	aliyavasÂni	anâgata bhayâni	muni gÂthÂ	mauneya sûte
A. C.	vinayasa	mukase (b)	aliyavasÂni	anÂgata bhayÂni	muni gÂthÂ	moneya sûte

Bur	upatisapasina	eva	lâghulo	[6] vÂde	musÂvÂdam	adhogichya
Wil	(u) patÂsa pasine	echa	lÂghulo	vÂda	musÂvÂ (cha) m	adhigachya
A. C.	Upatisa pasine	echa	Lâghulo	vÂde	musÂvÂdam (c)	adhigichya

Bur	bhagavatÂ	budhena	bhÂsite	etÂni	bhante	dhammapaliyÂyÂni
Wil	bhagavatÂ	budhena	bhÂsite	etÂni	bhante	dhamma paliyÂyÂni
A. C.	BhagavatÂ	Budhena	bhÂsite	etâni	bhante	dhamma paliyÂyÂni

Bur	ichhÂmi	[7] kitibihuke	bhikhapÂ	yechÂ	bhikhÂni	yechÂ	abhikhinam
Wil	ichhÂmi	kiti bahuke	bhikhapÂ	yecha	bhikhani	yecha	abhikhinam
A. C.	ichhÂmi	kinti bahuke	bhikhu (d) pÂ	yechÂ	bhikhuni	yecha	abhikhinam

Bur	sunayuchÂ	upadhÂleyayû	vÂ	[8] hevam	mevÂ	upÂsakÂ	chÂ	upÂsikÂ
Wil	sunayuchÂ	upadhÂleyeyu	cha	hevam	meva	upÂsakÂ	cha	upÂsika
A. C.	sunayuchÂ	upadhâleyeyû	chÂ	hevam	mevÂ	upÂsakÂ	chÂ	upÂsika

Bur	chÂ	eteni	bhunte	imam	likhÂpayÂmi	abhimati	me chÂ umtiti.
Wil	cha	etÂni	bhunte	ima (m)	likhÂ (pa) yÂmi	abhi heti	maja (nan) titi.
A. C.	chÂ	eteni	bhunte	imam	likhâpayÂmi	abhi peti	mejÂnantiti.

(*a*) The omission of the syllable *li* is no doubt the printer's fault, as Burnouf gives the word in full in the last word but one of the 6th line.

(*b*) I read *mukase*, and so did Captain Burt.

(*c*) Certainly *dam*, the curve is on the wrong side for *cham* as proposed by Wilson.

(*d*) The manner of attaching the vowel *u* at the foot of the *kh* was perhaps unknown to Burnouf and Wilson. It occurs again in *bhikhuni*.

No. 12.

KHANDAGIRI ROCK.

See Prinsep in Journal of the Bengal Asiatic Society, VI, 1080. (a)

1 J. P.	Namo	Arahantânam	namo	sava—	Sidhânam	Airena	mahârâjena
A. C.	Namo	Arahantânam	namo	sava—	Sidhânam	Airena	mahârâjena

J. P.	mahâmeghavâhanena	chetakâjate *	chhadanena	pasathasukela—	khanena
A. C.	mahâmeghavâhanena	chetarâmjava savam	dhanena	pasathasukela	khanena

J. P.	chaṭurantalatha	ganena	——— kalingâdhipatirâsi	sikhira	avalonam
A. C.	chaturamkalatha	gunena	* tena kalingâdhipatichâ	sâkâvâ	uvalena.

2 J. P.	pandarasa	vasâni	siri-kaḍara—	sariravatâ,	kidita-kumârakidika,	tato
A. C.	pandarasa	vasâni	siri-kaḍâra	sariravatâ	kiḍitâ-kumârakidikâ,	tato

J. P.	lekharûpa-gana-nâva—	vapâra	vidhi-visâra-dena	sava-vijâvadatena	navavasâni,
A. C.	lekhârûpâ-gaṇa-nâva—	vepâra	vidhi-visâra dena	sava-vijavadatenam	navavasâni,

J. P.	hota	râja	pansâsivase,	puna	chavavisati-vase	dânava	dhamena
A. C.	hota	vâja	pansâsivasa,	puna	chatuvinsati-vasesu	dânava	dhamena

J. P.	sesayavenâ	bhivijayo	tatiye.
A. C.	sesayovanâ	bhivijapo (b)	tatiye.

3 J. P.	kalinga-râja	vansa-puri	sanyuge,	mahârâjabbisechanam	pâpunâti
A. C.	kalinga-râja	vansa-puri	samyuge,	mahârâjabhise-chanam	pâpunâti

J. P.	Abhisita	mata	vapa dhamavase	vatavihatato	pura-pâhâra	nivesam
A. C.	Abhisita	mato	champadhamavase	vâtavihatato	pura-pâkâra	nivesanam

J. P.	paṭisankharayati.	Kalinga-nagari	khidhira	sitala	tadâga	pariyo	cha
A. C.	patisankhârayati.	Kalinga-nagari	khimbira	isitâla	taḍiya	pâḍiyo	cha

J. P.	bathupayasi	sava	yânipati	santhapa (nam) cha.
A. C.	thâpâ (?) payati	sava	yânampati	santhapanam cha.

4 J. P.	kârayati ;	panatisirâsihi (c)	satasahasehi	pakatiyo	ranjayati	datiya
A. C.	kârayati ;	pannítâsidhi	satasahasehi	pakâtiye	ijayata	datiye

J. P.	cha	vâse,	âchitayitâ	sotekâre	pachhimâ	disam,	haya
A. C.	cha	vâse,	achitayita	sotakâni	pachhima	disam	iha

J. P.	gaja	nara	radha	bahula	darin	pathâpayati	kansabanâgatâya
A. C.	yejam	nara	radha	bahulalanam te		pathapanati	sabânâgatâya

J. P.	dasanâya	vâtânam	sakanagara	vâsino	punavase
A. C.	ḍisenoya	vâtânanta	sakanagara	navâye	punavase

(a) The differences between Kittoe's text, which Prinsep used, and the text of the photograph of the plaster cast, are so numerous, that I have thought it better to give my own reading from the new text, than to note the many variations.

(b) Reading of last syllable doubtful.

(c) The last two letters of this word would appear to have been accidentally repeated by Kittoe. This is a very common occurrence with hand-made transcripts.

5 J. P. gandhava veda-budho-dampana tabhata vâditâ sandasanâhi usava
A. C. gandhava veda-budhâ dampana tagi (?) ta vâdita sandasanâhi usava

J. P. samaja kârâpanâhi cha kidapayati nâgari Tatha vivuthevase
A. C. samaja kârâpanâhi cha kâḍapayanti nagari Tatha vivuthevase

J. P. vijadharâdhivâse a (ra) hata puba Kalinga puva Râjâni vasati
A. C. vijadharâdhivasam a (no letter) hata puva Kalinga puva Râjân * * * ?

J. P. —— (gap) —— vata dhama (not rendered) —— —— —— ——
A. C. (about 10 letters) vata dhama ṭisapâta (?) ijati (?) te cha nikhita chhata (?)

6 J. P. (a) bhigârehi taratana sâpatena savarathika bhojasepâ devam dâpayati.
A. C. bhigarehi taratanam sâpataye savarathika bhojakepâ devam dasayati.

J. P. Pachachadânivase NANDA Raja tivasata ughatitam tanisaraliya
A. C. Panchapanchadânivase NANDA Raja tivasasata ughâṭitam tanamsuliyam

J. P. vaja panadi nagara pasesa —————— ——————
A. C. vâṭa panâdi nagara pavesa * viso (about 10 letters) sabhisori cha * * hâsa

J. P. —— —— —— —— ——
A. C. cha sandesam tosa vakara vane.

7 J. P. anugaha anekani sata-sahasani visajati porajanapadam satamanchatisam
A. C. anugaha anekâni sata-sahasâni visejati (*a*) orajânepadam satamachavesam

J. P. pasâsato vajaragharavodham satam gharini savata kaha dapanna
A. C. pasa sato vajarighavadhâsatima —— gharini savata koha dapana

J. P. narapa —— (gap) thame vase manam ——————ta—— ge —— giri ——
A. C. narapa ketana (about 18 letters) ye thame cha vase mananti mena * ya * * * tapabhate dare sâri idha.

8 J. P. ghâtâpayitâ râjâ gabham upapîdapayati: dhatinam cha kammupâdana
A. C. ghâtâpayita raja gambhu (*b*) upapidapayuti: dhatinam cha kammapâdana

J. P. panâdena pambâtasena vâhayati: pammuchita madhuram apanata
A. C. —— —— —— pamachitu madhuram apayato

J. P. —— —————— mora dadâti ——————————
A. C. navam ranâ ba (about 24 letters) mora dadâti ya (*c*) (5 letters) pira chako (6 letters) palavamake.

9 J. P. kapam ukha haya gaja (lulapa ?) sahâya sesa cha ghara vsâya,
A. C. kapam ukha haya gaja (2 letters) sahâya sesa cha ghara vasaya

J. P. anatika-gana nirâsasahanancha karâyitun, ba imanânam jatapa
A. C. anatika-gava ? yasuvâgahanancha kârayitum, ba imanonam japuha

J. P. paradadâti,
A. C. sâra dadâti arapato (about 40 letters).

(*a*) The initial letter may perhaps be a *p*, but as I can see no upturn to the right, it looks to me like an initial *o*.
(*b*) The reading of this word is doubtful.
(*c*) This letter *y* is placed above the line, and was evidently inserted afterwards.

10 J. P. • • • manati râja pandarasa mahavijaya pâsâdam kârayatī
A. C. venati manati raja pandarasa mahavijaya pâsâd kârayati

J. P. —— —— —— —— —— ——
A. C. atha hita dusavasahasohi dasâme chatuse • datibhisara (4 letters)

J. P. —— —— ——
A. C. karathavasa pa • na maha java (7 letters) râ chû bî yati (9 letters)

J. P. —— —— —— —— —— —— ——
A. C. thayi lana (3 letters) ja • saniji (3 letters) yatana soti yo ru • ni upa lebhâta

11 J. P. —— puve râja nivesâtam pîthu dâga dambha nagare
A. C. (10 letters) puve râja nivesâtam pithu ḍaga dambha nagalo (?)

J. P. nakâsayatta janapade, bhâvana châ terasa vaso satako
A. C. nakâsamyata janapuda bhâvana che terasu vase satâka

J. P. • • • amaradehasa pâta bârasa ——
A. C. bhidasitâmaradehasa pâta bârasa maḍava (21 letters) ho cha

J. P. —— siri pithirâjâno.
A. C. (4 letters) phahi vitisiyatâ utara patharâjâno.

12 J. P. —— —— —— —— —— —— —— —— ——
A. C. (11 letters) ma dhânam cha vipula (ya) bhayam janeto hathasam gangâya pâya

J. P. —— —— —— —— —— —— —— —— —— —— ——
A. C. yati • • ma cha râjânam baha sati sitapâ deva dâpam yati NANDA

J. P. —— —— —— —— —— —— —— —— ——
A. C. râjâni ta vâmaga jinasa (10 letters) ma ata (5 letters) rota na

J. P. —— —— —— —— ——
A. C. suḍiha marîga MAGADHA Vasasa yam ri (5 letters).

13 J. P. • • • ta jâlo ralakhila BÂRANASI hiramanivenayati
A. C. (11 letters) tu jiva ralakhilayo BÂRÂNASI hiranâni cha iyati

J, P. —— —— —— —— —— —— ——
A. C. sata vasadana thari hârenam asita masâriya che hathi • navena

J. P. —— —— —— —— —— —— anekâni
A. C. pariha • • ya (4 letters) na • piva maha ri rajine nibhayoka

J. P. dato mani ratanâni aharâpayati. —— —— ——
A. C. • tavana • ratanâni aharâpayati idha sante ribha.

14 J. P. • • • si novasikariti terasamava vasesu panchata (a) vijaya
A. C. • • • • novasikariti terasamava vasesu pavata vijaya

(a) In Kittoe's copy this word may be read as *pabuta*, thus agreeing with my reading of pavata.

J. P. chana kumâri pasange arahate punavasata pi kamani
A. C. chanam kumârî pavate (*a*) arahato punavasatâ hi (*b*) kayâni (*c*)

J. P. sidinaya yâpuravake ——— ——— ——— ——— ———
A. C. sidinaya yâpujake hirâ * ladatini chenam daveni nasa sitâni

J. P. ——— ——— ——— ——— ——— ——— ———
A. C. ujani kata uvâsâyo rava ladiranâ jivima * kapuri khita (7 letters)?

15 J. P. ——— ——— ——— vihitânancha sata disânam
A. C. (11 letters) sakata samelasa vihitenam cha suta dâsinam

J. P. ——— ——— ——— ——— ——— ——— sidiya samîpe
A. C. tanâpe simapusa isa pupanam cha hasani sidaya samîpa

J. P. subhare ——— ——— ——— aneke yajanâ ——— ———
A. C. subhâre va + bhasa matha ghisipâ anake yojanâ pítâ ghipa

J. P. ——— ——— dhanâni
A. C. * * pipe * * * ni * * * * vinsi lapi bhaghapatha * * * dhadayana

16 J. P. ——— patâlake chatara chetegheriya gabha thambhe pati (tha)
A. C. (10 letters) patâlake chatara chetegheriya gabhe thabhe pati tha

J. P. payati ——— ——— ——— ——— ———
A. C. payati pannantariyasa cha vasâ * * * ja * * ya kala che chinam

J. P. ——— ——— agisati katariyam napâdachhati agama râja savatha
A. C. chacho yatha agesati katariyam napâdayati agama râja savatha

J. P. râja, saurase (na) raja, * ma raja, pasata saghate ——— ranâni
A. C. râja sambhi? * * * ja nâma raja, pasata sanauto anubhivato + râṇâni

17 J. P. ——— u vi se kusalo sava pasanda pujan (iya)
A. C. (11 letters) ruṭa pano chhise (?) kusalo sava pathabhi (*d*) pujako

J. P. (17 letters ———) kârakâra * patihata lakivâhani bâlevâka
A. C. (7 letters) ta * * * makâraka * * padahata — chakovâhani thalo châko

J. P. dhagata chana pavata chako râjâsanka lavinaravato mahâvijaye
A. C. dharaguta— chako pivata — chako râjasavam sakula vini gato mahavijayo

J. P. râja khâravela sanda.
A. C. râjâ kharavela siriuo.

(*a*) This word is quite clear.

(*b*) Perhaps *parinavasanta.*

(*c*) This word is quite clear.

(*d*) The letters of this word are indistinct. I have given what they appear to be to my own eye; but Prinsep's reading may be right.

No. 13.

DEOTEK SLAB.

Left Inscription.

1	Sâmi	anyapạyeti		Chikambari	* * sa
var.					pa *
2	hanam	to	badham to	vâ * ta	saradam * * · nâtha
var.					sakadam kurâ * va
3	ame	cha	nala	* * * *	nam * na
var.	ama	châ			
4	dato	30. 4. 3.		He. Pa. I. Di. 14.	Budhe?
var.	dato	le * *			

Right Inscription.

1	Chikkamburi	* sa * *	
var.		sa dyi pu	
2	sa ja tra ? ————		
var.	pa ———		
3	Pûrurava ?	* * * cha	barya ya
var.	da. ma		banȳya ya
4	vanşa (pu)	trasya	* Rûdra.
var.		tasya	
5	Sena Râjuya	* *	dharmma
var.			* mina sy atta

CAVE INSCRIPTIONS.

BARÂBAR.

No. 1.

Sudâma Cave.

1	LÂjinÂ	PiyadasinÂ	duvÂdasa	vasÂbhisitenÂ
2	iyam	Nigoha kubhÂ	dinÂ	Âdivikembi (*a*)

No. 2.

Viswa Cave.

1	LajinÂ	PiyadasinÂ	duvÂ
2	dasa	vasÂbhisitenÂ	iyam
3	kubhÂ	Khalatika	pavatasi
4	dinÂ	Âdivikemhi (*b*)	

No. 3.

Karna Cave.

1	LÂja	Piyadasi	ekunevin—
2	—sati	vasÂbhisitenÂ	methÂ
3	adamathÂtima	iyam	kubhÂ
4	sumpiye	Khalanti	pavata di
5	nÂ (*c*)		

NAGARJUNI CAVES.

No. 4.

Vapiyaka Cave.

1	Vapiyake kubhÂ	Dasalathena	DevÂnampiyena
2	Ânantaliyam	abhisitenÂ	Âdivikemhi
3	Bhadantehi	vÂsanisidiyaye	misiṭhe
4	Âchandama	sûliyam.	

No. 5.

Gopika Cave.

1	GopikÂ kubhÂ	Dasalathena	DevÂnampi—
2	—yenÂ	Ânantaliyam	abhisitenÂ Âdi—
3	—vikemhi	Bhadantehi	vÂsanisidiyÂye
4	nisiṭhÂ	Âchandama	sûliyam.

(*a*) The last six letters of this inscription are not given in Kittoe's copy, (Bengal Asiatic Society's Journal XVI, Pl. IX, No. 5,) but they are quite legible, in spite of a determined attempt to obliterate them with a chisel. Burnouf sagaciously corrected Kittoe's reading of *Nigopa* to *Nigoha*, which is the name of the cave, that is, the *Nyagrodha*, or Banian Tree Cave.—"Le Lotus," Appendice, 780.

(*b*) My reading of this inscription agrees in every letter with that of Kittoe's copy and Burnouf's transcript.

(*c*) In the first line Kittoe read ***ekânevisiti***, which Burnouf corrected to ***ekonavisati***. The rest of this inscription is indistinct, and is so imperfectly given by Kittoe, that Burnouf could make nothing of it. The only part that I have been able to restore with certainty is the name of the *Khalati* or *Khalanti* hills, which occurs also in No. 2.—"Le Lotus," Appendice, 780.

No. 6.

Vadathika Cave.

1	Vadathikâ kubhâ	Dasalathena	Devânam—
2	—piyenâ	ânantaliyam	abhisitenâ â—
3	—divikemhi	Bhadantehi	vâsanisidiyâye
4	nisiṭhâ	âchandama	sûliyam.

These three inscriptions, which were first published by Prinsep, have had the advantage of Burnouf's critical correction. Prinsep's texts and versions will be found in the Bengal Asiatic Society's Journal, Vol. VI, 676; and Burnouf's revised texts and translations in Le Lotus de la Bonne Loi, 775-776. Dasaratha was the grandson of Asoka, and succeeded to the throne in B. C. 218, in which year these inscriptions are dated.

KHANDAGIRI.

No. 1.

Nameless Cave.

Pâda-mulikasa kusumasa leṅam.

No. 2.

Snake Cave.

Chulakammasa kotha jayâ cha.

No. 3.

Snake Cave.

Kamase	ra * * * khi
Nayacho	pasâde.

No. 4.

Tiger Cave.

J. P.	Ugara	svedasa	sasuvino	lonam
A. C.	Ugara	akhadasa	sabhûtino	lenam.

No. 5.

Nameless Cave.

J. P.	Mâpâmadâti	bâkâya	yanâkiyasa	lonam
A. C.	Mâpâmadâsa	bâuiyaya	nâkiyasa	lenam.

No. 6.

Pawan Cave.

J. P.	Chulakumasa	paseta	kothaja (ya).
A. C.	Chula kramasa	pasâto	kothâja.

No. 7.

Manikpura Cave.

J. P.	Verasa	mahârâjasa	Kalingadhi patano	ma * * * * *
A. C.	Airasa	mahârâjasa	Kalingadhipatino	ma (hamegha) vâha (na)

J. P.	* kaḋepa	sirino	lonam
A. C.	* depa	sirino	leuam

No. 8.

Manikpura Cave.

J. P.	kumâro	Vattakasa	lonam
A. C.	kumâro	Vaddakasa	lenam.

No. 9.

Vaikunta Cave.

J. P.	Arahanta	paṣâdânam	Kalinga •	ya • nânam	lona .	kâdatam
A. C.	Arahanta	pasâdânam	Kalingânam	Samanânam	lenam	kâritam

J. P.	rajinolasa • •	2 hethisahasam	panotasaya	• •
A. C.	Rajino Lâlakasa •	2 hathi sâhanam	panâtasa	cha tino

J. P.	Kalinga	• • • • • •	velasa	3 agamahi	pitâkadâ
A. C.	Kalinga	cha • • • • •	velasa	3 agamahi	piḍakâda

No. 13.

RAMGARH CAVES IN SIRGUJA.

I.—Sitá Bânjirá Cave.

line 1	Adipayanti	hadayam	sada	va garaka	vayo
	cha tayam				
„ 2	dule	vasantiyâ	hâ	sâvânû	bhûte
	kudastatam	evam	alangi.		

II.—Jogi Márá Cave.

„ 1	Sutanuka nama		
„ 2	Devadaṣinyi		
„ 3	Sutanuka nama	Deva	daṣinyi
„ 4	tam	kamayi ṭha	balanaṣeye
„ 5	Deva	dina nama	lupadakhe

N. B.—The texts of these cave inscriptions have been taken from Mr. Beglar's paper impressions. For Nos. 4 and 9, I have had the advantage of consulting the photographs of Mr. H. H. Locke's plaster-of-Paris casts; No. 1 is a new inscription.

PILLAR INSCRIPTIONS.

EDICT I.

(Delhi, North.)

D. S.	Devânampiye	Piyadasi	Lâja	hevam̃	âhâ :	Saḍḍavisativasa [2]	abhisitename
D. M.	—	—	—	—	—	—	—
A.	Devânampiye	Piyadasî	Lâjâ	hevam	âhâ :	Saḍḍavisativasâbhisitename	
L. A.	Devânampiye	Piyadasi	Lâja	hevam̃	âha :	Saḍḍavîsati vasâbhisitename	
L. N.	Devanampiye	Piyadasi	Lâja	hevam̃	âha :	Saḍḍavisati vasâbhisitename	

D. S.	iyam̃	dhammalipi	likhâpitâ	[3] hidatapâlate	dusam̃paṭipâdaye	Annata
D. M.	—	—	—	—	—	—
A.	iyam	dhammalipi	likhâpitâ	hidatapâlate	dusampaṭipâdâye	[3] Annata
L. A.	iyam̃	dhammalipi	[2] likhâpita	hidatapâlate	dusam̃paṭipâdaye	Annata
L. N.	iyam̃ [2]	dhammalipi	likhâpita	hidatapâlate	dusam̃paṭipadaye	Annata

D. S.	agâyâ	dhammakâmatâyâ	[4] agâya	palîkhâyâ,	agâya	susuśâyâ,	agena
D. M.	—	—	—	—	—	—	—
A.	agâya	dhammakâmatâya	agâya	palîkaya,	agâya	susûsâyâ,	agena
L. A.	agâya	dhammakâmatâya	agâya	palîkhâyo,	[3] agâya	susûsaya,	agena
L. N.	agâya	dhammakâmatâya	[3] agâya	palîkhaya,	agâya	sususaya,	agena

D. S.	bhayena,	[5] agena	usâhenâ,	esa	chukhomama	anusathiyâ	[6] dhamma pekhâ,
D. M.	—	—	—	—	—	—	—
A.	bhayena,	agena	usâhena	esa	chukhomama	anusathiyâ	[3] dhammapekhâ,
L. A.	bhayena,	âgena	usâhena	esa	chukhomama	anusathiya	dhammâpekha,
L. N.	bhay na,	agena	usâhena	esa	chukhomama	[4] anusathiya	dhammâpekha,

D. S.	dhamma kâmatâ	cha	suve	suve	vadḥitâ	vadḥisati	che vâ
D. M.	—	—	—	—	—	—	—
A.	dhammakâmatâ	cha	suve	suve	vadḥitâ	vadḥisati	che vâ
L. A.	[4] dhammakâmatâ	cha	suve	suve	vadḥitâ	vadḥisati	che vâ
L. N.	dhammakâmatâ	cha	suve	suve	vadḥita	vadhisati	che vâ

D. S.	[7] pulisâpi	cha	me	ukasâ	châ	gevayâ	châ	majhimâ châ
D. M.	—	—	—	—	—	—	—	—
A.	pulisâpi	*a*	me	ukasâ	cha	gevayâ	cha	majhimâ cha
L. A.	pulisâpi	*a*	me	ukasâ	cha	gevayâ	cha	majhimâ cha
L. N.	pulisâpi	*a*	me	ukasâ	cha	gevayâ	cha	majhimâ châ

D. S.	anuvidhîyañti	[8] sampaṭipâdayañti	châ	alañchapalañ	samâdapayitave	hemevâ
D. M.	—	—	—	—	—	—
A.	anuvidhîyanti	sampaṭipâdayanti	cha	[4] alanchapalau	samâdapayitave	hemevâ
L. A.	anuvidhîyañti	[5] sampaṭi pâdayañti	cha	alañchapalañ	samâdapayitave	hemeva
L. N.	anuvidhîyanti	sampaṭipâdayañti	cha	alañchapalañ	samâdapayitavo	[6] hemeva

(*a*) The word *cha* is omitted in these three texts.

D. S.	añta	[9] mahâmâtâpi	esahi	vidhi	yâ,	iyam̃	dham̃mena	pâlanâ,
D. M.	añta	mahâmâtâpi	——	——	——	——	——	——* nâ,
A.	auta	mahâmâtâpi	esâhi	vidhi	yâ	iyam	dhammena	pâlana,
L. A.	añta	mahâmâtâpi	esâhi	vidhi	yâ	iyam̃	dham̃mena	pâlana,
L. N.	añta	mahâmâtâpi	esâhi	vidhi	yâ	iyam̃	dham̃mena	pâlana,

D. S.	dham̃mena	vidhâne,	[10] dham̃mena	sukhiyanâ,	dham̃mena	gotîti	
D. M.	dham̃mena	vidhâne,	[10] dham̃mena	su ——	——	——	
A.	dhammena	vidhâne,	dhammena	sukhîyanâ,	dhammena	gotîti	cha.
L. A.	[6] dham̃mena	vidhâne,	dham̃mena	sukhiyana,	dham̃mena	gotîti	
L. N.	dhammena	vidhâne,	dham̃mena	sukhîyana,	[7] dham̃mena	gotîti	

EDICT II.

(Delhi, North.)

D. S.	Devânam̃piye	Piyadasi	Lâja	[11] hevam	âhâ	Dhammesâdhû,	kiyam̃cha
D. M.	[11] Devânam̃piye	Piyadasi	Lâja	he—	——	Dhammesâdhû,	kiyam̃cha
A.	[5] Devânampiye	Piyadasî	Lâjâ	hevam	âhâ	Dhammesâdhu,	kiyamchu (*a*)
L. A.	[7] Devânam̃piye	Piyadasi	Lâjâ	hevam̃	âha	Dham̃mesâdhu,	kiyam̃cha
L. N.	[8] Devânam̃piye	Piyadasi	Lâja	hevam̃	âha	Dhammesâdhu,	kiyam̃cha

D. S.	dham̃meti	apâsinave	bahukayâne	[12] dayâdâne	sache	sochaye	chakhudâne
D. M.	dhammeti	[12] apâsinave	bahukayâni	dayâdâne	sache	sochaye	chakhudâne
A.	dhammeti	apâsinave	bahukayâne	dayâdâne	sache	sochaye	chakhudâne
L. A.	dham̃meti	apâsinave	bahukayâne	dayadâne	sache	[8] socheyeti	chakhudâne
L. N.	dham̃meti	apâsinave	bahukayâne	[9] dayadâne	sache	socheyeti	chakhudâne

D. S.	pime	bahuvidhe	diñne,	dupada	[13] chatupadesu,	pakhi	vâlichalesu
D. M.	pime	[13] bahuvidhe	diñne,	dupâda	chatupadesu,	pakhi	vâlichalesu
A.	pime	[6] bahuvidhe	dinne	dupada	chatupadesu,	pakhi	vâlichalesu
L. A.	pime	bahuvidhe	dine,	dupada	chatupadesu,	pakhi	vâlichalesu
L. N.	pime	bahuvidhe	dine,	dupada	chatupadesu,	pakhi	[10] vâlichalesu

D. S.	vividhe me	anugahe	kaṭe ;	apâna	[14] dâkhinâye	aññânipicha	me
D. M.	————	[14] gahe	kaṭe ;	apâne	dâkhanâye	aññânipiche	me
A.	vividhe me	anugahe	kaṭe :	apâna	dakhinaye	anuânipicha	me
L. A.	vividha me	anugahe	kaṭe ;	[9] apâna	dakhinaye	aññânipicha	me
L. N.	vividhe me	anugahe	kaṭe ;	apâna	dakhinâye	aunânipicha	me

D. S.	bahuni	kayânâni	kaṭâni ;	etâye	me	athâye	iyam̃	dham̃mâlipi
D. M.	——	——	[15] kaṭâni ;	etâye	me	athâye	iyam̃	dham̃malipi
A.	bahûni	kayânâni	kaṭâni ;	[7] etâye	me	athâye	iyam	dhammalipi
L. A.	bahuni	kayânâni	kaṭâni ;	etâye	me	athâye	iyam̃	dham̃malipi
L. N.	bahûni	kayânâni	[11] kaṭâni ;	etâye	me	aṭhâye	iyam̃	dhammalipi

D. S.	likhâpitâ.	Hevam̃	anupaṭipajañtu	[16] chilanthiti	kâcha	hotûtiti :	yecha
D. M.	——	——	[16] anupaṭipajañtû	chilâthiti	kâcha	hot	——
A.	likhâpitâ.	Hevam	anupaipajanṭu	chilathitî	kâcha	hotûti :	yecha
L. A.	likhâpita.	Hevam̃	[10] anupaṭipajañtu	chilanthitî	kâcha	hotûti :	yecha
L. N.	likhâpita.	Hevam	anupaṭipajañtu	chilanthitî	kâcha	hotûti :	[12] yecha

(*a*) The vowel *u* is perhaps only a flaw in the stone.

D. S.	hevam̃	sam̃paṭi	pajîsati	se sukaṭam̃	kachhatîti.
D. M.	——	——	pajisati	so sukatha	kachhatiti.
A.	hevam	sampaṭi	pajisati	se sukaṭam	kachhatiti.
L. A.	hevam	sampaṭi	pajisati	se sukaṭam̃	kachhatiti.
L. N.	hevam	sampaṭi	pajisati	se sukaṭam̃	kachhati.

EDICT III.

(Delhi, North.)

D. S.	[17] Devânaṁpiye	Piyadasi	Lâja	hevam̃	ahâ:	kayânam̃	meva	dekhati
D. M.	[22] Devânaṁpiye	Piyadasi	Lâja	hevaṁ	âhâ:	kayânaṁ	meva	dekhati
A.	[8] Devanampiye	Piyadasî	Lâjâ	hevam	âhâ:	kayânam	meva	dekhati
L. A.	[11] Devanaṁpiye	Piyadasi	Lâja	hevaṁ	âha:	kayânaṁ	meva	dekhaṁti
L. N.	[13] Devânaṁpiye	Piyadasi	Lâja	hevaṁ	âhâ:	kayânaṁ	meva	dekhaṁti

D. S.	iyam̃	me	[18] kayâne	kaṭeti:	Nomina	pâpaṁ	dekhati	iyaṁ	me
D. M.	iyaṁ	me	kayâne	kaṭeti:	Nomina	pâpaṁ	dekhati	iyaṁ	me
A.	iyam	me	kayâne	kaṭeti:	Nomina	pâpakam	dekhati	iyam	me
L. A.	iyaṁ	me	kayâne	kaṭeti:	Nomina	pâpaṁ	dekhaṁti	iyaṁ	me
L. N.	iyaṁ	me	kayâne	kaṭeti:	Nomina	pâpaṁ	[14] dekhanti	iyaṁ	me

D. S.	pâpe	kaṭeti;	iyaṁ	vâ	âsinave	[19] nâmâti,	dupaṭivekhe	chukho
D. M.	pâpe	kaṭeti;	iyaṁ	va	[20] âsinave	nâmâti,	dupaṭivekhe	chukho
A.	pâpake	kaṭeti;	iyam	vâ	âsinave	nâmâti,	* * * (a)	* *
L. A.	pâpe	kaṭeti;	[12] iyaṁ	va	âsinave	nâmâti,	dupaṭi vekhe	chukho
L. N.	pâpe	kaṭeti;	iyaṁ	va	âsinave	nâmâti,	dupaṭi vekhe	chukho

D. S.	esâ	hevaṁ	chukhe	esa	dekhiye.	I meni	[20] âsinava	gâmîni nâma;
D. M.	esâ	hevaṁ	chukho	esa	dekhiye.	[21] I mâni	âsinava	gâmini nâma;
A.	*	* *	* *	*	* *	* *	* *	* *
L. A.	esa	hevaṁ	chukho	esa	dekhiye.	I mâni	âsinava	gâmîni nâmâti;
L. N.	esa	hevaṁ	chukho	esa	dekhiye.	[15] Imâni	asinava	gâmini nâmâti;

D. S.	atha	chaṁḍiye	nithûliye	kodhemâne	isyâ:	[21] kâlane navahakaṁ	mâ
D. M.	atha	chaṁḍiye	nithûliye	kodhe [22] mane	isya:	kâlane navâhakaṁ	mâ
A.	*	* *	——	——	——	——	——
L. A.	atha	chaṁḍiye	[13] nithûliye	kodhe mâne	isya:	kâlanenavahakaṁ	mâ
L. N.	atha	chaṁḍiye	nithûliye	kodhe mâne	isya:	kâlanenavahakaṁ	[16] mâ

D. S.	palibhasayisaṁ:	esa bâḍha	dekhiye	iyaṁ	me	[22] hidatikâye	iyaṁ
D. M.	palibhasayisaṁ:	esa bâḍha	[23] dekhiye	iyaṁ	me	hidatikâye	iyaṁ
A.	——	——	——	——	——	——	——
L. A.	palibhasayisaṁti:	esa bâdhaṁ	dekhiye	iyaṁ	me	hidatikaye	iyaṁ
L. N.	palibhasayisanti:	esa bâdham	dekhiye	iyaṁ	me	hidatikaye	iyam

D. S.	mana	me	pâlatikaye.
D. M.	(b)	me	pâlatikaye.
A.	——	——	——
L. A.	mana	me	pâlatikayeti.
L. N.	mana	me	pâlatikayeti.

(a) Here the Asoka inscription is cut away by Jahangir's barbarous record of his ancestry.

(b) Omitted in the original text.

EDICT IV.

(Delhi, North.)

D. S.	[1] Devânaṁpiye	Piyadasi	lâja	hevaṁ	âhâ :	Saḍḍavîsati	vasa [2] abhisitename
D. M.	—	—	—	—	—	—	—
A.	—	—	—	—	—	—	—
L. A.	[14] Devânaṁpiye	Piyadasi	lâja	hevaṁ	âha :	Saḍḍavîsati	vasâbhisitename
L. N.	[17] Devânaṁpiye	Piyadasi	lâja	hevaṁ	âhâ :	Saḍḍavîsati	vasâbhisitename

D. S.	iyaṁ	dhaṁmalipi	likhâpitâ.	Lajukâme	[3] bahûsu	pâna	sata	sahasesu
D. M.	—	—	—	—	—	—	—	—
A.	—	—	—	—	—	—	—	—
L. A.	iyaṁ	dhaṁmalipi	likhâpita.	Lajukâme	bahûsu	pâna	sata	sahasesu
L. N.	iyaṁ	dhaṁmalipi	likhâpita.	Lajukâme	[18] bahûsu	pâna	sata	sahasesu

D. S.	janasi	âyatâ	tesaṁ	ye	abhihâleva	[4] daṅdeva	atapatiye	me	kaṭe
D. M.	—	—	—	—	—	—	—	—	—
A.	—	—	—	—	—	—	—	—	—
L. A.	[15] janasi	âyata	tesâṁ	ye	abhihâleva	daṅdeva	atapatiye	me	kaṭe
L. N.	janasi	âyata	tesâṁ	ye	abhihâleva	daṅdevâ	atapatiye	me	kaṭe

D. S.	kinti	lajûkâ	aswatha	abhitâ	[5] kaṁmâni	pavatayevû :		janasa
D. M.	—	—	—	—	—	—	—	—
A.	—	—	—	—	—	—	—	—
L. A.	kinti	lajûka	aswatha	abhita	kaṁmâni	pavataye	vûti :	janasa
L. N.	kinti	lajûka	aswatha	[19] abhita	kammâni	pavataye	vûti :	janasa

D. S.	janapadasâ	hitasukhaṁ	upadahevu	anugahineva	cha	sukhiyana—
D. M.	—	—	—	—	—	—
A.	—	—	—	—	—	—
L. A.	janapadasa	[16] hitasukhaṁ	upadahevu	anugahinevu	cha	sukhiyana—
L. N.	janapâdasa	hitasukhaṁ	upadahevû	anugahinevu	cha	sukhîyana—

D. S.	dukhiyanaṁ	jânisanti :	Dhaṁmayatena	cha	[7] viyo	vidasanti.	Janaṁ
D. M.	—	—	—	—	—	—	—
A.	—	—	—	—	—	—	—
L. A.	dukhiyanaṁ	jânisaṅti :	Dhaṁmayatena	cha	viyo	vadisaṅti.	Janaṁ
L. N.	dukhîyanaṁ	[20] jânisanti :	Dhammayatena	cha	viyo	vadisaṅti.	Janaṁ

D. S.	janapadaṁ	kintihi	datam	cha	palitam	cha	[8] aladhayevuti	lajuka
D. M.	—	—	—	—	—	—	—	—
A.	—	—	—	—	—	—	—	—
L. A.	jânapadaṁ	kintihi	datam	cha	[17] pâlatam	cha	âlâdhayavu	lajukâ
L. N.	jânapadaṁ	kintihi	datam	cha	pâlatam	cha	âlâdhayevûti	lajukâ

D. S.	pilahanti ; (*a*)	paṭichalitaveman	pulisânipi me	[9] chhaṅdaṅnâni	paṭichalisanti,	tepi	cha
D. M.	—	—	—	—	paṭichalisanti,	[10] tepi	cha
A.	—	—	—	—	—	—	—
L. A.	pilaghanti	paṭichalitavemaṅ	pulisânipi me	chhaṅdaṅnâni	paṭichalisanti,	tepi	cha
L. N.	pilaghaṅti	[21] paṭichalitavemaṅ	pulisânipi me	chhandaṅnâni	paṭichalisanti.	tepi	cha

D. S.	kâni	viyo	vadisaṅti	yenamaṁ	lajûkâ	[10] chaghaṅti	âlâdhayitave.
D. M.	—	—	—	—	— kâ	chaghaṅtî	alâdha [11] yitave
A.	—	—	—	—	—	—	—
L. A.	kâni	viyo	vadisanti	yenamaṁ	[18] lajûka	chaghaṅti	âladheyatave.
L. N.	kâni	viyo	vadisanti	yenamaṁ	lajûka	chaghaṅti	âlâdhayitave.

(*a*) The two Lauriya Pillars read *pilaghanti*, with the rough guttural aspirate *gh*.

D. S.	Athâ	hi pajaṁ	viyatâye	dhâtiye	nisi jitu	[11] aswathe	hoti ;	viyata
D. M.	——	——	——	——	nisa jitû	aswatha	hoti ;	[12] viyata
A.	——	——	——	——	——	——	——	——
L. A.	Athâ +	hi pajaṁ	viyâṅtâye	dhâtiye	nisi jitu	aswathe	hoti	viyata
L. N.	[22] Athâ	hi pajaṁ	viyâtâye	dhâtiye	nisi jitu	aswathe	hoti	viyata

D. S.	dhâti	chaghaṅti	me pajaṁ ;	sukhaṁ	hali	hatane	[12] hevaṁ	mamâ
D. M.	——	——	——	——	li	haṅtave	hevaṁ	mama
A.	——	——	——	——	——	——	——	——
L. A.	dhâti	chaghaṅti	me pajaṁ ;	sukhaṁ	hali	hataveti :	[19] hevaṁ	mama
L. N.	dhâti	chaghaṅti	me pajam ;	sukhaṁ	hali	hataveti :	[23] hevaṁ	mama

D. S.	lajûkâ	kaṭâ	jânapadasa	hitasukhâye	yena	ete	abhitâ	[13] aswatha
D. M.	[13] lajukâ	——	——	—— ye	yena	ete	abhitâ	[14] aswatha
A.	——	——	——	——	——	——	——	——
L. A.	lajûkâ	kaṭe	jânapadasa	hitasukhaye	yena	ete	abhitâ	aswathâ
L. N.	lajûka	kaṭe	jânapadasa	hitasukhaye	yena	ete	abhita	aswathe

D. S.	saṅtaṁ	avimanâ	kaṁmâni	pavataye	vûti.	Etena	me	lajukânaṁ
D. M.	saṅ	——	——	vataye	vûti	Etena	me	[15] lajukânaṁ
A.	——	——	——	——	——	——	—	[16] ——(a)naṁ
L. A.	saṅtaṁ	avimana	kaṁmâni	pavataye	vûti.	Etena	me	lajûkânaṁ
L. N.	saṅtaṁ	avimana	kaṁmâni	pavataye	vûti.	[24] Etena	me	lajûkânaṁ

D. S.	[14] abhihâleva	daṅḍevâ	atapatiye	kaṭe.	Ichhitaviyehi	esâ	kiṅti ;
D. M.	——	——	atapatiye	kaṭe.	[16] Ichhitaviye	—	——
A.	abhihaleva	danḍeva	atapatiye	kaṭe	Ichhitaviyehi	esa	hiṅti
L. A.	abhihâleva	[20] danḍeva	atapatiye	kaṭe	Ichhitaviye	esa	kiṅti ;
L. N.	abhihâleva	danḍeva	antapatiye	kaṭe.	Ichhitaviye	esa	kinti ;

D. S.	[15] viyohâla	samatâ	cha	siya	daṅḍa	samatâ	cha ;	ava	ite
D. M.	——bâla	samatâ	cha	siyâ	[17] daṅḍa	samata	——	——	—
A.	[17] viyohâla	samatâ	cha	siyâ	danḍa	samatâ	cha	âva	ite
L. A.	viyohâla	samatâ	cha	siya	danḍa	samatâ	cha ;	âvâ	ite
L. N.	viyohâla	samatâ	cha	siya	danḍa	samatâ	cha ;	[25] âvâ	ite

D. S.	pichame	avuti.	[16] Bandhana	badhânaṁ	munisânaṁ	tîlita	danḍânaṁ ;
D. M.	—— me	âvuti.	Bandhana	badhânaṁ	[18] munisânaṁ	——	——
A.	pichame	âvuti.	Bandhana	badhânam	munisânam	tilita	danḍânam ;
L. A.	pichame	âvuti.	Bandhana	bâdhânam	[21] munisânam	tîlita	danḍânaṁ ;
L. N.	pichame	âvuti.	Bandhane	bandhânam	munisânam	tîlita	danḍânam ;

D. S.	pata	vadhânaṁ	tiṅni	divasâni	me [17] yote	dinne	nâti	kâvakâni
D. M.	——	vadhânaṁ	tinni	divasâni	me [19] yote	dinne	* *	* *
A.	pata	vadhânam	tinni	divasâni	(b) yote	dinne	[18] nati	kanakâni
L. A.	pata	vadhânam	tinni	divasâni	me yote	dinne	nâti	kâvakâni
L. N.	pata	vadhânam	tiṅni	divasâni	me yote	dinne	nâti	kâvakâni

D. S.	nijhapayisaṅti ;	jîvitaye	tânaṁ	[18] nâsaṅtaṁ	vâ	nijhapayitâ	dânaṁ
D. M.	jhapayisanti ;	jîvitâye	tânam	[20] nasaṅtaṁ	vâ	ni ——	——
A.	nijhapayisanti ;	jîvitâye	tânam	nâsantam	vâ	nijhapayitâ	dânam
L. A.	nijhapayisanti ;	jîvitaye	tânam̃	nasaṅtam	vâ	[22] nijhapayitave	dânam
L. N.	[26] nijhapayisanti ;	jivitâye	tânam	nâsantam	vâ	nijhapayitave	dânam

(a) Here the Allahabad text becomes legible, the lower halves of the letters of the 16th line being visible under the flowered border of Jahangir's inscription.

(b) Omitted in the original text.*

D. S.	dâhanti	pâlatikaṁ	upavâsam	va	kachhanti	[19] Ichhâhime	hevam
D. M.	—— ti	pâlatikaṁ	[21] upavâsam	va	ka———	* * * *	hevam
A.	dâhanti	pâlatikam	upavâsam	vâ	kachhanti	[19] Icchâhime	hevam
L. A.	dâhanti	pâlatikam	upavâsuṁ	va	kachhanti	Ichhâhi me	hevam
L. N.	dahanti	palatikam	upavâsuṁ	va	kachhanti	Ichhâhi me	hevam

D. S.	niludhasipi	kâlasi	pâlatam	alâdhaye	vûti	janasa cha	[20] vaḍhati
D. M.	niludhasipi	kâlasi	[22] pâlatam	âlâdhaye	——	———	vaḍhati
A.	niludhasipi	kâlasi	pâlatam	âlâdhaye	vû	janasa cha	vaḍhati
L. A.	niludhasipi	kâlasi	pâlatam	âlâdhaye	vûti	[22] janasa cha	vaḍhati
L. N.	[27] niludhasipi	kalasi	pâlatam	âlâdhaye	vûti	janasa cha	vaḍhati

D. S.	vividhe	dhammachalane,	sayame	dânasa	vibhâgeti
D. M.	vividhe	dhammachalane,	[23] sayame	dâna—	———
A.	vividho	dhammachalane,	sayame	dânasa	vibhâgeti
L. A.	vividhe	dhammachalane	sayame	dânasa	vibhâgeti
L. N.	vividhe	dhammachalane	sayame	dânasa	vibhâgeti.

EDICT V.

(Delhi, South.)

D. S.	[1] Devânampiye	Piyadasi	Lâja	hevam	ahâ:	Saḍḍavisativasa
D. M.	———	———	———	———	———	———
A.	[20] Devânampiye	Piyadasi	Lâjâ	hevam	âhâ:	Saḍḍavisativasâ—
L. A.	[2] Devânampiye	Piyadasi	Lâja	hevam	âha:	Saḍḍavisativasâ—
L. N.	[1] Devânampiye	Piyadasi	Lâja	hevam	âha:	Saḍḍavisativasâ—

D. S.	[2] abhisitename	imâni	jâtâni	avadhiyâni	kaṭâni	seyathâ,
D. M.	———	———	———	———	———	———
A.	—bhisitename	imâni	jâtâni	avadhiyâni	katâni	seyathâ,
L. A.	—bhisitesame (a)	imâni	jâtâni	avadhyâni	[3] kaṭâni	seyatha,
L. N.	—bhisitesame	(b) imânipi	[2] jâtâni	avadhyâni	katâni	seyatha,

D. S.	[3] suke,	sâlikâ,	alune,	chakavâke,	hanse,	nandimukhe	gelâṭe,
D. M.	———	———	———	———	———	———	———
A.	suke,	sâilkâ,	alune,	chakavâke,	hanse,	[21] nandimukhe	gelâṭe
L. A.	suko,	sâlika,	alune,	chakavâke,	hanse,	nandimukhe	gelâṭe
L. N.	suke,	sâlika,	alune,	chakavâke,	hanse,	[3] nandimukhe,	gelâṭe

D. S.	[4] jatûkâ,	ambâkapîlikâ,	daḍî,	anathi kamachhe,	vedaveyake,
D. M.	* *	———	———	———	———
A.	jatûkâ,	ambâkipilikâ,	dubhi, (c)	anathi kamachhe,	vedaveyake,
L. A.	jatûka,	[3] ambâkapilika,	daḍi,	anathi kamachhe,	vedaveyake,
L. N.	jatûka,	ambâkapilika,	duḍi, (c)	anathi kamachhe,	vedaveyake,

D. S.	[5] gangâpupuṭake,	sankujamachhe,	kaphata	sayake,	pannasasesimale,
D. M.	———	———	———	———	———
A.	gangâpuputake,	sankujamachhe,	kaphata	* * ke,	pannasasesimale
L. A.	gangâpupuṭake,	sankujamachhe,	kaphata	seyake,	[4] pannasasesimale
L. N.	[4] gangâpupuṭake,	sankujamachhe,	kaphata	seyake,	pannasasesimale,

(a) Sic in both of the Lauriya texts.

(b) The addition of *pi* at the end of the word imâni is peculiar to this text.

(c) The differences of reading in this name are curious. Perhaps *bh* was intended in all which by the omission of a single small stroke would have become a cerebral ḍ.

D. S.	[6] sanḍake,	okapinḍe, (*a*)	palasate,	setaka-pote,	gâmaka-pote,
D. M.	—	—	—	—	—
A.	sanḍake,	* *	* *	[22] takapote,	gâmakapote,
L. A.	sanḍake,	okapinḍe,	palasate,	setaka-pote,	gâmaka-pote,
L. N.	sanḍake,	okapinḍe,	[6] palasate,	setaka-pote,	gâmaka-pote,

D. S.	[7] save	chatupade,	ye paṭibhogam	no eti,	na	chakhâdiyati,	—— î,
D. M.	—	—	—	—	—	—	ajakanâni
A.	save	chatupade	ye paṭibhogam	no *	*	* *	* * nâ
L. A.	save	chatupade	[6] ye paṭi * *	no eti,	na	chakhâdiyati,	ajakânâni,
L. N.	save	chatupade	ye paṭibhogaṁ	no eti,	na	chakhâdiyati,	[6] ajakânâni

D. S.	[8] eḍakâchâ,	sûkalichâ,	gabhinîva	payaminâva :	avadhaya pâtake
D. M.	eḍakâcha,	—	[9] gabhin + va	payamenava :	avadhaya pâtake
A.	* * *	* * *	* * *	pâyami *	* * * * *
L. A.	eḍakâ-cha,	sûkalî-cha,	gabhinîva	pâyamînâva ;	[8] avadhya potake
L. N.	eḍakâcha,	sûkalîcha,	gambhinîva	pâyamînâva ;	avadhya potake

D. S.	[9] pichakâni	âsanmâsike	vadhikukuṭe (*b*)	no	kaṭaviye :	tase	sajîve
D. M.	pichakâni	[10] âsanmâsike	vadhikukuṭe	no	kaṭaviye :	tase	sajîve
A.	* * *	* * *	* * * *	*	* * *	* *	[23] sajîve
L. A.	chakâni	âsanmâsike	vadhikukute	no	kaṭaviye :	tase	sajîve
L. N.	chakâni	[7] âsanmâsike	vadhikukute	no	kataviye :	tase	sajîve

D. S.	[10] no jhâpetaviye ;	dâve	anaṭhâyevâ	vihisâyevâ	no jhâpetaviye
D. M.	[11] no jhapetaviye	dâve	anaṭhâyevâ	vihisâyevâ	no [12] jhapetaviye
A.	no jhâpe * *	—	—	—	—
L. A.	no jhâpayitaviye	dâve	[7] anaṭhâyeva	vihisayeva	no jhâpayitaviye
L. N.	no jhâpayitaviye	dâve	anaṭhâyeva	[8] vihisayeva	no jhâpayitaviye

D. S.	[11] jivenajive	no	pusitaviye	tîsu	châtun	mâsîsu	Tisâyam	punnamâsiyam
D. M.	jîvenajîve	no	pusitaviye	tîsu	châtun	mâsîsu	[13] Tisâyam	punnamâsiyam
A.	—	—	—	—	—	—	—	—
L. A.	jîvenajîve	no	pusitaviye	tîsu	châtun	mâsîsu	Tisayam	[8] punnamâsiyam
L. N.	jîvenajîve	no	pusitaviye	tîsu	châtun	mâsîsu	Tisiyam	[9] punnamâsiyam

D. S.	[12] tinni	divasâni,	châvudasam,	pannaḍasam,	paṭipadâye	dhuvâya châ
D. M.	tinni	divasâni,	châvudasam,	pannaḍasam,	[14] paṭipadâye	dhavâyecha
A.	* *	* * *	[24] châvudasam,	panchadasam,	—	—
L. A.	tinni	divasâni,	châvudasam,	pannaḍasam,	paṭipadam,	dhuvâyecha
L. N.	tinni	divasâni,	châvudasam,	pannaḍasam,	paṭipadam,	dhuvâyecha

D. S.	[13] anuposatha	machhe	avadhiye	nopiviketaviye	etâni	yevâ	divasâni
D. M.	anuposatham	machhe	avadhiye	no pi [15] viketaviye	etâni	yevâ	divasâni
A.	—	—	—	—	—	—	—
L. A.	anuposatham	machhe	avadhye	no pi [9] viketaviye	etâni	yeva	divasâni
L. N.	anuposatham	machhe	avadhye	[10] no piviketaviye	etâni	yeva	divasâni

D. S.	[14] nâgavanasi,	kevaṭabhogasi	yâni	annâni	pi	jîvanikâyâni
D. M.	nâgavanasi,	kevaṭabhogasi	[16] yâni	annâni	pi	jivanikâyâni
A.	—	—	—	—	—	—
L. A.	nâgavanasi,	kevaṭabhogasi,	yâni	annâni	pi	jîvanikâyâni
L. N.	nâgavanasi,	kevaṭabhogasi,	yâni	annâni	pi	[11] jîvanikâyâni

(*a*) I have changed Prinsep's *uka* to *oka*, as the vowel is the initial *o* in all the texts.

(*b*) Prinsep reads *kaku*, but all the texts agree as above in giving *kute*.

D. S.	[16] nohantaviyâni.	Aṭhami	pakhâye,	châvudasâye,	pannaḍasâye,	Tisâye,
D. M.	nohantaviyâni.	[17] Aṭhami	pakhâye,	châvudasâye,	pannaḍasaye,	Tisâye,
A.	——	——	——	——	——	——
L. A.	[10] nohantaviyâni.	Aṭhami	pakhâye,	châvudasâye,	pannaḍasâye,	Tisâye,
L. N.	nohantaviyâni.	Aṭhami	pakhâye,	châvudasâye,	pannaḍasâye,	Tisâye,

D. S.	[16] punâvasune,	tîsun —	châtun—	mâsisu,	sudivasâye,	gone	nonîlakhitaviye,
D. M.	[18] punâvasune,	tîsun	châtun—	mâsisu,	sudivasâye,	gone	[19] no nîlakhitaviye
A.	——	——	——	——	[20] sudivasaye,	gone	no nilakhitaviye
L. A.	punâvasune,	tîsu—	châtun—	mâsisu,	[11] sudivasâye,	gone	no nîlakhitaviye
L. N.	punâvasune,	[12] tîsu—	châtun—	mâsisu,	sudivasâye,	gone	no nîlakhitaviye

D. S.	[17] ajake,	eḍake,	sûkale,	evâpi	anne	nîlakhiyati	no	nîlakhitaviye
D. M.	ajako,	eḍake,	sûkalo,	evâpi	[20] anne	nîlakhiyâti	no	nîlakhitamviye
A.	ajake,	eḍa—	——	——	——	——	—	——
L. A.	ajako,	eḍake,	sûkalo,	evâpi	anno	nîlakhiyati	no	nîlakhitaviye
L. N.	ajake,	eḍake,	sûkale,	evâpi	anne	[13] nîlakhiyati	no	nîlakitaviye

D. S.	[18] tisâye,	punâvasune,	châtunmâsiye,	châtunmâsipakhâye,	aswasâ,	gonasâ
D. M.	tisâye,	punâvasune,	[21] châtunmasiye,	châtunmâsipakhaye,	aswasâ,	gonasâ,
A.	——	——	——	——	——	——
L. A.	[12] tisâye,	punâvasune,	châtunmâsiye,	châtunmâsipakhaye,	aswasa,	gonasa
L. N.	tisâye,	punâvasune,	châtunmâsiye,	châtunmâsipakhaye,	aswasa,	gonasa,

D. S.	[19] lakhune	nokhaṭaviye:	yâva	saḍḍavîsativasa abhisitename	etâye
D. M.	lakhune	[22] nokhaṭaviye:	yâva	saḍḍavîsativasa abhisitename	etâye
A.	[27] lakhune	nokaṭaviye,	yâva	saḍḍavîsativasâbhi———	——
L. A.	lakhane	nokaṭaiye:	[13] yâva	saḍḍavîsativasâbhisitename	etâye
L. N.	[14] lakhane	nokaṭaviye:	yâva	saḍḍavisativasâbhisitename	etâye

D. S.	[20] antalikâye	pannavîsati	bandhana	mokhâni	kaṭâni.
D. M.	[23] antalikâye	pannavîsati	bandhana	mokhâni	kaṭâni. (a)
A.	——	——	——	——	——
L. A.	antalikâye	pannavîsati	bandhana	mokhâni	kaṭâni.
L. N.	antalikâye	pannavîsati	[15] bandhana	mokhâni	kaṭâni.

EDICT VI.

(Delhi, East.)

D. S.	[1] Devânampiye	Piyadasi	Lâja	hevam	ahâ.	Duvâḍasa
A.	[28] Devânampiye	Piyadasi	Lâ*	* *	* *	* * *
L. A.	[14] Devânampiye	Piyadasi	Lâja	hevam	âhâ.	Duvâḍasa
L. N.	[16] Devânampiye	Piyadasi	Lâja	hevam	âha.	Duvâḍasa

D. S.	[2] vasa abhisitename	dhammalipi	likhâpitâ	lokasâ
A.	——	—— ——	——	——
L. A.	vasâbhisitename	dhammalipi	likhâpita	lokasa
L. N.	vasâbhisitename	dhammalipi	likhâpita	[17] lokasa

D. S.	[3] hitasukhâye;	setam	apahaṭâ,	taṁtaṁ	dhammavaḍhi	pâpovâ
A.	——	——	——	——	dhammavaḍhi	pâpovâ
L. A.	[15] hitasukhâye;	setam	apahaṭa,	taṁtaṁ	dhammavaḍhi	pâpovâ
L. N.	hitasukhâye;	setam	apahaṭa,	tamtam	dhammavadhi	pâpova

(a) The inscription on the Delhi-Mirat Pillar ends here, the rest being lost by the abrasion of the stone.

D. S.	[4] hevam	lokasâ	hitasukheti	paṭivekhâmi.	Atha	iyam	[5] nâtisu
A.	hevam	lokasâ	[29] hitasukheti	paṭivekhâmi.	Atha	* *	* *
L. A.	hevam	lokasâ	hitasukheti	paṭivekhâmi.	[16] Athâ	iyam	nâtisu
L. N.	hevam	lokasa	[18] hitasukheti	paṭivekhâmi.	Athâ	iyam	nâtisu

D. S.	hevam	patiyâsannesu,	hevam	apakaṭhesu	[6] kimankâni	sukham
A.	* *	patiyasannesu,	hevam	apakaṭhesu	kimankâni	su *
L. A.	hevam	patyâsannesu,	hevam	apakaṭhesu	kimankâni	sukham
L. N.	hevam	patyâsannesu,	hevam	apakaṭhesu	[19] kimankâni	sukham

D. S.	avahâmîti	tatha	cha	vidahâmi;	hemeva	[7] savanikâyesu
A.	* * *	* *	*	idahâmi	hevam meva	sava * kâyesu
L. A.	âvahâmîti	tathâ	cha	vidahâmi	[17] hemeva	savanikâyesu
L. N.	âvahâmîti	tathâ	chạ	vidahâmi	hemeva	savanikâyesu

D. S.	paṭivekhâmi;	sava	pâsanḍâ	pime	pujitâ	[8] vividhâya	pûjâyâ
A.	paṭivekhâmi	[30] sava	pâsanḍâ	pi me	pûjita	vividhaya	* jâyâ
L. A.	paṭivekhâmi;	sava	pâsanḍâ	pime	pujita	vividhâya	pujâya
L. N.	paṭivekhâmi;	[20] sava	pâsandâ	pime	pujita	vividhâya	pujâya

D. S.	echu	iyam	atanâ	pachûpagamane	[9] seme	mokhyamate
A.	echu	iyam	atanâ	pachupagamane	seme	mukhyamute
L. A.	echu	iyam	atana	pachûpagamane	[18] seme	mukhyamute
L. N.	echu	iyam	atana	pachupagamane	[21] seme	mokhyamute

D. S.	saḍḍavîsativasa abhisitename	[10] iyam	dhammalipi	likhâpitâ.
A.	sa * * * * * * *	* *	* lipi	likhâpitâti.
L. A.	saḍḍavisativasâbhisitename	iyam	dhammalipi	likhâpita.
L. N.	saḍḍavisativasâbhisitename	iyam	dhammalipi	likhâpita.

EDICT VII.

(Delhi, East.)

11 Devânampiye Piyadasi lâjâ hevam âhâ: ye atikantam

12 antalam lâjâne husa hevam ichhisu, katham jane

13 dhammavaḍhiyâ vaḍheyâ nochujane anulupâyâ dhammavadhiyâ

14 vadḥithâ etam. Devânampiye Piyadasi lâjâ hevam âhâ: esame

15 huthâ atâkantam-cha antalam hevam ichhisu lâjâne katham jane

16 anulupâyâ dhammavadḥiyâ vaḍheyâti nochajane anulupâyâ

17 dhammavaḍhiyâ vadḥithâ: se kina sujane anupaṭipajeyâ

18 kina sujane anulupâyâ dhammavadhiyâ vadheyâti; kina sukâni

19 abhyuṁ nâmayeham dhammavadhiyâti etam. Devânampiya Piyadasi lâjâ hevam

20 âhâ: esame huthâ dhammasâvanâni sâvâpâyâmi dhammanusathini

21 anusisâmi: etam jane sutu anupaṭîpajisati abhyum namisati

EDICT VIII.

(Delhi, around the Pillar.)

1 Dhamma vadhiyâ cha bâḍham vaḍhisati etâye me athâye dhamma sâvanâni sâvâpitâni dhammânusathini vividhâni ânapitâni (yâthatiyi) pâpibahune janasm̃ âyatâ ete paliyo vadisantipi pavithalisantipi lajukâpi bahukesu pâna sata sahasesu âyatâ tepime ânapitâ hevam cha hevam cha paliyo vadatha

2 janam dhammayatam. Devânampiye Piyadasi (*a*) hevam âhâ eta meva me anuvekhamâne dhamma thambhâni kaṭâni, dhammamahâmâtâ kaṭa, dhamma (kha——)kaṭe Devânampiye Piyadasi lâjâ hevam âhâ: magesu pi me nigohâni lopâ pitâni chhâyopagâni hasanti pasumunisânam ambâvaḍikyâ lopâpitâ aḍhakosikyâdî pi me udupânâni

3 khânâpâpitâni ninsi diyâcha kâlâpitâ âpânâni me bahukâni tata tata kâlâpitâni paṭibhogâye pâsumunisânam (sa * *) esa paṭîbhogenâma vividhâyahi sukhâyanâyâ puli me hipî (*b*) lâjihi mamayâcha sukhayite loke: imamchu dhammanupaṭîpatî pajantuti etadathâ me

4 esa kaṭe: Devânampiye Piyadasi (*b*) hevam âhâ: dhammamahâmâtâ pime ta bahu bidhesu aṭhesu anugahikesu viyâpaṭa se pavajîtânam̃ cheva gihithânam cha sava (pâsan)ḍesu picha viyâpaṭa se sanghaṭhasi pime kaṭe ime viyâpaṭâ hohantiti hemeva. Bâbhanesu âjîvikesu pime kaṭe.

(Delhi, around the Pillar.)

5 ime viyâpaṭâ hohautiti; niganthesu pime kaṭe, ime viyâpaṭâ hohanti: nân pâsandesu pime kaṭe ime viyâpaṭâ hohantiti: pativisitham paṭîvisitham tesutesu te te mahâmâtâ dhammamahâmâtâ chu me etesu cheva viyâpaṭâ, savesu cha annesu pâsanḍesu. Devânampiya Piyadasi lâjâ hevam âhâ:

6 ete cha anne cha bahukâ mukhâ dânavisagasi viyâpaṭâ se mama cheva devinam cha, savasi cha me olodhanasi (*c*) te bahu vidhena a * lena tâni tâni taṭhâ yatan(â)ni patî(ta * * *) hida cheva disâsu cha dâlakânam pi cha me kaṭe annânam cha devikumâlânam imedânavisagesu viyapaṭâ hohantiti

7 dhammâpadâna ṭhaye dhammânupaṭipatiye: esahi dhammâpadâne dhammapaṭîpati cha yâ iyam dayâdâne sache so chave madave sâdavecha lokasa hevam vaḍhisatiti. Devanamp(iye piyada)si lâjâ hevam âhâ yânibikânichi mamiya sâdhavâni kaṭâni tam loke anûpatîpanne tam cha anuvidhiyanti tena vaḍhitâ cha

8 vaḍhisanti cha mâtâpitisu sususâyâ gulusu sususâyâ vayo mahâlakânam anupaṭîpatiyâ Bâbhana Samanesu, kapanavalakesu, âvadâsa bhaṭakesu sampaṭîpatiyâ. Devânampiye (Piya)dasi lâjâ hevam âhâ: munisânam chu ya iyam dhammavadḥi vaḍhitâ duvehi yeva âkâlehi dhammaniyamena cha nijhatiya cha

9 tata chu lahuse dhamma niyame nijhatiyiva bhuye dhammaniyame chukho esa yeme iyam kate: imânicha imâni jâtâni avadhiyâni annâni pichu bahuk(——) dhammâniyamâni yâni me kaṭâni: nijhatiya va chu bhuye munisânam dhammavadḥi vadḥitâ avihinsâye bhutânam

10 anâlambhâye pânânam se etâye athâye iyam kaṭe puṭa papotike chanda masuliyike hotuti tathâ cha anupaṭîpajantuti hevam hi anupaṭi pajantam hidata(pâla)te âladhe hoti satavisativasâbhisitename iyam dhammalibi likhâpâpitâti etam Devânampiye âhâ: iyam

11 dhammalibi ata athi silâthambhânivâ silaphalakânivâ (*d*) tata kaṭaviyâ ena esa chilatitbike siyâ.

(*a*) The word *Lâja* is omitted in both of these places after Piyadasi; but it is present in all the after part of the inscription wherever the king's name is mentioned.

(*b*) Omitted by Prinsep.

(*c*) Prinsep reads *uludhanasi*, but the word begins with the initial *o*.

(*d*) Prinsep's last reading of this word was *dharika* (see Journal of the Asiatic Society of Bengal, VI, 1069), but the true reading is *phalakâni*, or "tablets," as given in the text.

ALLAHABAD PILLAR.

Separate Edicts.

No. 1.

Queen's Edict.

1 Devânampiyasâ vachanena savata mahamatâ

2 vataviyâ : eheta dutiyâye Deviye ḍâne

3 Ambâvaḍikâ vâ âlameva dânam eheva(?)etasi(?) anne(?)

4 Kichhigaotya titâye Deviye senâni pi vathâ(?)

5 dutiyâye Deviyeti tî valamâtu kâluvâkiye.

No. 2.

Kosambi Edict.

1 Devânampiye ânapayati Kosambiyamahâmata

2 ——— ——— mari • • sanghasi nila hiyo

3 I——— ——— ti bhiti • bhanti nita chi

4 ba——— pinam dhapayita a • tasa • am vasayi.

SANCHI PILLAR.

1 J. P. ———
• • • • • • • • maga • •
A. C. • va 1 2 3 4 5 6 maga • •

2 J. P. ———
A. C. • seni • bhi • • nam châti petaviya

3 J. P. ———
A. C. • vika Chandagiriye koye sangham

4 J. P. bhakhati bhikhunâbhi khamavase dâtâ
A. C. bhakhati Bhikhu cha Bhikhuni yi khu dâtâ

5 J. P. ———
A. C. ———nidusapi savam • payita ana •

6 J. P. Sasijala petaviye ichhahime (idi)
A. C. sasi visa petaviye ichhani me san —

7 J. P. —si : sampesimate chilathitike siyâti
A. C. —ti sanghasamage chilathititke siyâti.

TRANSLATIONS.

ROCK INSCRIPTIONS.

EDICT I.

Prinsep.

"The following edict of religion is promulgated by the heaven-beloved king *Piyadasi*:

"'In this place the putting to death of anything whatever that hath life, either for the benefit of the puja, or in convivial meetings, shall not be done. Much cruelty of this nature occurs in such assemblies. The heaven-beloved king *Piyadasi* is (as it were) a father (to his people). Uniformity of worship is wise and proper for the congregation of the heaven-beloved *Piyadasi* Raja.

"'Formerly, in the great refectory and temple of the heaven-beloved king *Piyadasi*, daily were many hundred thousand animals sacrificed for the sake of meat food. So even at this day while this religious edict is under promulgation, from the sacrifice of animals for the sake of food, some two are killed, or one is killed; but now the joyful chorus resounds again and again—that henceforward not a single animal shall be put to death.'"

Wilson.

"This is the edict of the beloved of the gods Raja *Priyadasi*:

"'The putting to death of animals is to be entirely discontinued, and no convivial meeting is to be held; for the beloved of the gods, the Raja *Priyadasi*, remarks many faults in such assemblies. There is but one assembly, indeed, which is approved of by the Raja *Priyadasi*, the beloved of the gods, which is that of the great kitchen of Raja *Priyadasi*, the beloved of the gods. Every day hundreds of thousands of animals have been there slaughtered for virtuous purposes, but now, although this pious edict is proclaimed that animals may be killed for good purposes; and such is the practice, yet as the practice is not determined, these presents are proclaimed that hereafter they shall not be killed.'"

EDICT II.

Prinsep.

"Everywhere within the conquered province of Raja *Piyadasi*, the beloved of the gods, as well as in the parts occupied by the faithful, such as *Chola*, *Pida*,* *Satiyaputra*, and *Ketalaputra*, even as far as *Tambapanni* (Ceylon); and, moreover, within the dominions of ANTIOCHUS, the *Greek*

Wilson.

"In all the subjugated (territories) of the king *Priyadasi*, the beloved of the gods, and also in the bordering countries, as *(Choda)*, *Palaya* * (or *Paraya*), *Satyaputra*, *Keralaputra*, *Tambapani*, (it is proclaimed), and ANTIOCHUS by name the *Yona* (or *Yavana*) raja, and those princes

* The true readings of these important names of the countries bordering on the dominions of Asoka are as follows: Choḍa, Panḍiya, Satiyaputra, Ketalaputra, and Tambapani. The first two are well known as *Chola* and *Pândya*, being the extreme southern provinces of India, while *Tambapani* is the Island of Ceylon, the Taprobane of the Greeks. *Keṭalaputra* is the district of *Kerala*, on the western coast between the Krishna River and Mysore. No represéntative of Satiyaputra has yet been proposed except by Lassen, who considered it as the Buddhist name of the King of Pida (or Pândya). But it seems to me that this name is capable of the same exact identification as the others. In Ptolemy's map we have the name of *Sadinî*, a people on the coast to the west of *Baithâna*, or Paithan on the Godâvari. They are said to be pirates; and as the name of the *Andri Pirate* is also found in the same place, I believe that we have the same people designated by two different names—*first*, as SADINI, or *Sâdavahans* or *Sâtakarnis*, and *second*, as ANDRI or *Andhras*. That the Andhras were a powerful nation in the time of Asoka, I have already established by reading their name in 13th Edict of the Shahbazgarhi and Khâlsi texts. The name of *Satakarni* is written *Sâdavâhana* in one of the Nâsik Inscriptions (West No. 6), and Ptolemy's form would be obtained by the elision of the *k* in *Sadakani*. Another form of the name is preserved in the Periplus as *Saraganos*, in which, according to a common Indian practice, the *t* and *d* are changed to *r* in pronunciation.

Prinsep.

(of which Antiochus' generals are the rulers), everywhere the heaven-beloved Raja *Piyadasi's* double system of medical aid is established—both medical aid for men, and medical aid for animals, together with the medicaments of all sorts, which are suitable for men, and suitable for animals. And wherever there is not (such provision), in all such places they are to be prepared, and to be planted: both root-drugs and herbs, wheresoever there is not (a provision of them), in all such places shall they be deposited and planted.

" And in the public highways wells are to be dug, and trees to be planted, for the accommodation of men and animals."

Wilson.

who are nearer to (or allied with) that monarch, universally (are apprised) that (two designs have been cherished by *Priyadasi*, one design) regarding men, and one relating to animals; and whatever herbs are useful to men or useful to animals wherever there are none, such have been everywhere caused to be conveyed and planted, (and roots and fruits wherever there are none, such have been everywhere conveyed and planted; and on the roads) wells have been caused to be dug, (and trees have been planted) for the respective enjoyment of animals and men."

EDICT III.

Prinsep.

"Thus spake the heaven-beloved king *Piyadasi:* 'By me, after the twelfth year of my anointment, this commandment is made. Everywhere in the conquered (provinces) among the faithful, whether (my own) subjects or foreigners, after every five years, let there be (a public) humiliation for this express object, yea, for the confirmation of virtue and for the suppression of disgraceful acts.

"'Good and proper is dutiful service to mother and father; towards friends and kinsfolks, towards Brahmans and Sramans, excellent is charity:—prodigality and malicious slander are not good.

"'All this the leader of the congregation shall inculcate to the assembly, with (appropriate) explanation and example.'"

Wilson.

" King *Priyadasi* says: 'This was ordered by me when I had been twelve years inaugurated. In the conquered country, and among my own subjects as well as strangers, that every five years expiation should be undergone with this object, for the enforcement of such moral obligations as were declared by me to be good: such as duty to parents, (and protection of) friends and children, (relations,) Brahmans and Sramans:—good is liberality, good is non-injury of living creatures, and abstinence from prodigality and slander are good. Continuance in this course (the discharge of these duties) shall be commanded both by explanation and by example.'"

EDICT IV.

Prinsep.

"'In times past, even for many hundred years, has been practised the sacrifice of living beings, the slaughter of animals, disregard of relations, and disrespect towards Brahmans and Sramans.

"'This day, by the messenger of the religion of the heaven-beloved king *Piyadasi,* (has been made) a proclamation by beat of drum, a grand announcement of religious grace, and a display of equipages, and a parade of elephants, and things to gratify the senses, and every other kind of heavenly object for the admiration of mankind, such as had never been for many hundred years, such as were to-day exhibited.

Wilson.

"'During a past period of many centuries, there have prevailed—destruction of life, injury of living beings, disrespect towards kindred, and irreverence towards Sramans and Brahmans. But now, in conformity to moral duty, the pious proclamation of king *Priyadasi,* the beloved of the gods, is made by beat of drum, in a manner never before performed for hundreds of years, with chariot and elephant processions, and fireworks and other divine displays of the people exhibiting the ceremonies (and this) for the promulgation of the law of king *Priyadasi,* &c., that non-destruction of life, non-

Prinsep.

" 'By the *religious ordinance* of the heaven-beloved king *Piyadasi*, the non-sacrifice of animals, the non-destruction of living beings, proper regard to kindred, respect to Brahmans and Sramans, dutiful service to spiritual pastors—through these and many other similar (good acts) doth *religious grace* abound; and thus, moreover, shall the heaven-beloved king *Piyadasi* cause religion to flourish, and the same shall the sons, the grandsons, and the great-grandsons of the heaven-beloved king *Piyadasi* cause to abound exceedingly.

" 'As long as the mountains shall endure, so long in virtue and in strict observances shall the religion stand fast. And through good acts of this nature, that is to say, through these ordinances and the strict practice of religion, laxness of discipline is obviated. Moreover in this object, it is proper to be intelligent, and no wise neglected. For the same purpose is this (edict) ordered to be written. Let all take heed to profit of this good object, and not to give utterance to objections.'

"By the heaven-beloved king *Piyadasi*, after the twelfth year of his announcement, is this caused to be written."

Wilson.

injury to living beings, respect to relations, reverence of Brahmans and Sramans, and many other duties, do increase, and shall increase; and this moral law of the king *Priyadasi* the sons, grandsons, and great-grandsons of king *Priyadasi* shall maintain. Let the moral ordinance of king *Priyadasi* be stable as a mountain for the establishment of duty; for in these actions duty will be followed, as the law which directs ceremonial rites is not the observance of moral duties. It were well for every ill-conducted person to be attentive to the object of this injunction. This is the edict (writing) of king *Priyadasi*. Let not any thought be entertained by the subject-people of opposing the edict.' This has been caused to be written by the king *Priyadasi*, in the twelfth year of his inauguration."

Burnouf has also given a full translation of this edict, which I annex.*

" 'Dans le temps passé, pendant de nombreuses centaines d'années, onvit prospèrer uniquement le meurtre des êtres vivants et la méchanceté à l'égard des créatures, le manque de respect pour les parents, le manque de respect pour les Bâmhanas et les Samanas (les Brahmanes et les çramanas). Aussi, en ce jour, parce que *Piyadasi*, le Roi chéri des Dêvas, pratique la loi, le son de tambour (a retenti) ; oui, la voix de la loi (s'est fait entendre) après que des promenades des chars de parade, des promenades d'éléphants, des feux d'artifice, ainsi que d'autres représentations divines ont été montrées aux regards du peuple. Ce que depuis bien des centaines d'années on n'avait pas vu auparavant, on l'a vu prospèrer aujourd'hui, par suite de l'ordre que donne *Piyadasi*, le Roi chéri des Dêvas, de pratiquer la loi. La cessation du meurtre des êtres vivants et des actes de méchanceté à l'égard des créatures, le respect pour les parents, l'obéissance aux père et mère, l'obéissance aux anciens (*Thera*), voilà les vertus, ainsi que d'autres pratiques de la loi de diverses espèces, qui ici sont accrues. Et *Piyadasi*, le Roi chéri des Dêvas, fera croître encore cette observation de la loi; et les fils, et les petits-fils, et les arrière-petits-fils de *Piyadasi*, le Roi chéri des Dêvas, feront croître cette observation de la loi jusqu'au *Kalpa* de la destruction. Fermes dans la loi, dans la morale, ils ordonneront l'observation de la loi; car c'est la meilleure des actions que d'en joindre l'observation de la loi. Cette observation même de la loi n'existe pas pour celui qui n'a pas de morale. Il est bon que cet objet prospère et ne dépérisse pas: c'est pour cela qu'on a fait écrire cet édit. Si cet objet s'accroît, on n'en devra jamais voir le dépérissement.' *Piyadasi*, le Roi chéri des Dêvas, a fait écrire cet édit, la douzième année depuis son sacre."†

---

* Le Lotus de la Bonne Loi—Appendice, p. 781.

† Burnouf's remarks in justification of his own translation and reading of the text are much too long to be quoted here. See Le Lotus de la Bonne Loi, Appendice, p. 781. He very naturally takes exception to Wilson's explanation of *Bahmanas* and *Samanas* as "Brâhmans and (Brahmanical) ascetics," and shows that these two terms are intended to designate two classes of persons, the Brahmans and the Buddhists, in the same way that they are discriminated in the legends of the Divya Avadâna.

EDICT V.

Prinsep.

"Thus spake the heaven-beloved king *Piyadasi* :—

"'Prosperity (cometh) through adversity, and truly each man (to obtain) prosperity causeth himself present difficulty; therefore by me (nevertheless) has much prosperity been brought about, and therefore shall my sons and grandsons, and my latest posterity, as long as the very hills endure, pursue the same conduct; and so shall each meet his reward! While he, on the other hand, who shall neglect such conduct, shall meet his punishment in the midst of the wicked (in the nethermost regions of hell).

"'For a very long period of time there have been no ministers of religion appointed, who intermingling among all unbelievers (may overwhelm them) with the inundation of religion, and with the abundance of the sacred doctrines. Through Kam (bocha, Gan) dhâra, Narâstika,* Petenika, and elsewhere, finding their way unto the uttermost limits of the barbarian countries, for the benefit and pleasure of (all classes)...... and for restraining the passions of the faithful, and for the regeneration of those bound in the fetters (of sin) (?)...... are they appointed. Intermingling equally among the dreaded, and among the respected both in Pâtaliputa and in foreign places, teaching better things, shall they everywhere penetrate; so that they even who (oppose the faith shall at length become) ministers of it.'"

Wilson.

"The beloved of the gods king *Priyadasi* thus proclaims: 'Whoever perverts good to evil will derive evil from good; therefore much good has been done by me, and my sons and grandsons, and others my posterity, (will) conform to it for every age. So they who shall enjoy happiness, and those who cause the path to be abandoned shall suffer misfortune. The chief ministers of morality have for an unprecedentedly long time been tolerant of iniquity; therefore in the tenth year of the inauguration have ministers of morality been made, who are appointed for the purpose of presiding over morals among persons of all the religions for the sake of the augmentation of virtue, and for the happiness of the virtuous among the people of Kamboja, Gandhara, Naristika, and Petenika. They shall also be spread among the warriors, the Brahmans, the mendicants, the destitute, and others, without any obstruction, for the happiness of the well-disposed, in order to loosen the bonds of those who are bound, and liberate those who are confined, through the means of holy wisdom disseminated by pious teachers; and they will proceed to the outer cities and fastnesses of my brother and sister, and wherever are any other of my kindred: and the ministers of morals, those who are appointed as superintendents of morals, shall, wherever the moral law is established, give encouragement to the charitable and those addicted to virtue. With this intent this edict is written, and let my people obey it.'"

EDICT VI.

Prinsep.

"Thus spake *Piyadasi,* the heaven-beloved king :—

"'Never was there in any former period a system of instruction applicable to every season, and to every action, such as that which is now established by me.

"'For every season, for behaviour during meals, during repose, in domestic relations, in the nursery, in conversation, in general deportment, and on the bed of death—everywhere instructors (or Pativedakas) have been appointed. Accordingly do ye (instructors) deliver instruction in what concerneth my people.

Wilson.

"The beloved of the gods, king *Priyadasi,* thus declares: 'An unprecedentedly long time has past since it has been the custom at all times, and in all affairs, to submit representations. Now it is established by me that, whether at meals, in my palace, in the interior apartments, in discourse, in exchange of civility, in gardens, the officers appointed to make reports shall convey to me the objects of the people. I will always attend to the objects of the people; and whatever I declare verbally, whether punishment or reward, is further intrusted to the supervisors of morals (or eminent persons):

* The *sa* belongs to the preceding name *Gandharanam,* and the word thus becomes *Râstika,* which is a well-known name of Surashtra.

Prinsep.

"'And everywhere in what concerneth my people do I myself perform whatsoever with my mouth I enjoin (unto them); whether it be by me (esteemed) disagreeable, or whether agreeable. Moreover, for their better welfare, among them an awarder of punishment is duly installed. On this account, assembling together those who are dwelling in the reputation of much wisdom, do ye, meanwhile, instruct them as to the substance of what is hereby ordained by me for all circumstances, and for all seasons. This is not done by me in any desire for the collection of worldly gain, but in the real intention that the benefit of my people shall be effected; whereof, moreover, this is the root, the good foundation, and the steady repose in all circumstances: there is not a more effectual mode of benefiting all mankind than this on which I bestow my whole labour.

"'But upon how many living beings (I will pass over the mention of other things) do I confer happiness here:—hereafter, likewise, let them hope ardently for heaven!—Amen!

"'For this reason has the present religious edict been written. May it endure for evermore, and so may my sons, and my grandsons, and my great-grandsons uphold the same for the profit of all the world, and labour therein with the most reverential exertion!'"

Wilson.

for that purpose let those who reside in the immediate vicinage even become informers at all times, and in all places, so it is ordained by me. The distribution of wealth which is to be made is designed by me for the benefit of all the world; for the distribution of wealth is the root of virtues to the good of the world, for which I am always labouring. On the many beings over whom I rule I confer happiness in this world;—in the next they may obtain Swarga. With this view, this moral edict has been written. May it long endure, and may my sons, grandsons, and great-grandsons after me continue with still greater exertion to labour for universal good!'"

EDICT VII.

Prinsep.

"The heaven-beloved king *Piyadasi* everywhere ardently desireth that all unbelievers may be brought to repentance and peace of mind. He is anxious that every diversity of opinion, and every diversity of passion, may shine forth blended into one system, and be conspicuous in undistinguishing charity. Unto no one can be repentance and peace of mind until he hath attained supreme knowledge, perfect faith which surmounteth all obstacles, and perpetual assent."

Wilson.

"The beloved of the gods, the Raja *Priyadasi*, desires that all unbelievers may everywhere dwell (unmolested), as they also wish for moral restraint and purity of disposition. For men are of various purposes and various desires, and they do injury to all or only to a part. Although, however, there should not be moral restraint or purity of disposition in any one, yet wherever there is great liberality (or charity), gratitude will acknowledge merit even in those who were before that reputed vile."

The following is Burnouf's translation of this Edict* :—

"*Piyadasi*, le roi chéri des Dêvas, désire en tous lieux que les ascètes de toutes les croyances résident (tranquilles) : ils désirent tous l'empire qu'on exerce sur soi-même, et la pureté de l'âme; mais le peuple a des opinions diverses et des attachements divers, (et) les ascètes obtiennent, soit tout, soit une partie seulement (de ce qu'ils demandent). Cependant, pour celui-même auquel n'arrive pas une large aumône l'empire sur soi-même, la pureté de l'âme, la reconnaissance et une dévotion solide qui dure toujours, cela est bien."

---

* Le Lotus de la Bonne Loi, Appendice, p. 755.

EDICT VIII.

Prinsep.

"In ancient times, festivals for the amusement of sovereigns consisted of gambling, hunting the deer (or antelope), and other exhilarating pleasures of the same nature. But the heaven-beloved king *Piyadasi*, having attained the tenth year of his anointment, for the happiness of the wise, hath a festival of religion (been substituted) and this same consists in visits to Brahmans and Sramans, and in alms-giving, and in visits to the reverend and aged; and the liberal distribution of gold, the contemplation of the universe and its inhabitants, obeying the precepts of religion, and setting religion before all other things, are the expedients (he employs for amusement); and these will become an enjoyment without alloy to the heaven-beloved king *Piyadasi* in another existence."

Wilson.

"In past times kings were addicted to travelling about, to companions, to going abroad, to hunting and similar amusements, but *Piyadasi*, the beloved of the gods, having been ten years inaugurated, by him easily awakened, that moral festival is adopted, (which consists) in seeing and bestowing gifts on Brahmans and Sramans; in seeing and giving gold to elders, and overseeing the country and the people; the institution of moral laws, and the investigation of morals:—such are the devices for the removal of apprehension, and such are the different pursuits of the favourite of the gods, king *Piyadasi*."

Burnouf has not given a connected translation of this Edict, but his remarks on its general scope are of special importance. According to his explanation Asoka obtained *sambodhim*, or "la science complète de la Bodhi," or, in other words, "la connaissance de ce qu'enseigne le Buddha," after he had reigned ten years. He refers to Lassen as evidently holding the same opinion: "Quoique Lassen n'a pas traduit littéralement cette partie de votre inscription, il est facile de voir, par l'usage qu'il en a fait dans ses *Antiquitès Indiennes*, qu'il entend comme je propose de le faire. Voici les propres paroles de Lassen: 'C'est seulement la dixième année depuis son couronnement qu'il obtint la vue complète. Evidemment Lassen a lu comme moi *sambodhim*, 'la vue ou la science complète,' et compris de même ayâya."*

EDICT IX.

Prinsep.

"Thus spake King *Piyadasi*, beloved of the gods:

"'Each individual seeketh his own happiness in a diversity of ways, in the bonds of affection, in marriage, or otherwise, in the rearing of offspring, in foreign travel: in these, and other similar objects, doth man provide happiness of every degree. But there is great ruination—excesses of all kinds when (a man) maketh worldly objects his happiness. On the contrary, this is what is to be done,—(for most certainly that species of happiness is a fruitless happiness—) to obtain the happiness which yieldeth plentiful fruit, even the happiness of virtue; that is to say: kindness to dependants, reverence to spiritual teachers, are proper; humanity to animals is proper:—all these acts, and others of the same kind, are to be rightly denominated the happiness of virtue!

"'By father and by son, and by brother; by master, (and by servant) it is proper that these

Wilson.

"The beloved of the gods *Priyadasi Raja*, thus says: 'Every man that is celebrates various occasions of festivity, as on the removal of incumbrances, on invitations, on marriages, on the birth of a son, or on setting forth on a journey:—on these and other occasions a man makes various rejoicings. The benevolent man also celebrates many and various kinds of pure and disinterested festivities;—and such rejoicing is to be practised. Such festivities are fruitless and vain, but the festivity that bears great fruit is the festival of duty—such as the respect of the servant to his master: reverence for holy teachers is good; tenderness for living creatures is good; liberality to Brahmans and Sramans is good. These, and other such acts, constitute verily the festival of duty; and it is to be cherished as father by son, a dependant by his master. This is good, this is the festival to be observed: for the establishment of this

---

* Burnouf, Le Lotus, Appendice, p. 759, quoting Lassen *Ind. Alterthum*, II, 227, n. 3.

Prinsep.

things should be entitled happiness, and further, for the more complete attainment of this object, secret charity is most suitable :—yea, there is no alms, and no loving-kindness, comparable with the alms of religion, and the loving-kindness of religion, which ought verily to be upheld alike by the friend, by the good-hearted; by kinsman and neighbour, in the entire fulfilment of pleasing duties.

" 'This is what is to be done :—this is what is good. With those things let each man propitiate heaven. And how much ought (not) to be done in order to the propitiation of heaven?' "

Wilson.

object virtuous donations are made; for there is no such donation or benevolence as the gift of duty, or the benevolence of duty: that (benevolence) is chaff (which is contracted) with a friend, a companion, a kinsman, or an associate, and is to be reprehended. In such and in such manner this is to be done. This is good: with these means let a man seek Swarga. This is to be done: by these means it is to be done, as by them Swarga has been gained.' "

EDICT X.

Prinsep.

"The heaven-beloved king *Piyadasi* doth not deem that glory and reputation (are) the things of chief importance; on the contrary, (only for the prevention of sin,) and for enforcing conformity among a people praiseworthy for following the four rules of virtue, and pious, doth the heaven-beloved king *Piyadasi* desire glory and reputation in this world; and whatsoever the heaven-beloved king *Piyadasi* chiefly displayeth heroism in obtaining, that is all (connected with) the other world.

"For in every thing connected with his immortality, there is, as regards mortal things in general, discredit. Let this be discriminated with encouragement or with abandonment, with honor or with the most respectful force; and every difficulty connected with futurity shall, with equal reverence, be vanquished."

Wilson.

"The beloved of the gods, the Prince *Piyadasi*, does not esteem glory and fame as of great value; and, besides, for a long time it has been my fame and that of my people, that the observance of moral duty, and the service of the virtuous, should be practised: for this is to be done. This is the fame that the beloved of the gods desires: and inasmuch as the beloved of the gods excels, (he holds) all such reputations as no real reputation, but such as may be that of the unrighteous—pain and chaff; for it may be acquired by crafty and unworthy persons; and by whatever further effort it is acquired, it is worthless and a source of pain."

Burnouf, after quoting the above translations by Prinsep and Wilson, gives his own translation as follows :*

"*Piyadasi*, le roi chéri des Dêvas, ne pense pas que la gloire ni la renommée produisent de grands avantages, sauf la gloire (qu'il désire) pour lui-même, savoir que mes peuples pratiquent longtemps l'obéissance à la loi et qu'ils observent la règle de la loi. C'est pour cela seulement que *Piyadasi*, le roi chéri des Dêvas, désire gloire et renommée. Car tout ce que *Piyadasi*, le roi chéri des Dêvas, déploie d'heroïsme, c'est en vue de l'autre vie. Bien plus, toute gloire ne donne que peu de profit; ce qui en résulte, au contraire, c'est l'absence de vertu. Toutefois c'est en effet une chose difficile (que le travailler pour le ciel) pour un homme médiocre comme pour un homme élevé, si ce n'est quand, par une heroïsme suprême, on a tout abandonné; mais cela est certainement difficile pour un homme élevé."

* Le Lotus de la Bonne Loi, Appendice, p. 659.

EDICT XI.

Prinsep.

"Thus spake *Piyadasi*, the king, beloved of the gods:—

"'There is no such charity as the charity which springeth from virtue,—(which is) the intimate knowledge of virtue, the inheritance of virtue, the close union with virtue. And in these maxims it is manifested—kindness towards servants and hirelings: towards mother and father dutiful service is proper: towards a friend's offspring, to kindred in general, to Brahmans and Sramans almsgiving is proper: avoiding the destruction of animals' life is proper.

"'And this (saying) should be equally repeated by father and son, (?) by hireling, and even so by neighbours in general.

"'This is excellent:—and this is what ought to be done!

"'And whoso doeth thus is blessed of the inhabitants of this world: and in the next world endless moral merit resulteth from such religious charity.'"

Wilson.

"Thus says the beloved of the gods, king *Priyadasi*: 'There is no gift like the gift of virtue; whether it be the praise of virtue, the apportionment of virtue, or relationship of virtue. This (gift) is, the cherishing of slaves and dependants; pious devotion to mother and father; generous gifts to friends and kinsmen, Brahmans and Sramans; and non-injury of living beings is good. In this manner, it is to be lived by father and son, and brother, and friend, and friend's friend (?), and by a master (of slaves), and by neighbours. This is good: this is to be practised; and thus having acted, there is happiness in worldly existence, and hereafter great holiness is obtained by this gift of virtue.'"

EDICT XII.

Prinsep.

"The heaven-beloved king *Piyadasi* propitiateth all unbelievers, both of the ascetic and of the domestic classes: by charitable offerings, and by every species of *puja* doth he (strive to) propitiate them. Not that the beloved of the gods deemeth offerings or prayers to be of the same (value) with true glory. The promotion of his own salvation promoted, in many ways, the salvation of all unbelievers; of which, indeed, this is the root, and the whole substance.

"Again, the propitiation of the converted heretic, and the reproof of the unconverted heretic, must not be (effected) by harsh treatment:—but let those who enter into discussion (conciliate them) by restraint of their own passions, and by their mild address. By such and such conciliatory demeanours shall even the unconverted heretics be propitiated. And such conduct increaseth the number of converted heretics, while it disposeth of the unconverted heretic, and effecteth a revolution of opinion in him. And (he) encourageth the converted heretic, while he disposeth completely of the unconverted heretic, whosoever propitiateth the converted heretic, or reproveth the unconverted heretic, by the pecuniary support of the converted heretic. And who so, again, doth so, he purifieth in the most

Wilson.

"The beloved of the gods, king *Priyadasi*, honours all forms of religious faith, whether professed by ascetics or householders; he honours them with gifts and with manifold kinds of reverence: but the beloved of the gods considers no gift or honour so much as the increase of the substance (of religion):—his encouragement of the increase of the substance of all religious belief is manifold. But the root of his (encouragement) is this:—reverence for one's own faith, and no reviling nor injury of that of others. Let the reverence be shown in such and such a manner as is suited to the difference of belief; as when it is done in that manner, it augments our own faith, and benefits that of others. Whoever acts otherwise injures his own religion, and wrongs that of others; for he who in some way honours his own religion, and reviles that of others, saying, having extended to all our own belief, let us make it famous;—he who does this throws difficulties in the way of his own religion: this, his conduct, cannot be right. The duty of a person consists in respect and service of others. Such is the wish of the beloved of the gods; for in all forms of religion there may be many scriptures (Sutras), and many holy texts, which are to be

Prinsep.

effectual manner the heretic;—and of himself such an act is his very breath, and his well-being.

"Moreover, 'hear ye the religion of the faithful, and attend thereto': even such is the desire, the act, the hope of the beloved of the gods, that all unbelievers may speedily be purified, and brought into contentment speedily.

"Furthermore, from place to place this most gracious sentiment should be repeated: 'The beloved of the gods doth not esteem either charitable offering or *puja*, as comparable with true glory. The increase of blessing to himself is (of) as much (importance) to all unbelievers.'

"For this purpose, have been spread abroad ministers of religion, possessing fortitude of mind, and practices of every virtue. May the various congregations co-operate (with them) for the accomplishment therefor! For the increase of converts is, indeed, the lustre of religion."

Wilson.

thereafter followed through my protection. The beloved of the gods considers no gift or reverence to be equal to the increase of the essence of religion: and as this is the object of all religions,—with a view to its dissemination, superintendents of moral duty, as well as over women, and officers of compassion, as well as other officers, (are appointed); and the fruit of this (regulation) will be the augmentation of our own faith, and the lustre of moral duty."

This Edict has been fortunate in attracting the attention of Burnouf, whose translation here follows: *

"*Piyadasi*, le roi chéri des Dêvas, honore tous les croyances, ainsi que les mendiants et les maîtres de maison, soit par des aumônes, soit par des diverses marques de respect. Mais le roi chéri des Dêvas honore tous les croyances, ainsi que les mendiants et les maîtres de maison, soit par des aumônes, soit par des diverses marques de respect. Mais le roi chéri des Dêvas n'estime pas autant les aumônes et les marques de respect que l'augmentation de ce qui est l'essence de la renommée. Or, l'augmentation de ce qui est essentiel [en ce genre] pour toutes les croyances, est de plusieurs espèces: cependant le fonds en est pour chacune d'elles la louange en paroles. Il y a plus: on doit seulement honorer sa propre croyance, mais non blâmer celle des autres: il y aura ainsi peu le tort de produit. Il y a même telle et telle circonstance où la croyance des autres doit aussi être honorée; en agissant ainsi selon chacun de ces circonstances, on augmente sa propre croyance et on sert celle des autres. Celui qui agit autrement diminue sa propre croyance et fait tort aussi à celle des autres. L'homme, quelqu'il soit, qui honore sa propre croyance et blâme celle des autres, le tout par dévotion pour sa croyance, et bien plus, en disant: 'Mettons notre propre croyance en lumière.' L'homme, dis-je, qui agit ainsi, ne fait que nuire plus gravement à sa croyance propre. C'est pourquoi le bon accord seul est bien. Il y a plus; que les hommes écoutent et suivent avec soumission chacun la loi les uns des autres; car tel est le désir du roi chéri des Dêvas. Il y a plus: puissent [les hommes de] toutes les croyances abonder en savoir et prospèrer en vertu! Et ceux qui ont foi à telle et telle religion, doivent répéter ceci: Le roi chéri des Dêvas n'estime pas autant les aumônes et les marques de respect que l'augmentation de ce qui est l'essence de la renommée et la multiplication de toutes les croyances. A cet effet ont été établis des grands ministres de la loi et des grands ministres surveillants des femmes, ainsi que des inspecteurs des lieux secrets, et d'autres corps d'agents. Et le fruit de cette institution, c'est que l'augmentation des religions ait promptement lieu, ainsi que la mise en lumière de la loi."

EDICT XIII.

Prinsep.

"......Whose equality, and exertion towards that object, exceeding activity, judicious conduct.......... afterwards in the Kalinga provinces not to be obtained by wealth.........the decline of religion,

* Le Lotus de la Bonne Loi, Appendice, p. 762.

Prinsep.

murder, and death, and unrestrained license of mankind; when flourished the (precious maxims) of Devânampiyo, comprising the essence of learning and of science:—dutiful service to mother and father; dutiful service to spiritual teachers: the love of friend and child; (charity) to kinsfolk, to servants (to Brahmans and Sramans, &c., which) cleanse away the calamities of generations: further also in these things unceasing perseverance is fame. There is not in either class of the heretics of men, not so to say, a procedure marked by such grace,.........nor so glorious nor friendly, nor even so extremely liberal as Devânampiyo's injunctions for the non-injury, and content of living creatures.........and the Greek King besides, by whom the Kings of Egypt, Ptolemaios and Antigonos,(?) and Magas,............ both here and in foreign (countries), everywhere the religious ordinances of Devânampiyo effect conversion, wherever they go;.........conquest is of every description: but further the conquest which bringeth joy springing from pleasant emotions, becometh joy itself; the victory of virtue is happiness: the victory of happiness is not to be overcome, that which essentially possesses a pledge of happiness,——such victory is desired in things of this world and things of the next world!

"And this place is named the WHITE ELEPHANT, conferring pleasure on all the world." *

EDICT XIV.

Prinsep.

"This religious edict is caused to be written by the heaven-beloved king Piyadasi. It is (partly) (written) with abridgment; it is (partly) with ordinary extent; and it is (partly) with amplification: not incoherent (or disjointed) but throughout continuous (and united) it is powerful in overcoming the wise; and it is much written and caused to be written, yet it is always but the same thing repeated over and over again.

"For the persuasive eloquence which is lavished on each separate subject shall man the rather render obedience thereunto!

"Furthermore, at one time even unto the conclusion is this written, incomparable in manner, and conformable with the copy, by Relachepu the scribe and pandit."

Burnouf.†

"Ce texte de la loi a été écrit par l'ordre de Piyadasi, le roi chéri des Devas. Il se trouve sous une forme abrégée, il se trouve sous une forme de moyenne étendue, il se trouve enfin sous une forme développée: et cependant le tout n'est certainement pas mutilé. Des grands hommes aussi ont fait des conquêtes, et ont beaucoup écrit; et moi je ferai aussi écrire ceci. Et s'il y a ici autant de répétitions, c'est à cause de la douceur de chacune des pensées qui sont répétées. Il y a plus! puisse le peuple y conformer sa conduite! Tout ce qui peut, en quelques endroits, avoir été écrit sans être achevé, sans ordre, et sans qu'on ait un égard au texte qui fait autorité, tout cela vient uniquement de la faute de l'écrivain."

* This last sentence should follow Edict XIV. Professor Kern translates it differently—"the White Elephant whose name is "Bringer of happiness to the whole world," and adds "that by this term Sákya is implied there can be no doubt, since the legend says that the Bodhisattva, the future Buddha, left heaven to bring happiness to men, and entered his mother's womb as a White Elephant." See Indian Antiquary, V, 257, 258.

† As no translation of this Edict has been given by Wilson, it is fortunate that we possess another version from the learned and careful pen of Burnouf in Le Lotus de la Bonne Loi, p. 752.

TRANSLATIONS.

No. 6.

DHAULI AND JAUGADA.

No. 1. SEPARATE EDICT.

Prinsep.

Journal of the Bengal Asiatic Society, VII. 442.

"By command of Devánampiya (the beloved of the gods)! In (the city of) Tosalî, the public officers in charge of the town are to be enjoined (as follows) :—

"Whomsoever I ascertain to be a murderer, him do I desire to be imprisoned. This I publicly proclaim, and I will carry into effect however difficult :—for this my supreme will is irresistible! On this account the present *Tope* (Stupa) is denominated the tope of commandment.

"From amongst many thousand souls, oh ye my chosen people! repair ye (hither) to the holy men. Every righteous man is my (true) subject, and for my subjects I desire this only, that they may be possessed of every benefit and happiness as to things of this world and of the world beyond.........and furthermore I desire ye do not purify the wicked until.......................

"In this country and not anywhere else is to be seen such a stupa (?) in which is provided proper rules of moral conduct.

"When one man relieves (his fellow-creature) from the bondage and misery (of sin), it necessarily follows that he himself is released from bondage; but again despairing at the number of human beings in the same state (whom he is unable to relieve) he is much troubled.

Thence is this stupa so desirable (as an asylum); that in the midst of virtuous regulations we may pursue our obedient course!

And through these classes (of deeds) are people rendered disobedient, *viz.*, by enviousness, by the

Burnouf.

Le Lotus de la Bonne Loi, 672-683.

"Au nom du (roi) chéri des Dêvas, le grand ministre de Tosali, gouverneur de la ville, doit s'entendre dire : Quoique ce soit que je décréte, je désire qu'il en soit l'exécuteur. Voilà ce que je lui fait connaître, et je recommence deux fois, parce que cette répétition est regardée par moi comme capitale. C'est dans ce dessein que ce *Tupha* (*Stûpa*) a été dressé; ce Stûpa de commandement en effet a été destiné aujourd'hui à de nombreux milliers d'êtres vivants, comme un présent et un bouquet de fleurs pour les gens de bien. Tout homme de bien est pour moi un fils. Et pour mes fils, ce que je désire, c'est qu'ils soient en possession de toute espèce d'avantages, et de plaisirs, tant dans ce monde que dans l'autre. Ainsi je désire le bonheur du peuple, et puissiez-vous ne pas éprouver de malheur, jusqu'à (*lacune de* 10 *lettres*) un seul homme pense. En effet, ce *Stûpa* regarde ce pays tout entier qui nous est soumis; sur ce *Stûpa* a été promulguée la règle morale. Que si un homme (4 *lettres*) est soumis soit à la captivité, soit à de mauvais traitements, à partir de ce moment (il sera délivré) à l'instant par lui de cette captivité et des autres (2 *lettres*). Beaucoup de gens du pays souffrent dans l'esclavage; c'est pourquoi ce *Stûpa* a dû être désiré. Puissions-nous, me suis-je dit, (leur) faire obtenir la liqueur enivrante de la morale! Mais la morale n'est pas respectée par ces espèces (de vices): l'envie, la destruction de la vie, les injures, la violence, l'absence d'occupation, la paresse,

Burnouf.

Journal of the Bengal Asiatic Society, VII, 442.

practice of destroying life, by tyranny, by cruelty, by idleness, by laziness, by waste of time. That morality is to be desired which is based on my ordinances (?) and in all these the roots (or leading principles) are,—the non-destruction of life, and the non-infliction of cruelty. May the desire of such moral guidance endure unto the end of time! and may these (principles) continuing to rise (in estimation) ever flourish, and in as much as this benefit and love should be ever had in remembrance, my desire is that in this very manner, these (ordinances) shall be pronounced aloud by the person appointed to the Stupa; and adverting to nothing else but precisely according to the commandment of Devánampiya, let him (further) declare and explain them.

"Much longing after the things of (this life) is a disobedience I again declare: not less so is the laborious ambition of dominion by a prince, (who would be) a propitiator of heaven. Confess and believe in God, who is the worthy object of obedience! for equal to this (belief), I declare unto you, ye shall not find such a means of propitiating heaven. Oh strive ye to obtain this inestimable treasure!

"And this edict is to be read at (the time of) the lunar mansion Tisa, at the end of the month of Bhâtun: it is to be made heard (even if) by by a single (listener). And thus (has been founded) the Kálanta stupa for the spiritual instruction of the congregation. For this reason is this edict here inscribed, whereby the inhabitants of the town may be guided in their devotions for ages to come—and as of the people insensibly the divine knowledge and insensibly the (good works) increase so the god of passion no longer yieldeth them gratification (?).

"For this reason also I shall cause to be, every five years, a general nikhama, (or act of humiliation?) (on which occasions) the slaughter (of no animal of any kind?) shall take place. Having learnt this object, it shall be so carried into effect according to my commandment.

"And the young prince of Ujein, for the same purpose, shall cause a religious observance of the self-same custom: and he shall not allow any transgression of this custom for the space of three years—so that when .... functionaries have admitted to initiation the penitent, then should any not leave off his (evil) practices—if even there be hundreds (in the same predicament) it shall be certainly done unto him according to the commandment of the râja.

Prinsep.

Le Lotus de la Bonne Loi, 672-683.

la fainéantise. La gloire qui doit être désirée, est que ces (3 *lettres*) puissent exister pour moi. Or elles ont toutes pour fondement l'absence de meurtre, et l'absence de violence. Que celui qui, désirant suivre la règle, serait dans la crainte, sorte de sa profonde détresse et prospère; l'utile et l'agréable sont les seules choses qui doivent être obtenues. Aussi est-ce là ce qui doit être proclamé par le gardien du *Stûpa* qui ne regardera rien autre chose (*ou bien,* aussi cet édit a dû être exprimé au moyen du *Prâkrita* et non dans un autre idiome). Et ainsi le veut ici le commandement du roi chéri des Dêvas. J'en confie l'exécution au grand ministre. Avec de grands desseins ,je fais exécuter ce qui n'a pas été mis à exécution; non en effet, cela n'est pas. L'acquisition du ciel, voilà en réalité ce qu'il est difficile d'obtenir, mais non l'acquisition de la royauté. J'honore extrêmement les *Richesses* aussi accomplis, mais (je dis): Vous n'obtiendrez pas ainsi le ciel. Efforcez-vous d'acquérir ce trésor sans prix.

"Et cet édit doit être entendu au *Nakhata Tisa* (Nakchatra Tichya) et à la fin du mois *Tisa* (4 *lettres*) au *Nakhata,* même par une seule personne il doit être entendu. Et c'est ainsi que ce *Stûpa* doit être honoré jusqu'à la fin des temps pour le bien de l'Assemblée.

"C'est pour cela que cet édit a été écrit ici afin que les gouverneurs de la ville s'appliquent continuellement (5 *lettres*) pour le peuple une instruction instantanée, instantané aussi * * * comblant les désirs pour nous * * voilà.

"Et pour cela, tous les cinq ans je ferai exécuter (la confession) par les ministres de la loi celui qui dissimulant ses péchés (2 *lettres*) celui là sera impuissant dans son effort.

"Ayant connu cet objet * * * car tel est mon commandement. Et le Prince Royal d'Udjdjayini devra aussi à cause de cela exécuter (4 *lettres*) une cérémonie parelle: et il ne devra pas laisser, passer plus de trois ans; et de même ainsi à *Takhasila* (*Takchaçila*) même. Quand (4 *lettres*) les grands ministres exécuteront la cérémonie de la confession, alors, sans faire abandonner son métier à aucun des gens du peuple, ils le feront pratiquer au contraire par chacun. C'est là l'ordre du roi."

No. 7.

DHAULI AND JAUGADA.

No. II. SEPARATE EDICT.

Prinsep.

Journal of the Bengal Asiatic Society, VII, 446.

"By command of Devânampiya! It shall be signified to the prince and the great officers in the city of Tosale.

"Whomsoever I ascertain to be .... and this my supreme will is irresistible! On this account is the present Stupa .... and for my loving subjects do I ardently desire to this effect:—that they may be filled with every species of blessing and happiness both as to the things of this world and the world beyond! .... may be of countless things as yet unknown .... I ardently desire .... they may partake! Thus hath said Devânampiya ....may repose .... and take pleasure, while the removal of affliction is in like manner the chief consequence of true devotion. (?) Devânampiya hath also said;—fame (consisteth in) this act, to meditate with devotion on my motives, and on my deeds (of virtue) and to pray for blessings in this world and the world to come. For this purpose do I appoint another (?) Stupa by the which I cause to be respected that which is (above) directed and proclaimed and my promise is imperishable! However bitter (or hard) it shall be carried into effect by me, and consolation (will accrue to him who obeys?) by which is exceeding virtue—so be it."

"Like as love itself, so is Devânampiya worthy of respect! and as the soul itself so is the unrelaxing guidance of Devânampiya worthy of respect! and according (to the conduct of) the subject, so is the compassion of Devânampiya: wherefore I myself, to accomplish his commands, will become the slave and hireling of Devânampiya. For this reason the Dubalâhi Tupha (is instituted) for undisturbed meditation, and for

Burnouf.

Le Lotus de la Bonne Loi, 693-707.

"Au nom du (roi) chéri des Dêvas, le prince royal et le grand ministre de Tosali, gouverneur de la ville, doit s'entendre dire." p. 693.

"Ainsi je désire qu'ils puissent ne pas éprouver de terreur." p. 695.

"Qu'ils écoutent, voilà, et qu'ils se consolent, qu'ils obtiennent aussi du bonheur." p. 695.

"Le roi chéri des Dêvas a dit."

"Qu'ils obtiennent le bonheur en ce monde et dans l'autre." p. 696.

"C'est dans ce dessein que je commande, le *Stûpa* exprime mes ordres." p. 696.

"Conséquemment je proclame et ce qui est ordonné, et toute autre chose que cela dont il a été donne connaissance." p. 697.

"Et la promesse de moi, imperissable elle (est)." p. 698.

"Aussi une œuvre difficile doit-elle être accomplie?" p. 698.

"Comme un ami, ainsi est Devânampiya certainement."

(ou)

"Comme un père, ainsi est Devânampiya."* p. 698.

"Et comme un enfant, ainsi moi (qui parle) je dois être châtié par Devânampiya." p. 700.

* Burnouf adopted this alternative reading of *pita* "father" from Kittoe's copy, in preference to Prinsep's reading of *piye*. As the *Jaugada* text has *pita* there can be no hesitation in adopting his correction.

Prinsep.

Journal of the Bengal Asiatic Society, VII, 446.

(securing every) blessing and happiness as to the concerns of this world and the world beyond! and thus to the end of time (is this) *Tupha* for the propitiation of heaven."

"Accordingly strive ye to accomplish each and all of my desires. For this object is this edict here inscribed, whereby (the spot) shall be caused by me to receive the name of *mahámátá swasatam*, or (place of meditation of the officers). Let it so remain for a perpetual endowment by me and for the furtherance of religion.

"And this edict shall be read aloud in the course of the month of Bhâtun (Bhadún?) (when the moon is) in the nakhatra (or lunar mansion) of Tisa:—and, as most desirable, also it shall be repeatedly read aloud in the last month of the year, in the lunar mansion Tisa, even if one person be present; thus to the end of time to afford instruction to the congregation of the *Tupha*."

Burnouf.

Le Lotus de la Bonne Loi, 693-707.

"Je serai l'esclave et la serviteur à gages de Devânampiya." p. 700.

"C'est pourquoi le *Stûpa* (*Le Dubalahi*) pour la consolation ainsi que pour l'avantage, et le bonheur a été, tant dans ce monde que dans l'autre." p. 702.

"Et ainsi jusqu'à la fin des temps le *Stûpa* fera obtenir le ciel." p. 704.

"Et cet édit a été inscrit ici dans ce dessein même que les grands ministres s'appliquent à la consolation (du peuple), et à la pratique de la loi." p. 704.

"Et cet édit doit être entendu tous les quatres mois, au *Nakhata Tisa* (Nakchatra Tichya)." p. 705.

"Et même dans l' intervalle, à tel moment que cela sera désiré, l'édit pourra être lu par un seul Tissa." p. 706.

"C'est ainsi qu' on doit pourvoir à ce que le *Stupa* soit honorer jusqu'à la fin des temps." p. 707.

No. 8.

ROCK AT SAHASARAM.

Translation by DR. G. BÜHLER.

See *Indian Antiquary*, 1877, page 156.

"The beloved of the gods speaketh thus: [*It is more than thirty-two*] years [*and a half*] that I am a worshipper [of *Buddha*], and I have not exerted myself strenuously. [*It is*] a year and more [*that I have exerted myself strenuously*]. During this interval those gods that were [*held to be*] true gods in Jambudrîpa have been made [*to be regarded as*] men* and false. For through strenuous exertion comes this reward, and it ought not to be said to be an effect of [*my*] greatness—For even a small man who exerts himself can gain for himself great rewards in heaven. Just for this purpose a sermon has been preached:

"'Both small ones and great ones should exert themselves, and in the end they should also obtain [*true*] knowledge. And this spiritual good will increase; it will even increase exceedingly; it will increase one [*size*] and a half, at least one [*size*] and a half.' And this sermon [*is*] by the DEPARTED.—Two-hundred [*years*] exceeded by fifty-six, 256, have passed since; and I have caused this matter to be incised on the hills; or where those stone pillars are, there too I have caused it to be incised."

* This phrase probably alludes to the Buddhist belief that the *Devas* also have shorter or longer terms of existence.

No. 9.

ROCK AT RUPNATH.

Translation by Dr. G. Buhler.

See *Indian Antiquary*, 1877, page 156.

"The beloved of the gods speaketh thus: [*It is*] more than thirty-two years and a half that I am a hearer [*of the law*], and I did not exert myself strenuously. But it is a year and more that I have entered the community [*of ascetics*], and that I have exerted myself strenuously. Those gods who during this time were considered to be true [*gods*] in Jambudvîpa have now been abjured. For through exertion [*comes*] this reward, and it cannot be obtained by greatness. For a small [*man*] who exerts himself somewhat can gain for himself great heavenly bliss. And for this purpose this sermon has been preached: 'Both great ones and small ones should exert themselves, and should in the end gain [*true*] knowledge, and this manner [*of acting*] should be what? Of long duration. For this spiritual good will grow the growth, and will grow exceedingly, at the least it will grow one [*size*] and a half.' And this matter has been caused to be written on the hills; [*where*] a stone pillar is, [*there*] it has been written on a stone pillar. And as often as [*man brings*]. to this writing ripe thought, [*so often*] will he rejoice, learning to subdue his senses.* This sermon has been preached by the Departed. 256 [*years have* elapsed] since the departure of the Teacher."

No. 10.

SECOND BAIRAT ROCK.

TRANSLATIONS.

Burnouf.

Le Lotus de la Bonne Loi, p. 725.

" Le roi Piyadasa, à l'Assemblée du Magadha qu'il fait saluer, a souhaité et peu de peines et une existence agréable.

" Il est bien connu, seigneurs, jusqu'où vont et mon respect et ma foi pour le Buddha, pour la Loi, pour l'Assemblée.

" Tout ce qui, seigneurs, a été dit par le bienheureux Buddha, tout cela seulement est bien dit. Il faut donc montrer, seigneurs, quelles (en) sont les autorités; de cette manière, la bonne loi sera de longue durée: voilà ce que moi je crois necessaire.

" En attendant, voici, seigneurs, les sujets qu' embrasse la loi; les bornes marquées par le *Vinaya* (ou la discipline), les facultés surnaturelles des Ariyas, les dangers de l'avenir, les stances du solitaire, le *Suta* (le *Sutra*) du solitaire, la spécu-

Wilson.

Journal of the Royal Asiatic Society, XVI, 366.

"Piyadasi, the King, to the venerable assembly of Mâgadhâ commands the infliction of little pain, and indulgence to animals.

" It is verily known, I proclaim, to what extent my respect and favour (are placed) in Buddha, in the law, and in the assembly.

" Whatsoever (words) have been spoken by the divine Buddha, they have all been well said, and in them verily I declare that capability of proof is to be discerned—so that the pure law (which they teach) will be of long duration, as far as I am worthy (of being obeyed).

" For these I declare are the precepts of the law of the principal discipline (Vinaya) having overcome the oppressions of the Aryas, and future perils, (and refuted) the songs of the Munis, the Sûtras of the Munis, (the practices)

---

* The original has a double meaning. The other meaning is "And as often as [*a man seasons his*] boiled rice with this condiment he will be satisfied, falling into a state of *Samvara, i.e.*, that state of intense satisfaction and repletion, in which he closes his eyes from pleasure, and suspends the activity of the senses generally."

Prinsep.

Le Lotus de la Bonne Loi, p. 725.

lation d'Upatissa (Câriputra) seulement, l'instruction de Lâghula (Râhula), en rejetant les doctrines fausses.

" (Voilà) ce qui a été dit par le bienheureux Buddha. Ces sujets qu'embrasse la loi, seigneurs, je désire, et c'est la gloire à laquelle je tiens le plus, que les Religieux et les Religieuses les écoutent et les méditent constamment, aussi bien que les fidèles des deux sexes.

" C'est pour cela, seigneurs, que je (vous) fais écrire ceci : telle est ma volonté et ma declaration."

Wilson.

Journal of the Royal Asiatic Society, XVI, 366.

of inferior ascetics, the censure of a light world, and (all) false doctrines.

" These things, as declared by the divine Buddha, I proclaim, and I desire them to be regarded as the precepts of the law.

" And that as many as there may be, male and female mendicants, may hear and observe them, constantly, as well also as male and female followers (of the laity).

" These things I affirm, and have caused this to be written (to make known to you) that such will be my intention."

The following improved translation of this important inscription has lately appeared in the Indian Antiquary, Vol. V, p. 257, from the very competent pen of Professor Kern :—

" King *Priyadarsin* (that is, the Humane) of *Magadha* greets the Assembly (of Clerics)* and wishes them welfare and happiness. Ye know, Sirs, how great is our reverence and affection for the Triad which is called *Buddha* (the Master), *Faith*, and *Assembly*. All that our Lord Buddha has spoken, my Lords, is well spoken : wherefore, Sirs, it must indeed be regarded as having indisputable authority ; so the true faith shall last long. Thus, my Lords, I honour (?) in the first place these religious works :—*Summary of the Discipline*, *The Supernatural Powers of the Master* (or of the Masters), *The Terrors of the Future*, *The Song of the Hermit*, *The Sûtra on Asceticism*, *The Question of Upatishya*, and *The Admonition to Râhula concerning Falsehood*, uttered by our Lord Buddha. These religious works, Sirs, I will that the Monks and Nuns, for the advancement of their good name, shall uninterruptedly study and remember, as also the laics of the male and female sex. For this end, my Lords, I cause this to be written, and have made my wish evident."

No. 10.

KHANDAGIRI ROCK.

TRANSLATION.

Prinsep.†

LINE 1.—" Salutation (or glory) to the *arhantas*, glory to all the saints ; (or those who have attained final emancipation).

" By *Aira*, the great king, borne on his mighty cloud-chariot,—rich in possession of the purest wealth of heart and desire,—of exceeding personal beauty,—having an army of undaunted courage.

" By him (was made) the excavation of the 83 rocky peaks of *Kalingadwipa*" (or) " by him, the king of Kalinga, was this rock excavation (made)."

LINE 2.—" (By him) possessed of a comely form at the age of 15 years,—then joining in youthful sports,—afterwards for nine years engaged in mastering the arts of reading and writing, arithmetic, navigation, commerce, and law ;—and resplendent in all knowledge,—(the former Raja being then in his 85th year) thus, at the age of 24, full of wisdom and uprightness, and on the verge of manhood, (lit. the remainder of youth) (through him) does a third victory in the battle of the city of the *Kalinga* royal family, sanctify the accession (anointment) of the mahârâja.

LINE 3.—" Upon his accession, choosing the Brahmanical faith he causes to be repaired the city, walls, and houses, (that had been) destroyed by a storm.

---

* Or, " greets the Assembly of Magadha."

† Journal of the Bengal Asiatic Society, VI, 1080.

"For the poor (or ascetics) of *Kalinga* a reservoir of cool water and a ghât (?), also presents of every necessary and equipages he makes permanent endowment of."

LINE 4.—"With 83,000 *panas** he gains the affection of his people, and in a second house (which) the architect has prepared on the western side (for) horses, elephants, men, carriages, a number of chambers he caused to be established (or he transferred them thither). for those coming from *Kansa* forest to see; the balcony * * * of the

LINE 5.— inhabitants of *Sákanagara;* he, inclining to virtue, skilled in the science of music, causing to be sounded the *dampana* and the *tabhata* (drums?) with beautiful and merry dancing girls, causes diversions.

"In like manner turning his mind to law, in an establishment of learned men, he (called together) the Buddhist priests of Eastern *Kalinga*, who were settled there under the ancient kings."

LINE 6.—* * "act of devotion * * jewel * * all equipages * * * he gives to god."

"Afterwards inclining to charity, the hundred houses (?) of *Nanda Raja* destroyed,† and himself expelled; all that was in the city of *Vajapanddi*" (here we may fill up "he converted the plunder to the charitable purposes alluded to," and this sense is borne out by the beginning of the following or 7th line).

LINE 7.—"He munificently distributes in charity many hundred thousands (*panas*)—the town territory."‡ * * *

LINE 8.—"(To) the prince who caused (its) destruction, he ordains the pain of the cavern (imprisons in one of the caves?)—and causes the murderer to labour by a generous requital * * seated on the hill * * * and lavishes bland speeches and obedience."

LINE 9.—"Apes, bulls, horses, elephants, buffaloes (?) and all requisites for the furniture of the house;—to induce the practice of rejecting improper persons, he farther bestowed (or appointed) attendants of the *baiman* caste (Brahman?).

[*From this point the commencement of each line is lost.*]

LINE 10.—"*rája* causes to be made the palace (or fort) of 15 victories"

LINE 11.—"finding no glory in the country which had been the seat of the ancient princes,—a city abounding in envy and hypocrisy,—and reflecting in the year 1300"—(a break follows and leaves us in the dark as to what era (if any) is here alluded to) * * * falling of heavenly form * * * twelve * * * §.

LINE 12.—|| * * * * * * * *

LINE 13.—"He distributes much gold at Benares * * * * he gives as charity innumerable and most precious jewels."

LINE 14.—"In the year 1300 married with the daughter of the so-called conqueror of the mountains (a hill râja), (the rest is obscure, but seemingly declaratory of some presents to priests).

LINE 15.—(Few words intelligible.)

LINE 16.—"He causes to be constructed subterranean chambers, caves containing a *chetiya* temple and pillars." * * * *

LINE 17.—"For whom the happy heretics continually pray * * slayer, having a lakh of equipages * * the fearless sovereign of many hills, by the sun (cherished, or some such epithet) the great conqueror Raja *Khâravela Sanda* (or "the king of the Ocean shore," reading *Khâravelasya*, and supposing the two final strokes not to be letters)."

I read the last name as *Khâravela Sri*, and just preceding it there seems to be a cluster of geographical names, ending with "all the râjas of the hill districts," *pavata-chako râja savam.*

---

* There is no word for 83 in the original, Prinsep having got two letters too many in the term *pannatisidhi*, which he reads *pannatasirasihi*. Apparently the sum is 100,000, *satasahasehi* according to Prinsep's own reading of the following word.

† Here Prinsep reads *porajanapadam*, which may be correct, but the initial letter in the photograph looks like ○.

‡ Here my correcter reading of the text will necessitate a fresh translation, which will considerably alter the meaning.

§ At the end of this line where Prinsep reads *Siri pithi râjâno* I read *utara-patha-râjâno*, or "the king of the northern region," an expression which recals the *Dakshinapatha* or southern region of Samudra Gupta's inscription.

|| Prinsep has not attempted to read any portion of this line, but I observe the name of *Nanda Raja*, and I think also that of *Magadha vasasa*.

TRANSLATIONS

OF

CAVE INSCRIPTIONS.

BARABAR CAVES.

No. 1.

Burnouf.

"Par le roi Piyadasi, la douzième année de son sacre, cette caverne du *Nigoha* (le figuier Indién) a été donnée (le reste manque)."

A. C.

"By the King Piyadasi, in the 12th year of his inauguration, this cave of the Nyagrodha Tree (the banian) has been given to the mendicants."

As Burnouf found Kittoe's copy of this inscription incomplete, he left his translation as above. But as I have been able to complete the text by the addition of the words (*di*)*ná adivikemhi,* I have added the translation of the same phrase "aux mendiants," as given by Burnouf in another place.*

No. 2.

Burnouf.

"Par le roi Piyadasi, la douzième année de son sacre, cette grotte dans la montagne *Khalatika* a été donnée par les mendiants."

A. C.

"By the King Piyadasi, in the 12th year of his inauguration, this cave in the *Khalatika* hills has been given to the mendicants."

Burnouf has an interesting note on the name of *Khalatika,* which he ingeniously identifies with the Sanskrit *skhalatika,* "slippery."† In my descriptive account of these caves in the early part of this volume I have suggested that this name may be connected with Thsang's *Kie-lan-to,* and with the Kallatii or Kalantii Indians of Herodotus and Hekatæus.

No. 3.

Burnouf.

"Le Roi Piyadasi * la dix-neuvième année depuis son sacre * * * cette caverne" * *

A. C.

"The King Piyadasi, in the 19th year after his inauguration * * this cavern * * in the Khalanti hill" * *

Burnouf felt unable to suggest even a conjectural reading for the imperfect portion of this inscription.‡ I have recovered the words *Khalati* or *Khalanti pavata,* but I can make nothing of the remaining portion.

NAGARJUNI CAVES.

No. 4.

Prinsep.

"The Brahman girl's cave, excavated by the hands of the most devoted sect of Bauddha ascetics for the purpose of a secluded residence,

Burnouf.

"La caverne des Tisserands a été destinée par le roi *Dasalatha,* le bien aimé des Dêvas, aussitôt après sa consecration au trône, à être un lieu

* Le Lotus de la Bonne Loi, Appendice, 779-780.

† Le Lotus, Appendice, 779.

‡ Le Lotus de la Bonne Loi, Appendice, 780.

Prinsep.

was appointed their habitation in perpetuity by *Dasaratha*, the beloved of the gods, immediately on his ascending the throne." *

Burnouf.

d'habitation pour les respectables mendiants, tant que dureront le soleil et la lune." †

This cave, as well as the two next mentioned, were excavated by King Dasaratha, the grandson of Asoka, in the first year of his reign, B. C. 215, as a residence for *Bhadantas.* I have formerly suggested that the term *Vapiyaka*, which is the name of the cave, was derived from *Vápi*, a well or *reservoir*, and that the cave was so called because there is a fine large well immediately in front of it. The well is 9 feet in diameter and 23 feet deep.‡

No. 5.

Prinsep.

"The *Milkmaid's* cave, excavated by the hands of the most devoted sect of Bauddha ascetics for the purpose of a secluded residence, was appointed their habitation in perpetuity by Dasaratha, the beloved of the gods, immediately on his ascending the throne."§

Burnouf.

"La caverne de la *Bergère* a été destinée par le *Dasalatha*, le bien-aimé des Dêvas, aussitôt après sa consecration au trône, à être un lieu d'habitation pour les respectables mendiants, tant que dureront le soleil et la lune." ||

Burnouf suggests that these caves probably existed before the time of Dasaratha as natural caverns, and were already known as the "Milkmaid's cave," &c. This explanation seems a very natural one, but I do not think that it can be true, as all these caves have been hewn out of solid masses of rock, where the outer face presents a clean and unfissured front. Apparently Burnouf was not quite satisfied with the translation of *Gopika Kubhâ* as "la caverne de la Bergère," for he gives the alternative version of "la caverne des Bergers," by making *gopika* an adjective agreeing with *kubha*.

No. 6.

Prinsep.

Prinsep has not proposed any rendering of the word *Vaḍathika*, which forms the name of the cave.

Burnouf.

"La caverne de celui qui a cru en richesses a été destinée par le roi Dasalatha," &c., as in Nos. 4 and 5.¶

In this translation Burnouf has taken *vadathika* as the equivalent of the Sanskrit *vriddhartha*, "celui qui a fait croître ses richesses."

UDAYAGIRI.

No. 1.—*The Snake Cave.*

*Prinsep.***

"The impregnable (or unequalled) Chamber of *Chulakarma*" * * continued in—

No. 2.—*The Snake Cave.*

"and the appropriate temple (or palace) of *Karma*" * (Rishi?)

No. 3.—*The Tiger Cave.*

"Excavated by *Ugra Aveda*" (the antivedist?) the *Sasuvin*."

"The cave of *Sabhuti* of Ugara Akhada,"††

---

* Journal of the Bengal Asiatic Society, VI, 678.

† Le Lotus de la Bonne Loi, Appendice, 775.

‡ Archæological Survey of India, I, 49.

§ Journal of the Bengal Asiatic Society, VI, 678.

|| Le Lotus de la Bonne Loi, Appendice, 775-776.

¶ Ditto ditto, 778.

** These translations are taken from the Journal of the Bengal Asiatic Society, VI, 1073-1074.

†† My reading of the text of this inscription is taken from a photographic picture of a cast made by Mr. H. H. Locke.

Prinsep.

No. 4.—*Nameless Cave.*

" The excavation of Yanâkiya for *

No. 5.—*The Pawan Cave.*

(Similar to No. 1.)

No. 6.—*Manikpura Cave.*

" The excavation of the mighty (or of *Vira*) sovereign, the lord of Kalinga, &c., * * * of Kadepa (?) the worshipper of the Sun."

" Cave of *Aira* Maharaja, lord of Kalinga, the great cloud-borne" * * *

No. 7.—*Manikpura Cave.*

" The excavation of the Prince *Vattaka.*"

" Cave of Prince Vaḍḍaka."

As this last record is placed over a small door of the same cave in which No. 6 is found, it would seem that Prince Vaddaka must have been a son of Raja Aira.

No. 8.—*The Vaikanta Cave.*

Prinsep.

" Excavation of the Rajas of Kalinga enjoying the favour of the Arhantas" (Buddhist Saints) (the rest is too much mutilated to be read with any degree of confidence).

" Cave made by * * * Raja Lalâka for the benefit (or use) of the Arhantas" and Sramanas of Kalinga, &c., * "

TRANSLATIONS.

PILLAR INSCRIPTIONS.

See *Journal of Bengal Asiatic Society*, Vol. VI, p. 581, by Prinsep.

Delhi Pillar—North Side.

EDICT I.

Prinsep.

" Thus spake king Devânampiya Piyadasi :—' In the twenty-seventh year of my anointment, I have caused this religious edict to be published in writing. I acknowledge and confess the faults that have been cherished in my heart. From the love of virtue, by the side of which all other things are as sins, from the strict scrutiny of sin, and from fervent desire to be told of sin, by the fear of sin and by very enormity of sin ;—by these may my eyes be strengthened and confirmed (in rectitude).

" ' The sight of religion, and the love of religion, of their own accord increase and will ever increase : and my people, whether of the laity (*grihist*) or of the priesthood (ascetics), all mortal beings, are knit together thereby, and prescribe to themselves the same path : and, above all, having obtained the mastery over their passions, they become supremely wise. For this is indeed true wisdom : it is upheld and bound by (it consists in) religion ; by religion which cherishes, religion which teaches pious acts, religion that bestows (the only true) pleasure.' "

EDICT II.

" Thus spake king Devânampiya Piyadasi :—' In religion is the chief excellence ; but religion consists in good works : in the non-omission of many acts :—mercy and charity, purity and chastity ;—(these are) to me the anointment of consecration. Towards the poor and the afflicted, towards bipeds and quadrupeds, towards the fowls of the air and things that move in the waters, manifold have been the benevolent acts performed by me. Out of consideration for things inanimate even many other excellent things have been done by me. To this purpose is the present edict promulgated ; let all pay attention to it (or take cognizance thereof), and let it endure for ages to come :—and he who acts in conformity thereto, the same shall attain eternal happiness, (or shall be united with Sugato).' "*

EDICT III.

" ' Thus spake king Devânampiya Piyadasi :—' Whatever appeareth to me to be virtuous and good, that is so held to be good and virtuous by me, and not the less if it have evil tendency, is it accounted for evil by me or is it named among the *asinave* (the nine offences ?). Eyes are given (to man) to distinguish between the two qualities (between right and wrong) : according to the capacity of the eyes so may they behold.

" ' The following are accounted among the nine minor transgressions :—mischief, hard-heartedness, anger, pride, envy. These evil deeds of nine kinds shall on no account be mentioned. They should be regarded as opposite (or prohibited). Let this (ordinance) be impressed on my heart, let it be cherished with all my soul.' "†

* Burnouf has criticised this translation in Le Lotus de la Bonne Loi, p. 667.

† The translation of this Edict has been criticised by Burnouf in Le Lotus de la Bonne Loi, p. 669.

EDICT IV.

West Side.

"Thus spake king Piyadasi, beloved of the gods:—'In the twenty-seventh year of my anointment, I have caused to be promulgated the following religious edict. My devotees, in very many hundred thousand souls, having (now) attained unto knowledge, I have ordained (the following) fines and punishments for their transgressions. Wherever devotees shall abide around (or circumambulate) the holy fig-tree for the performance of pious duties, the benefit and pleasure of the country and its inhabitants shall be (in making) offerings: and according to their generosity or otherwise shall they enjoy prosperity or adversity: and they shall give thanks for the coming of the faith. Whatever villages with their inhabitants may be given or maintained for the sake of the worship, the devotees shall receive the same, and for an example unto my people they shall follow after (or exercise solitary) austerities. And likewise, whatever blessings they shall pronounce, by these shall my devotees accumulate for the worship (?). Furthermore, the people shall attend in the night the great myrobalan-tree and the holy fig-tree. My people shall foster (accumulate) the great myrobalan. Pleasure is to be eschewed, as intoxication (?).

"'My devotees doing thus for the profit and pleasure of the village, whereby they (coming) around the beauteous and *holy fig-tree* may cheerfully abide in the performance of pious acts. In this also are fines and punishments for the transgressions of my devotees appointed. Much to be desired is such renown! According to the measure of the offence (the destruction of *viya* or happiness ?) shall be the measure of the punishment, but (the offender) shall not be put to death by me. Banishment (shall be) the punishment of those malefactors deserving of imprisonment and execution. Of those who commit murder on the high road (dacoits ?) even none, whether of the poor or of the rich, shall be injured (tortured) on my three especial days (?) Those guilty of cruelly beating or slaughtering living things, having escaped mutilation (through my clemency) shall give alms (as a deodand) and shall also undergo the penance of fasting. And thus it is my desire that the protection of even the workers of opposition shall tend to (the support of) the worship; and (on the other hand) the people, whose righteousness increases in every respect, shall spontaneously partake of my benevolence.'"

EDICT V.

South Side.

"Thus spake king Devânampiya Piyadasi:—'In the twenty-seventh year of my anointment the following animals shall not be put to death: the parrot, the maina (or thrush), the wild duck of the wilderness, the goose, the bull-faced owl, the vulture, the bat, the *ambaka-pillika*, the raven, and the common crow, the *vèdavéyaka*, the adjutant, the *sankujamava*, the *kaphatasayaka*, the *panasasesimala*, the *sandaka*, the *okapada*, those that go in pairs, the white dove, and the domestic pigeon. Among all four-footed beasts the following shall not be for food, they shall not be eaten: the she-goat of various kinds, and the sheep, and the sow, either when heavy with young or when giving milk. Unkilled birds of every sort for the desire of their flesh shall not be put to death. The same being alive shall not be injured: whether because of their uselessness or for the sake of amusement they shall not be injured. Animals that prey on life shall not be cherished. In the three four-monthly periods (of the year) on the evening of the full moon, during the three (holy) days, namely, the fourteenth, the fifteenth, and the first day after conjunction, in the midst of the uposatha ceremonies (or strict fasts), unkilled things (or live fish ?) shall not be exposed for sale. Yea, on these days, neither the snake tribe, nor the feeders on fish (alligators), nor any living beings whatsoever shall be put to death.

"'On the eighth day of the paksha (or half month) on the fourteenth, on the fifteenth, on (the days when the moon is in the mansions of) trisha or punarvasu,—on these several days in the three four-monthly periods, the ox shall not be tended: the goat, the sheep, and the pig, if indeed any be tended (for domestic use) shall not then be tended. On the tirsha and the punarvasu of every four months, and of every paksha or semilunation of the four months, it is forbidden to keep (for labour) either the horse or the ox.

"'Furthermore, in the twenty-seventh year of my reign, at this present time, twenty-five prisoners are set at liberty.'"

EDICT VI.

East Side.

"Thus spake king Devânampiya Piyadasi :—'In the twelfth year of my anointment, a religious edict (was) published for the pleasure and profit of the world; having destroyed that (document) and regarding my former religion as sin, I now for the benefit of the world proclaim the fact. And this (among my nobles, among my near relations, and among my dependants, whatsoever pleasures I may thus abandon,) I therefore cause to be destroyed; and I proclaim the same in all the congregations; while I pray with every variety of prayer for those who differ from me in creed, that they following after my proper example may with me attain unto eternal salvation: wherefore the present edict of religion is promulgated in this twenty-seventh year of my anointment.'"

EDICT VII.

"Thus spake king Devânampiya Piyadasi :—'Kings of the olden time have gone to heaven under these very desires. How then among mankind may religion (or growth in grace) be increased? Yea, through the conversion of the humbly-born shall religion increase.'"

"Thus spake king Devânampiya Piyadasi :—'The present moment and the past have departed under the same ardent hopes. How by the conversion of the royal-born may religion be increased? Through the conversion of the lowly-born if religion thus increaseth, by how much (more) through the conviction of the high-born, and their conversion, shall religion increase? Among whomsoever the name of God resteth (?) verily this is religion, (or verily virtue shall there increase).'"

"Thus spake king Devânampiya Piyadasi :—'Wherefore from this very hour I have caused religious discourses to be preached; I have appointed religious observances that mankind having listened thereto shall be brought to follow in the right path and give glory unto God'" (Agni?)

EDICT VIII.

"Moreover, along with the increase of religion, opposition will increase: for which reason I have appointed sermons to be preached, and I have established ordinances of every kind; through the efficacy of which, the misguided, having acquired true knowledge, shall proclaim it on all sides (?) and shall become active in upholding its duties. The disciples, too, flocking in vast multitudes (many hundred thousand souls). Let these likewise receive my command, 'In such wise do ye, too, address on all sides (or address comfortably?) the people united in religion.'"

"King Devânampiya Piyadasi thus spake :—'Thus among the present generation have I endowed establishments, appointed men very wise in the faith, and done............for the faith.'"

"King Devânampiya Piyadasi again spake as follows :—'Along the high roads I have caused fig-trees to be planted, that they may be for shade to animals and men; I have (also) planted mango trees: and at every half coss I have caused wells to be constructed, and (resting places?) for nights to be erected. And how many taverns (or serais) have been erected by me at various places for the entertainment of man and beast! So that as the people, finding the road to every species of pleasure and convenience in these places of entertainment, these new towns, (vayapuri?) rejoiceth under my rule, so let them thoroughly appreciate and follow after the same (system of benevolence). This is my object, and thus I have done.'"

"Thus spake king Devânampiya Piyadasi :—'Let the priests deeply versed in the faith (or let my doctrines?) penetrate among the multitudes of the rich capable of granting favours, and let them penetrate alike among all the unbelievers, whether of ascetics or of householders, and let them penetrate into the assemblies (?) for my sake. Moreover, let them for my sake find their way among the Bráhmans and the most destitute: and among those who have abandoned domestic life, for my sake let them penetrate; and among various unbelievers for my sake let them find their way :—yea use your utmost endeavours among these several classes, that the wise men, these men learned in the religion (or these doctrines of my religion) may penetrate among these respectively, as well as among all other unbelievers.'"

"Thus spake king Devânampiya Piyadasi :—'And let these (priests) and others the most skilful in the sacred offices penetrating among the charitably disposed of my queens and among all my secluded women discreetly and respectfully use their most persuasive efforts (at conversion), and acting on the heart and on the eyes of the children, for my sake penetrate in like manner among the charitably disposed of other queens and princes for the purpose (of imparting) religious enthusiasm and thorough religious instruction. And this is the true religious devotion, this the sum of religious instruction, *viz.*, that it shall increase the mercy and charity, the truth and purity, the kindness and honesty of the world.' "

"Thus spake king Devânampiya Piyadasi :—'And whateversoever benevolent acts have been done by me, the same shall be prescribed as duties to the people who follow after me: and in this (manner) shall their influence and increase be manifest,—by doing service to father and mother; by doing service to spiritual pastors; by respectful demeanour to the aged and full of years, and by kindness and condescension to Brahmans and Sramans, to the orphan and destitute, to servants and the minstrel tribe.' "

"King Devânampiya Piyadasi again spake :—'And religion increaseth among men by two separate processes, by performance of religious offices and by security against persecution. Accordingly, that religious offices and immunities might abound among multitudes, I have observed the ordinances myself as the apple of my eye (?) (as testified by) all these animals which have been saved from slaughter, and by manifold other virtuous acts performed on my behalf. And that the religion may be from the persecution of men, increasing through the absolute prohibition to put to death living beings, or to sacrifice aught that draweth breath. For such an object is all this done, that it may endure to my sons and their sons' sons as long as the sun and moon shall last. Wherefore let them follow its injunctions and be obedient thereto and let it be had in reverence and respect. In the twenty-seventh year of my reign have I caused this edict to be written; so sayeth (Devânampiya). Let stone pillars be prepared and let this edict of religion be engraven thereon, that it may endure unto the remotest ages.' "*

SEPARATE EDICTS.

ALLAHABAD PILLAR.

No. 1.

Queen's Edict.

Prinsep.

"By the mandate of *Devânampiya* the ministers everywhere are to receive notice. These also (namely) mango trees† and other things are the gift of the second princess (his) queen, and these for * * * of *Kichhigani*, the third princess, the general (daughter's * * ?). Of the second lady thus let the act redound with triple force."‡

In his remarks on this inscription Turnour has identified the "second queen" with the attendant of the former queen Asandhimitrâ, whom Asoka married in the 34th year of his reign.§ But as a "third queen" is mentioned in the inscription, the second queen must have been *Asandhimitrâ* herself, and the "third queen," who was married in the 34th year of Asoka, must have been the queen *Kichhigani* of the inscription. By this reckoning the first queen would have been the predecessor of Asandhimitrâ and the mother of Kunâla. The names of at least two other queens are known: *1, Tishya-rakshitâ,* by whose contrivance Prince Kunâla was blinded; and

---

* This last passage was afterwards slightly altered by Prinsep as follows :—"In order that this religious edict may stand (remain), stone pillars and stone slabs (or receptacles) shall be accordingly prepared, by which the same may endure unto remote ages."—Bengal Asiatic Society Journal, VI, 1059. The word translated stone slabs is read as *sila-dhârikani,* instead of *phalakani* or "tablets," as pointed out by me some twelve years ago.

† *Ambavadika* means a "mango garden."

‡ Journal of the Bengal Asiatic Society, VI, 967. The words immediately following the name of Devânampiya, "the ministers everywhere are to receive notice," are taken from Prinsep's corrected reading in Vol. VI, p. 448.

§ Turnour's Mahawanso, p. 122.

2, *Padmávati*, the mother of Kunâla.* It is probable therefore that the titles of first, second, and third queens must denote their relative rank, and not their sequence in order of time. It is certain at least that *Tishya-rakshitá* was the "first" queen, as she is distinctly called so in the *Asoka avadâna*.†

No. 2.

Kosambi Edict.

As this inscription has only lately been discovered by myself, there is of course no translation available, and I am afraid that it is in too mutilated a state to be of much use. But the first line is complete, and may be rendered:

"Devânampiya commands the rulers of Kosambi."

The same word *annapayati* occurs in the Deotek inscription.

Sanchi Pillar.

Of this inscription Prinsep remarks that it is in "too mutilated a state to be restored entirely, but from the commencement of the third line, it may be concluded that some provision was made by a 'charitable and religiously disposed person for hungry priests,' and this is confirmed by the two nearly perfect lines at the foot: 'It is also my desire that camphorated (cool?) water should be given to drink. May this excellent purpose endure for ever!'"

A comparison of Prinsep's reading of the text with my version, which has been made afresh during a recent visit to Sânchi, shows some important differences which will necessitate a revised translation of the last two lines. My reading of the fourth line also differs from Prinsep's, but in a less degree. The words *Bhikhu cha Bhikhuni* seemed to me to be quite clear.

---

* Burnouf: Introduction à l'Histoire du Buddhism, Indien, 149, 403, 405.

† Burnouf, p. 405: "La première des femmes d'Acoka."

INDEX.

	PAGE.
Aira Raja—Inscription on Khandagiri Rock	27, 98, 132
——— in Khandagiri Caves	104, 136
Alexander II, of Epirus—Rock Edict XIII	4, 87, 126
Allahabad Pillar	4, 37
——— Texts of Asoka's Edicts	106
——— Translations of Asoka's Edicts	137
——— Two additional Edicts, texts	116
———, translations	140, 141
——— Samudra Gupta's Inscription	38
——— Raja Birbal's Inscription	39
Alphabetical characters of Asoka's period	49
——— Arianq-Pâli alphabet	50
——— Indian-Pâli alphabet	49, 51
——— Indigenous origin of Indian alphabet	52
Andhras, a people, coupled with the Pulindas	11, 87, 126
Antigonus [Gonnatas of Macedonia] Rock Edict XIII	11, 87, 126
Antiochus [II Theos, of Syria] Rock Edict II	11, 66, 177
——— Rock Edict XIII	87, 126
Asoka—Chronology of his reign	Preface vii
——— Reigned 41 years	" vi
——— Date of accession, B. C. 264	" vi
——— Date of inauguration, B. C. 260	" vi
Bairât Rock Inscription	22
——— Text of	96
——— Second Rock Inscription	24
——— Text of	97
——— Translation of	131
Barâbar Caves—Inscriptions	30, 103, 134
Bârânasi, or Benares—Khandagiri Rock Edict	100, 30, 103, 135
Bhadanta—Buddhist title corrupted to Bhantê	25, 26
Bhoja, a country, coupled with Pitenika—Rock edict XIII	87, 126
Buddha, name of, in 2nd Bairât Inscription	25, 97, 131
——— Date of death, or Nirvâna, B. C. 478	Preface iii
Bühler, Dr. G.—Text and translation of Sahasarâm Inscription	94, 130
——— Text and translation of Rûpnâth Inscription	95, 131
Burnouf—Translation of Rock Edict IV	119
——— VII	121
——— X	123
——— XII	125
——— XIV	126
——— of first separate Edict, Dhauli	127
——— of second " "	129
——— of second Bairât Rock Inscription	131
——— of Nâgârjuni Cave Inscriptions	134
Cave Inscriptions	30
——— at Barâbar	30, 103, 134
——— at Nâgârjuni	31, 103, 134

PAGE.

Cave Inscriptions at Khandagiri and Udayagiri . . . 52, 104
——— at Râmgarh, in Sirguja . . . 33, 105
Chandra Gupta Maurya . . . 4
Chikambari, name of country, Deotek Slab . . . 102
Choda, or Chola, Rock Edict II . . . 66, 116

Dasaratha, inscriptions of, at Nâgârjuni . . . 103, 134
Date of Asoka . . . Preface vi, vii
——— Buddha's death, or Nirvâna, B. C. 478 . . . " iii
——— Chandra Gupta Maurya . . . " vi
——— Mahâvira . . . " iv
Delhi Pillar, from Siwâlik . . . 3
———, from Mirat . . . 3
——— Texts of Inscriptions . . . 106
——— Translations of Inscriptions . . . 137
——— Two additional Edicts, VII and VIII . . . 116, 140
Deotek Slab Inscription . . . 2, 102
Devânampriya, title of Asoka . . . *passim.*
———, title of Dasaratha, Nâgârjuni Caves . . . 103, 134
Dhauli Rock Inscription . . . 15, 65, 118
——— first separate Edict . . . 20, 89, 127
——— second separate Edict . . . 20, 92, 129

Gândhâra—Rock Edict V . . . 72, 120
Gâya Inscription, dated in era of Nirvâna . . . Preface v
Girnâr Rock Inscription . . . 14
——— Text . . . 65
——— Translation . . . 117
Gotama-swâmi, or Indrabhûti, disciple of Mahâvira . . . Preface iv
Greek Kings, names of, in Asoka's Rock Edicts II and XIII . . . 9, 66, 86

Inscription on Shâhbâzgarhi Rock . . . 8, 65, 118
——— Khâlsi Rock . . . 12, 65, 118
——— Girnâr Rock . . . 14, 65, 118
——— Dhauli Rock . . . 15, 65, 118
——— Jaugada Rock . . . 17, 65, 118
——— first separate, on Dhauli and Jaugada Rocks . . . 20, 89, 127
——— second " " " " . . . 20, 92, 129
——— on Sahasarâm Rock . . . 20, 94, 130
——— on Rûpnâth Rock . . . 21, 95, 131
——— on Bairât . . . 22, 96
——— on second Bairât Rock . . . 24, 97, 131
——— on Deotek Slab . . . 28, 102
——— in Ramgarh Caves . . . 33, 105
——— in Barâbar Caves . . . 30, 103, 134
——— in Nâgârjuni Caves . . . 31, 103, 134
——— on Khandagiri Rock . . . 27, 98, 132
——— in Khandagiri and Udayagiri Caves . . . 32, 104, 135
——— on Delhi Pillar from Siwâlik . . . 34, 106, 137
——— on Delhi Pillar from Mirat . . . 37, 106, 137
——— on Allahabad Pillar . . . 37, 106, 137
——— on Lauriya Ararâj Pillar . . . 39, 106, 137
——— on Lauriya Navandgarh Pillar . . . 41, 106, 137
——— separate Edicts on Allahabad Pillar . . . 38, 116, 140
——— on Sânchi Pillar . . . 42, 116, 141

Jaugada—Fort and Rock Inscription . . . 17, 19
——— Text of Inscription . . . 65

PAGE.

Jaugada—Translation of Inscription . . . 118
————Text of separate Edicts . . . 89, 92
————Translation of separate Edicts . . . 127, 129

Kalinga—Rock Edict XIII . . . 84, 125
——— Khandagiri Rock Inscription . . . 99, 132
——— Khandagiri Caves . . . 104, 105, 136
Kâmboja—Rock Edict V . . . 72, 120
Kern, Professor—Translation of second Bairât Inscription . . . 132
Ketalaputra, or Kerala—Rock Edict II . . . 66, 117
Khalati, or Khalanti Hills—Barâbar Cave Inscriptions . . . 32, 103, 134
Khâlsi—Rock Inscription . . . 12
——— Text of Inscription . . . 65
——— Translation of Inscription . . . 118
Khandagiri Rock Inscription . . . 27
———— Text of Inscription . . . 98
———— Translation of Inscription . . . 132
———— and Udayagiri Caves . . . 32, 104, 135
Khepingala hills, in Dhauli and Jaugada Inscriptions . . . 19, 65
Kosâmbi, Edict of, on Allahabad Pillar . . . 38, 116, 141

Language of Inscriptions . . . 43
Lauriya Ararâj Pillar . . . 39
———- Navandgarh Pillar . . . 41
———- Text of both Inscriptions . . . 65
———- Translation of ditto . . . 117

Mahâvira—Date of his Nirvâna, B. C. 527 . . . Preface iv
Mahindo, or Mahendra, son of Asoka . . . 17
Masson—His copy of Shâhbâzgarhi Inscription . . . 8

Nâgârjuni Cave Inscriptions . . . 31
Nanda Raja—Khandagiri Rock Inscription . . . 99, 133
Nirvâna of Mahâvira, B. C. 527 . . . Preface iv
———— of Buddha, Sâkya Muni, B. C. 478 . . . iv
———— era, used in Gâya Inscription . . . iv

Panda, or Pandionis Regio—Rock Edict II . . . 10, 66, 117
Pillar at Allahabad . . . 37
——— at Delhi from Siwâlik . . . 34
——— at Delhi from Mirat . . . 37
——— at Lauriya Ararâj . . . 39
——— at Lauriya Navandgarh . . . 41
——— at Sânchi . . . 42
Pitenika, name of district, coupled with Bhoja, Edict XIII . . . 87, 117
Prinsep, James—Notes on Indian Pâli Alphabet . . . 51
——— Summary of contents of Edicts . . . 5
——— Remarks on Khandagiri alphabet . . . 27
——— Remarks on language of Asoka's Inscription . . . 47
——— Texts of Rock Inscriptions . . . 65
———————— of separate Rock Edicts . . . 89
———————— of Khandagiri Rock Inscription . . . 98
———————— of Cave Inscriptions . . . 103
—————— Texts of Delhi and other Pillar Inscriptions . . . 106
—————— Translations of Rock Edicts . . . 117
———————————— of Khandagiri Rock Inscription . . . 127, 129
———————————— of Cave Inscriptions . . . 134
———————————— of Pillar Edicts . . . 137

PAGE.

Queen's Edict on Allahabad Pillar . . . 116, 140

Râhula, or Lâghula, in second Bairât Inscription . . . 26, 27, 67, 132
Râmgarh Caves, in Sirguja—Inscriptions . . . 33, 105
Râshtika, a country, same as Surashtra—Edict V . . . 72, 120
Rock Inscription, at Shâhbâzgarhi . . . 8
——— at Khâlsi . . . 12
——— at Girnâr . . . 14
——— at Dhauli . . . 15
——— at Jaugada . . . 17
——— Separate, at Dhauli and Jaugada . . . 20
——— at Sahasarâm . . . 20
——— at Rûpnâth . . . 21
——— at Bairât . . . 22
——— Second, at Bairât . . . 24
——— at Khandagiri . . . 27
Rûpnâth Rock Inscription . . . 21
——— Text of, by Dr. Bühler . . . 95
——— Translation ,, . . . 131

Sahasarâm Rock Inscription . . . 20, 12
——— Text of Inscription by Dr. Bühler . . . 94
——— Translation of ,, ,, . . . 130
Sâkanagara, city, mentioned in Khandagiri Rock Inscription . . . 98, 133
Samâpâ, city, mentioned in Jaugada—Separate Edicts . . . 19, 89
Sânchi Pillar Inscription . . . 42, 116, 141
Shâhbâzgarhi Rock Inscription . . . 8
———, the Po-lu-sha of Hwen Thsang . . . 9
———, the Bazaria of Arrian . . . 9
——— Text of Inscription . . . 65
——— Translation of Inscription . . . 117
Separate Edicts on Dhauli Rock . . . 16, 89, 127, 129
——— on Jaugada Rock . . . 19, 89, 127, 129
——— of Queen on Allahabad Pillar . . . 38, 116, 140
——— of Kosâmbi on ,, . . . 38, 116, 141
——— on Delhi Siwâlik Pillar . . . 36, 114, 115

Takhasila, or Taxila—First separate Edict, Dhauli . . . 91, 128
Tambapanni, Pâli name of Ceylon—Rock Edict II . . . 66, 117
Texts of Rock Inscriptions . . . 65
——— first separate Edict at Dhauli and Jaugada . . . 89
——— second ,, ,, ,, ,, . . . 92
——— Khandagiri Rock Inscription . . . 98
——— Sahasarâm Rock Inscription . . . 94
——— Rûpnâth Rock ,, . . . 95
——— Bairât Rock ,, . . . 96
——— Second Bairât Rock ,, . . . 97
——— Deotek Slab ,, . . . 102
——— Pillar Inscriptions . . . 106
——— Separate Pillar Inscriptions . . . 114, 115, 116
——— Cave Inscriptions . . . 103
Tosali, name of a town and district, in Dhauli—Separate Edicts . . . 16, 127, 129
Translations of Rock Edicts by Prinsep and Wilson . . . 117, 126
——— of first separate Rock by Prinsep and Burnouf . . . 127
——— of second ,, ,, ,, ,, . . . 129
——— of Sahasarâm Rock Inscription, by Dr. Bühler . . . 130
——— of Rûpnâth ,, ,, ,, . . . 131
——— of second Bairât Inscription, by Burnouf and Wilson . . . 131

PAGE.

Translation of second Bairât Inscription, by Professor Kern 132
—— of Khandagiri Rock Inscription, by Prinsep 132
—— of Khandagiri and Udayagiri Cave Inscriptions 135
—— of Barâbar Cave Inscriptions 134
—— of Nâgârjuni Cave Inscriptions 134
—— of Pillar Edicts, by Prinsep 137, 139
—— of separate Edicts on Delhi Pillar, by Prinsep 139
—— of „ „ on Allahabad Pillar 140
—— of Sânchi Pillar Inscriptions 141

Upatissa, or Sâriputra—Second Bairât Rock Inscription 97, 132

Vira, or Aira, Raja—Khandagiri Rock and Cave Inscriptions 98, 132, 104, 136

Wilson, H. H.—His criticism on Prinsep's translations 7
—— Remarks on second Bairât Inscription 26
—— Translation of „ „ 131
—— Remarks on language of Asoka's Inscriptions 44
—— Translations of Rock Edicts 117, 125

Yona, country, coupled with Kâmboja 10, 72
——. kings, Antiochus, &c—Rock Edict II 66, 117
—— „ „ „ „ „ XIII 86, 126

INSCRIPTIONS of ASOKA

PLATE I.

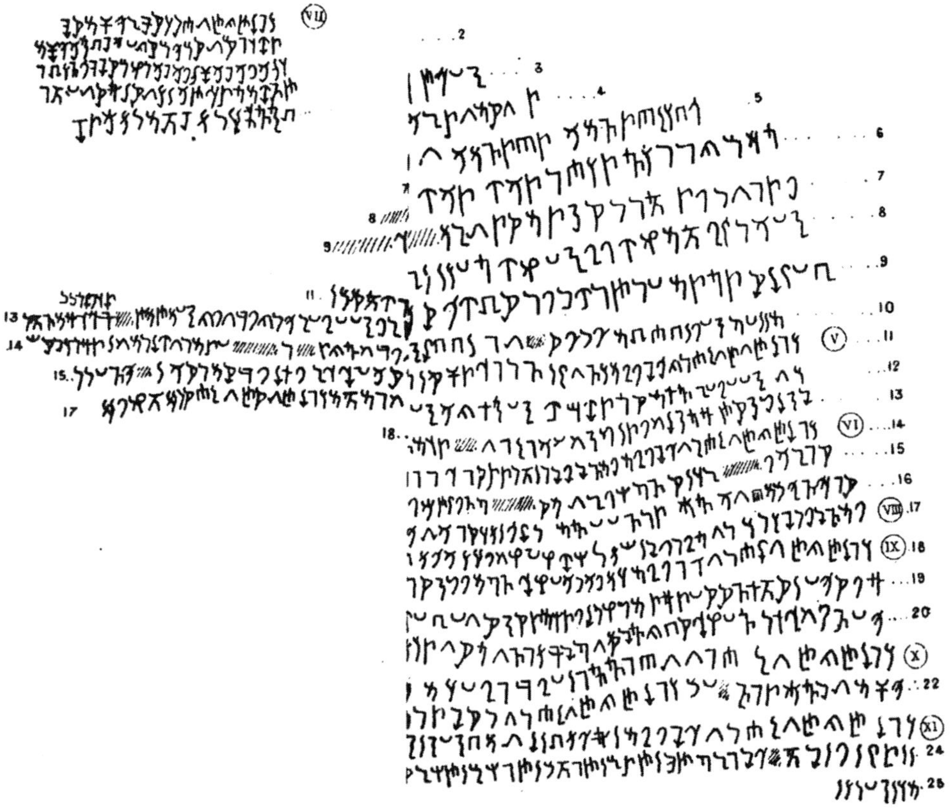

A. Cunningham, del.

Photozincographed at the Surveyor General's Office Calcutta

INSCRIPTIONS of ASOKA

PLATE I.

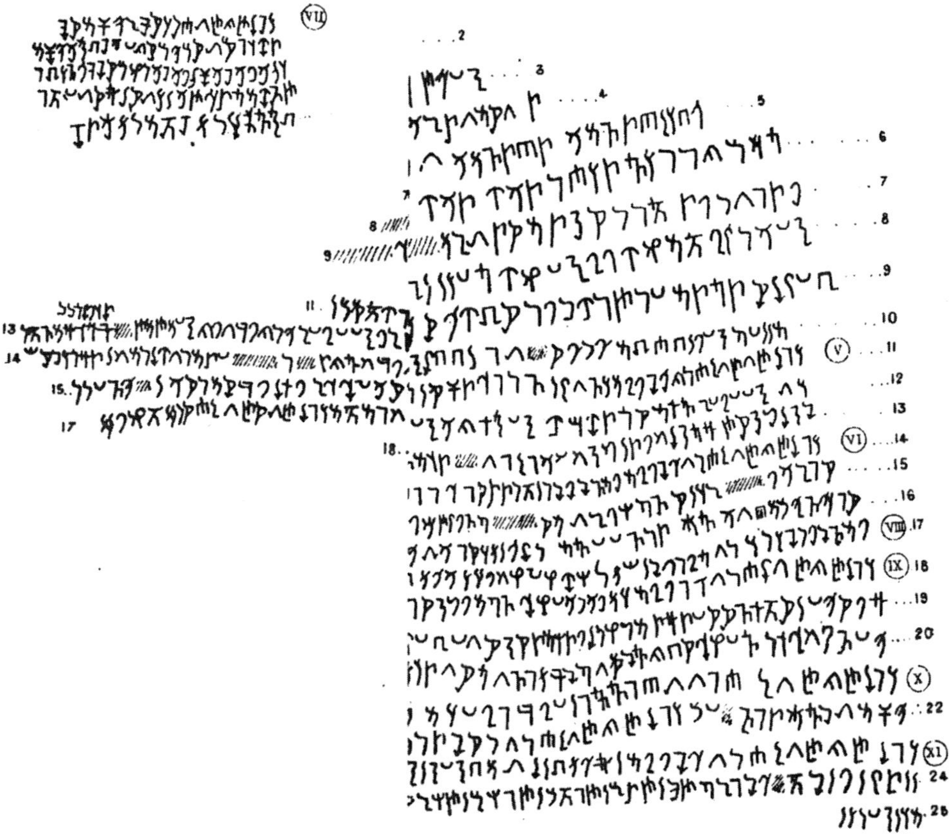

A. Cunningham, del.

Photozincographed at the Surveyor General's Office, Calcutta

INSCRIPTIONS of ASOKA.

PLATE II.

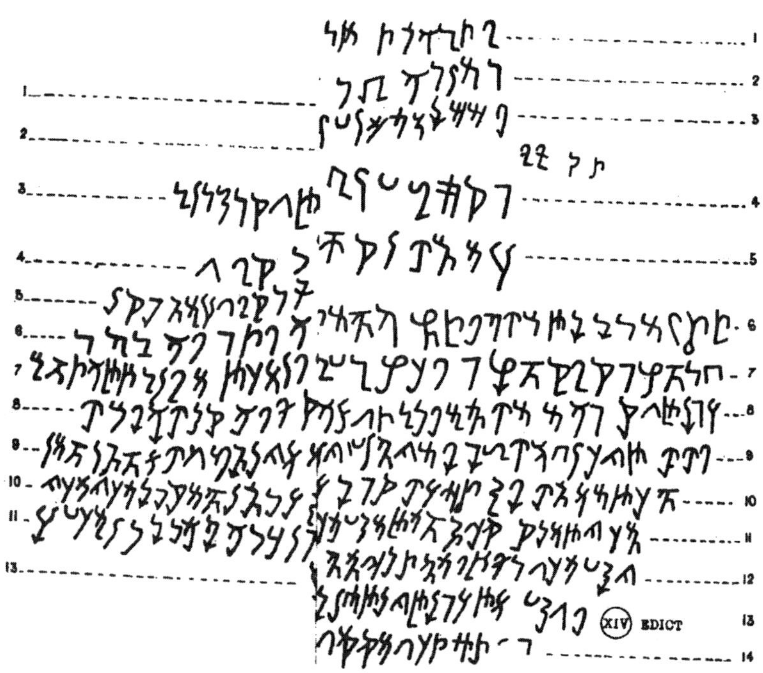

A. Cunningham, del.

Photozincographed at the Surveyor General's Office Calcutta.

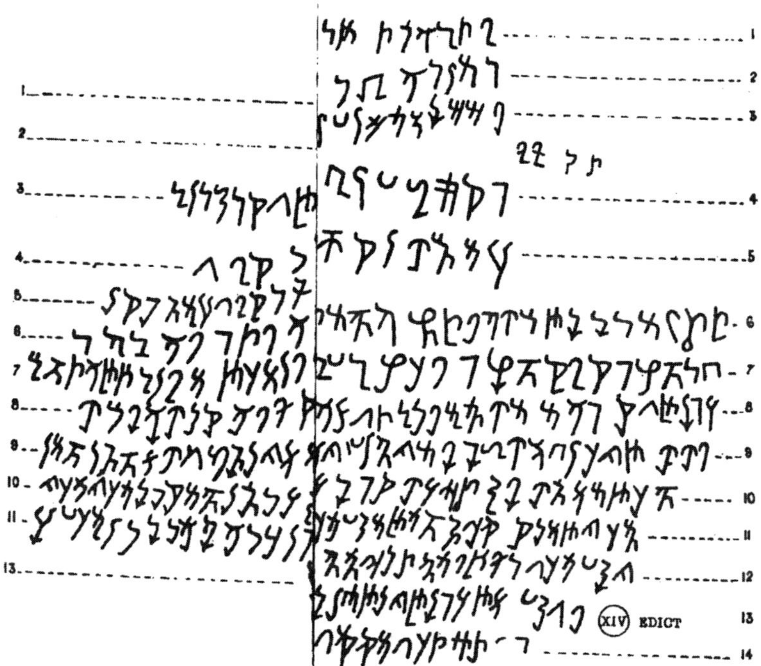

A. Cunningham, del.

Photozincographed at the Surveyor General's Office Calcutta.

INSCRIPTIONS of ASOKA. PLATE III.

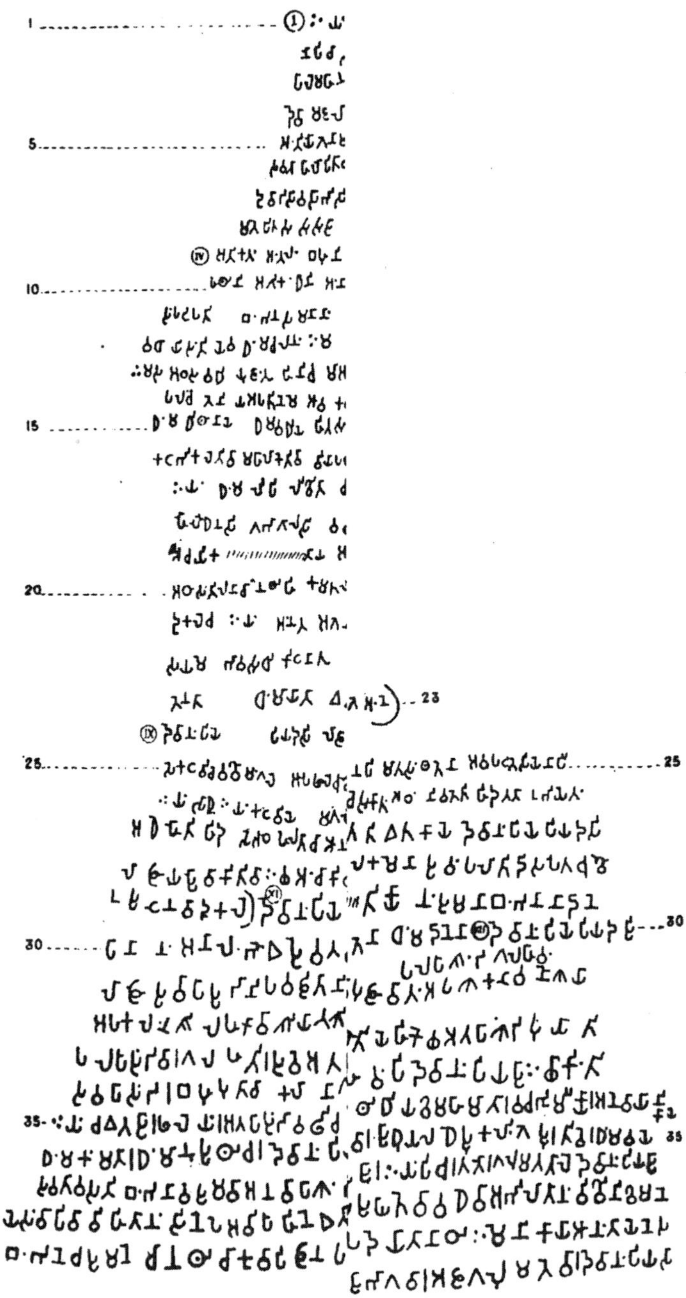

A Cunningham, del.

Photozincographed at the Surveyor General's Office Calcutta.

INSCRIPTIONS of ASOKA. PLATE IV.

KHALSI ROCK

N. Face.

S. Face.

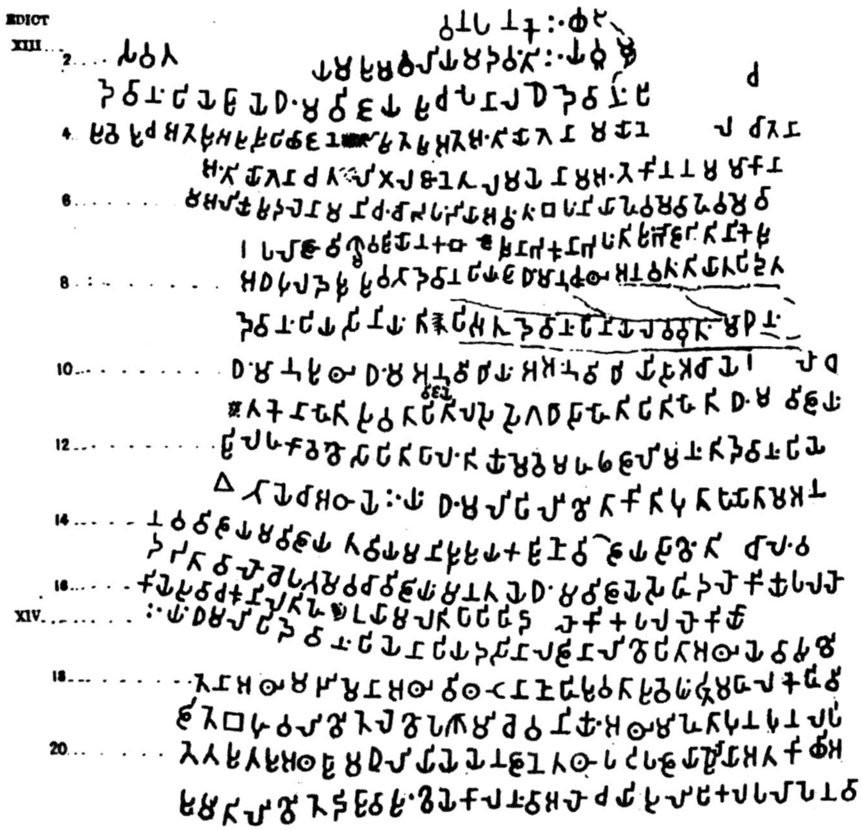

One-sixth of the Original.

A. Cunningham, del.

Photozincographed at the Surveyor General's Office Calcutta.

INSCRIPTIONS of ASOKA

PLATE V.

ROCK AT GIRNÂR
in Kathiâwâd

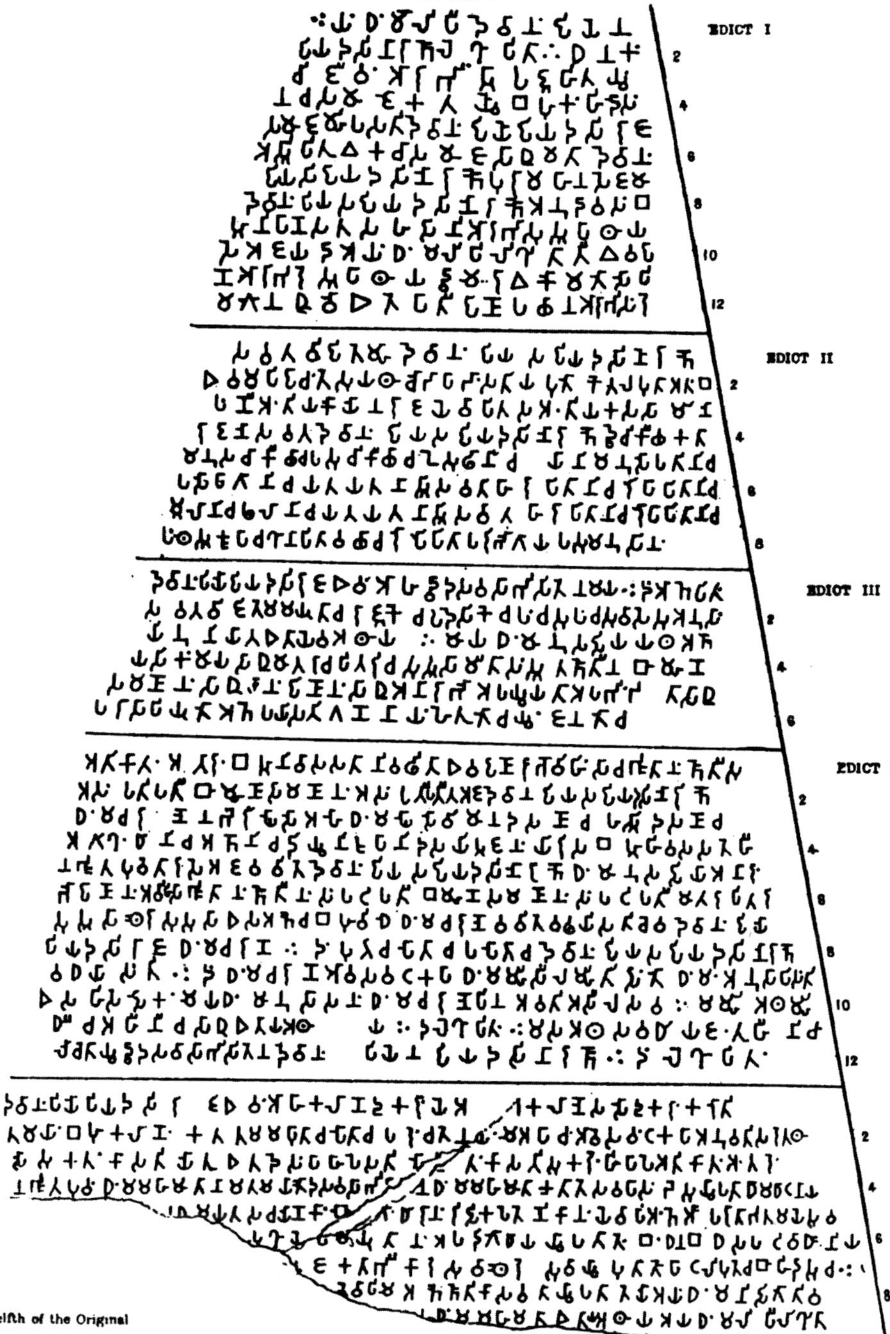

One-twelfth of the Original

A. Cunningham, del.

Photozincographed at the Surveyor General's Office Calcutta

GIRNÂR ROCK
in Kâthiâwâd.

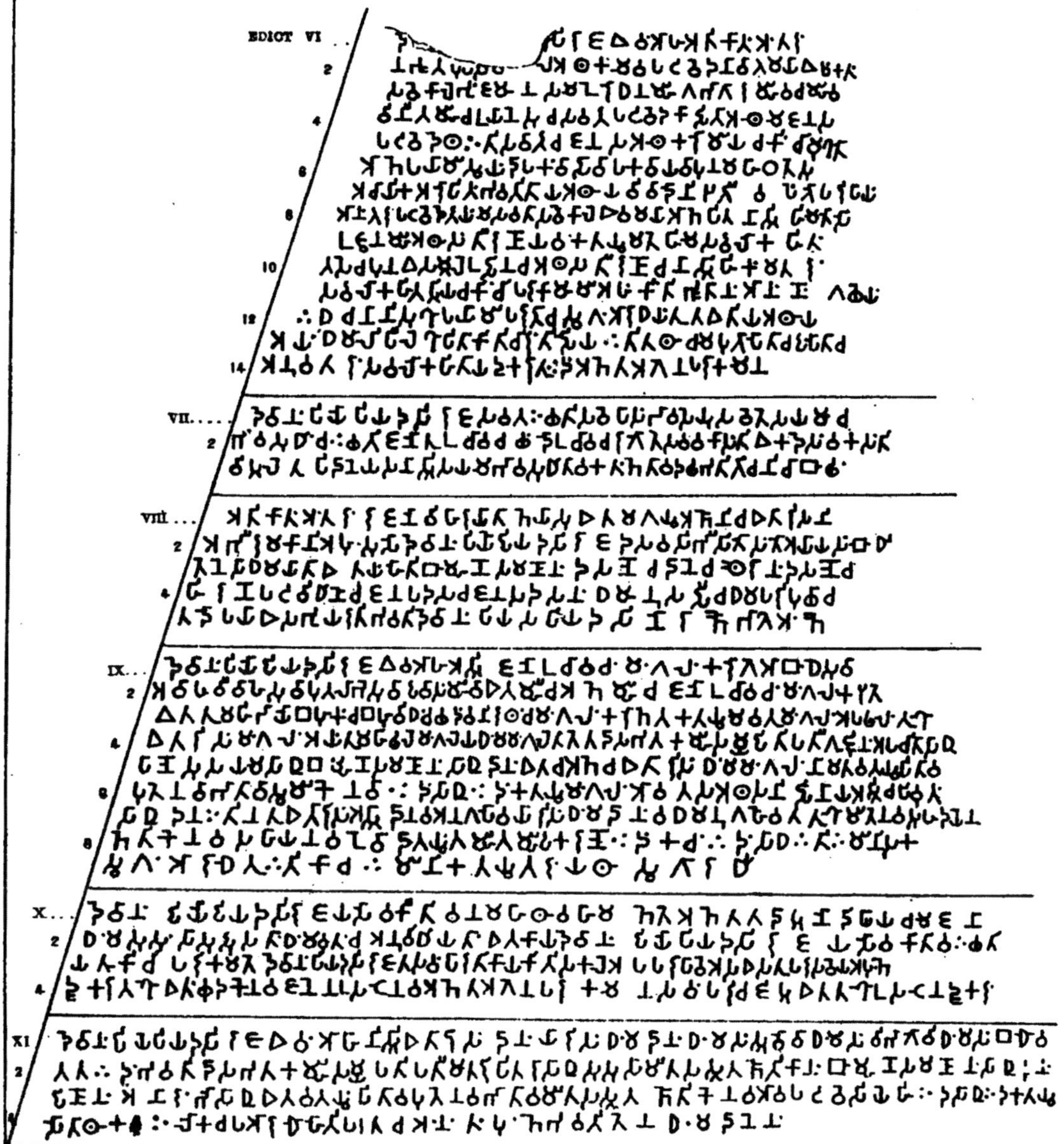

One-twelfth of the Original

A. Cunningham, del.

Photozincographed at the Surveyor General's Office, Calcutta

INSCRIPTIONS of ASOKA PLATE VII.

GIRNÂR ROCK
in Kâthiâwâd

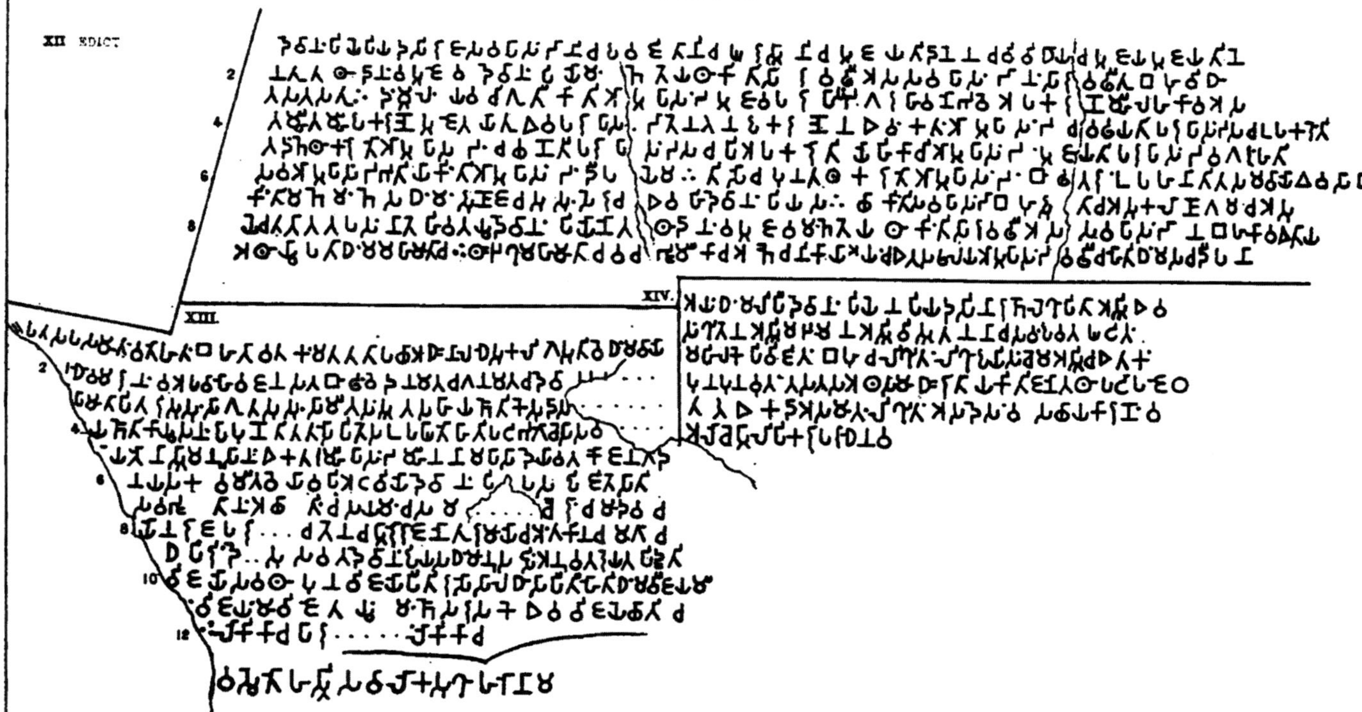

One-twelfth of the Original

A. Cunningham, del.

Photozincographed at the Surveyor General's Office Calcutta.

INSCRIPTIONS of ASOKA. PLATE VIII.

DHAULI ROCK
Left Face.

FIRST SEPARATE EDICT.

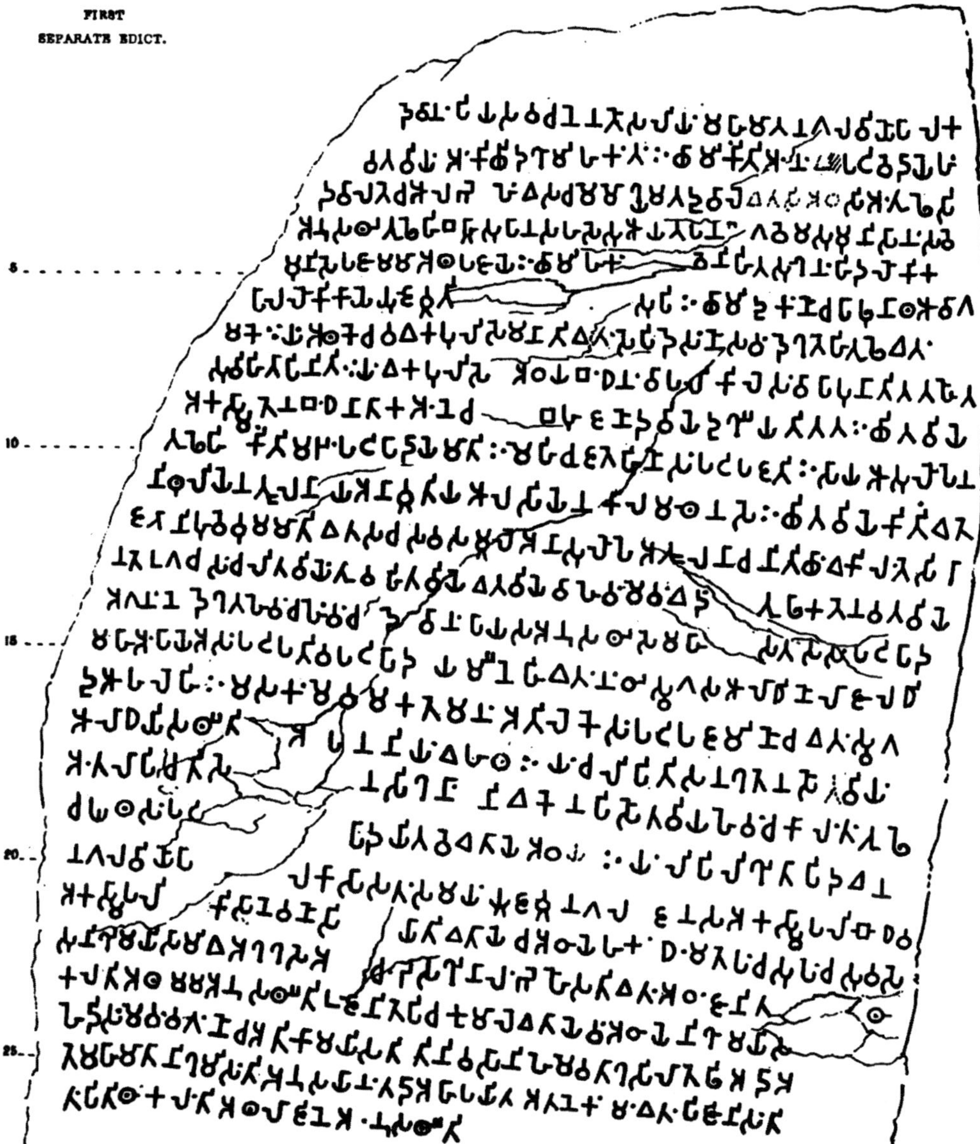

A. Cunningham, del.

Photozincographed at the Surveyor General's Office, Calcutta.

INSCRIPTIONS of ASOKA. PLATE IX.

DHAULI ROCK
Middle Face.

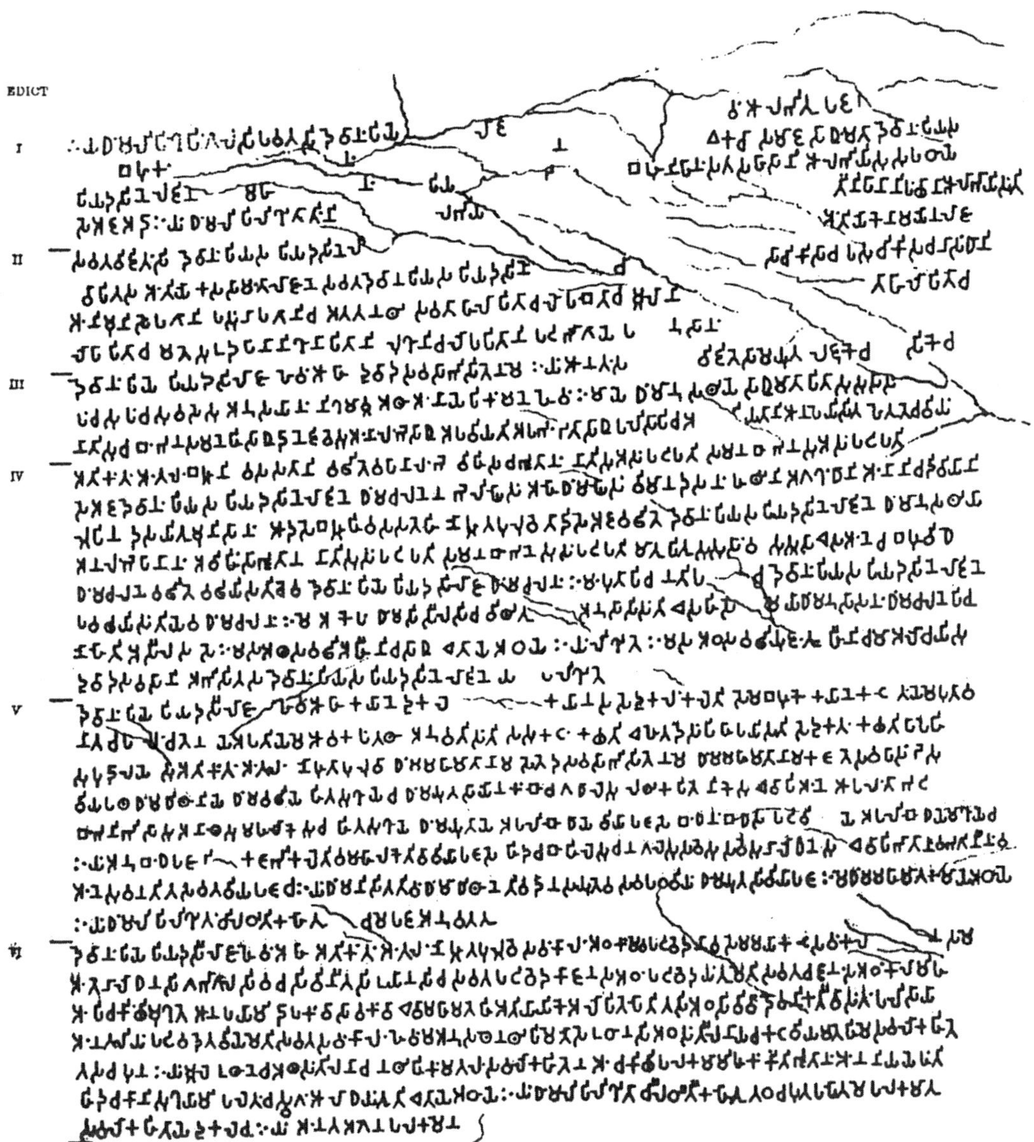

A. Cunningham, del.

Photozincographed at the Surveyor General's Office, Calcutta.

INSCRIPTIONS of ASOKA. PLATE X.

DHAULI ROCK
Right Face:

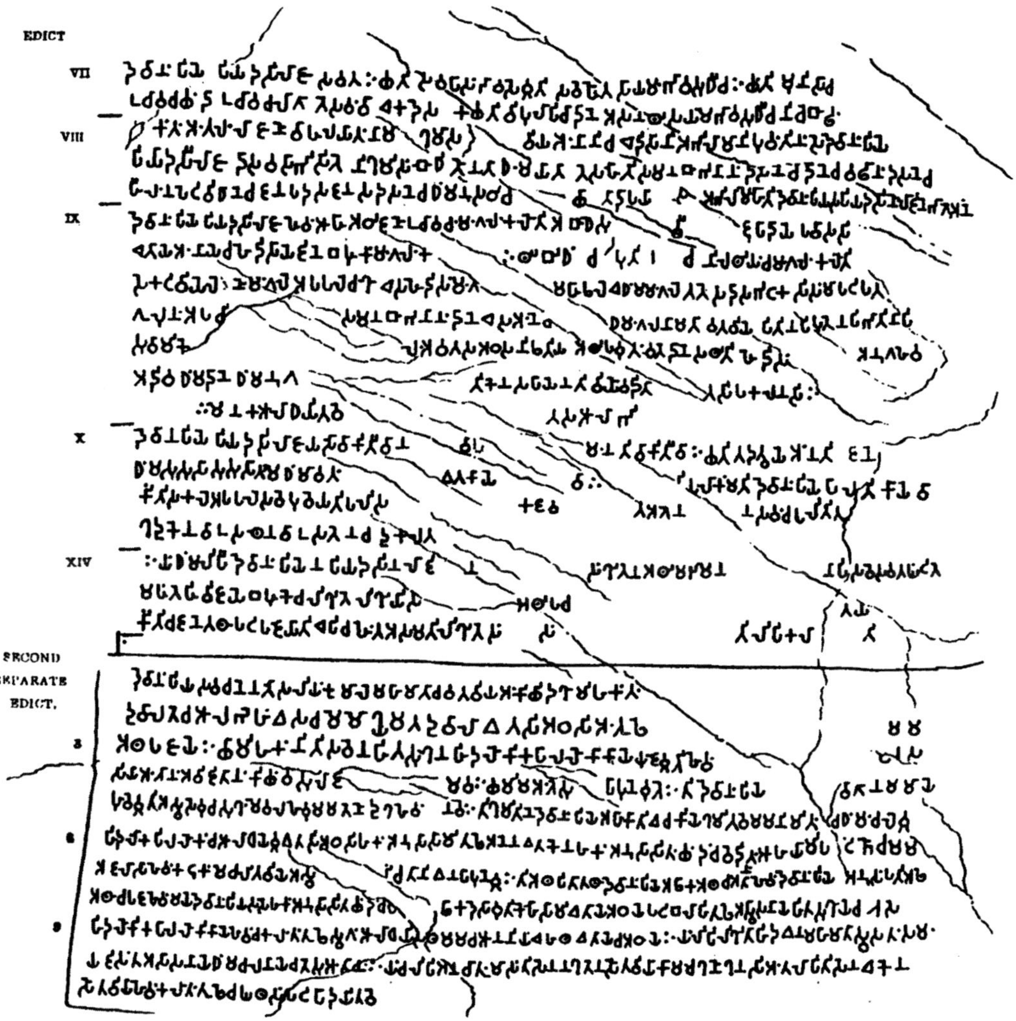

A. Cunningham, del. Photozincographed at the Surveyor General's Office, Calcutta

INSCRIPTIONS OF ASOKA — PLATE XI.

ROCK OF JAUGADA IN GANJAM.

A. Cunningham, del.

ROCK OF JAUGADA
in Ganjam.

EDICT VI. VII. VIII. IX. X. XIV.

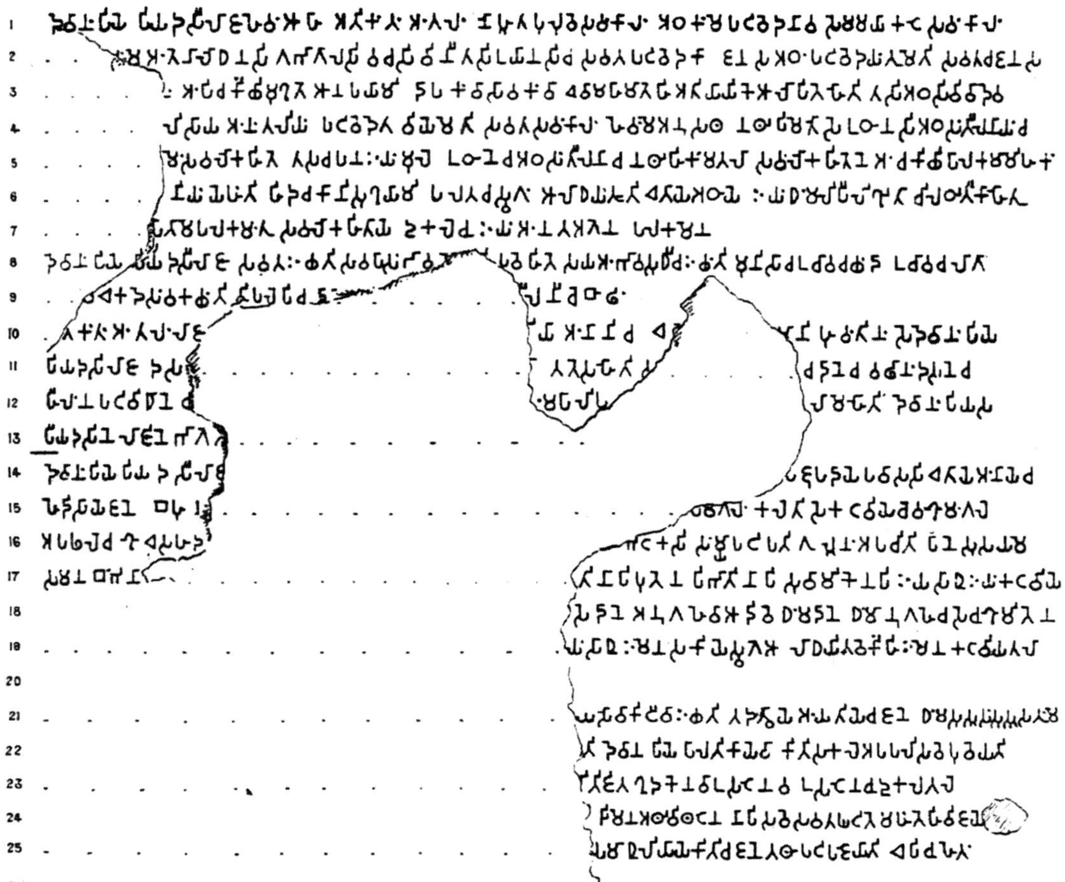

One-tenth of the Original

A. Cunningham, del.

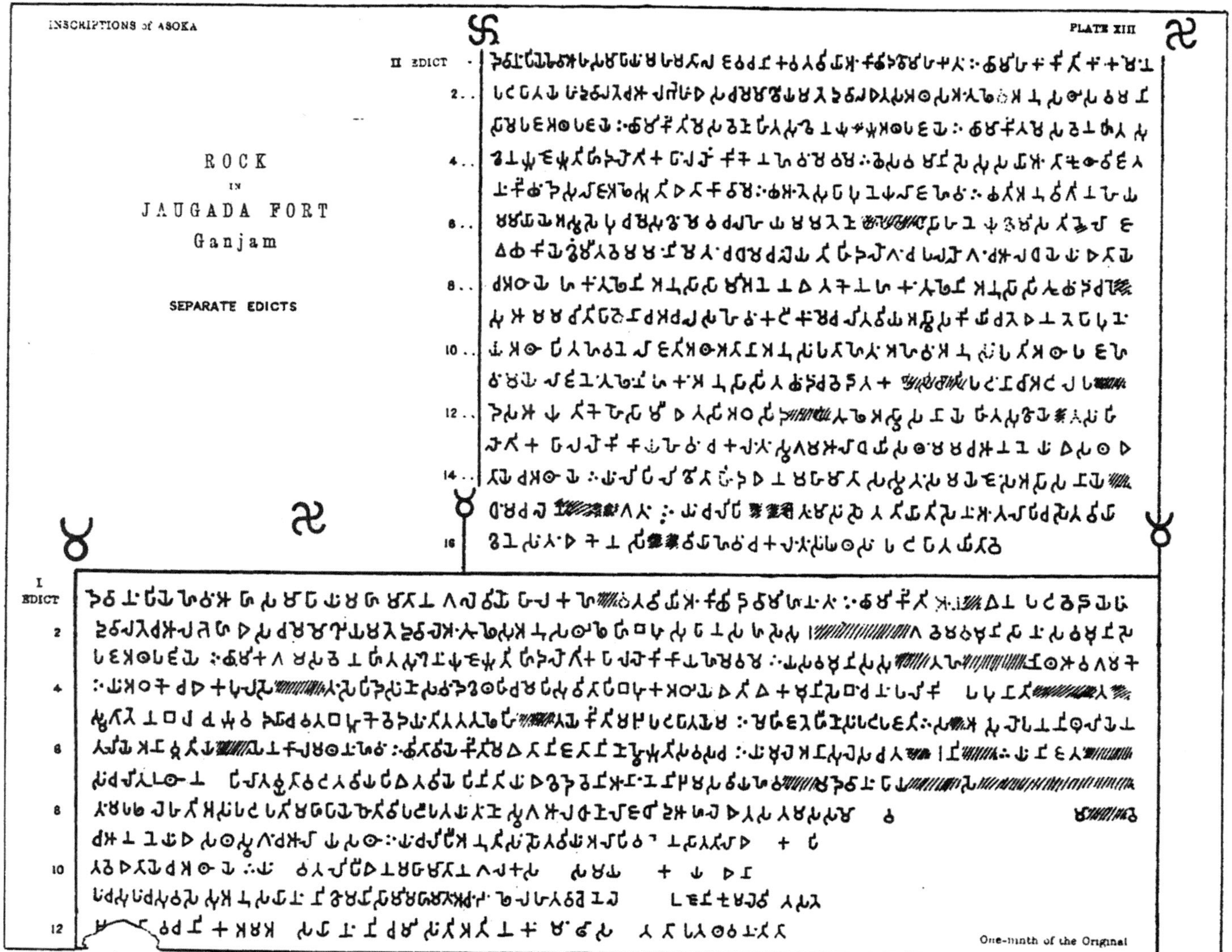

A. Cunningham, del.

Photozincographed at the Surveyor General's Office, Calcutta

VIII.

ROCK AT SAHASARÂM
near Patna.

IX.

ROCK AT RUPNÂTH
near Jabalpur.

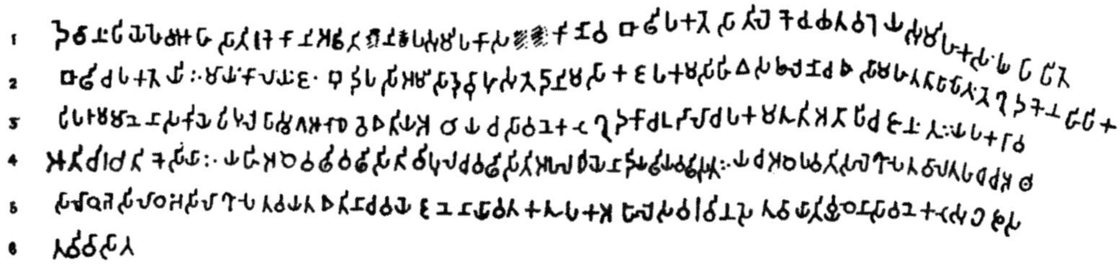

X.

ROCK AT BAIRÂT
near Jaypur.

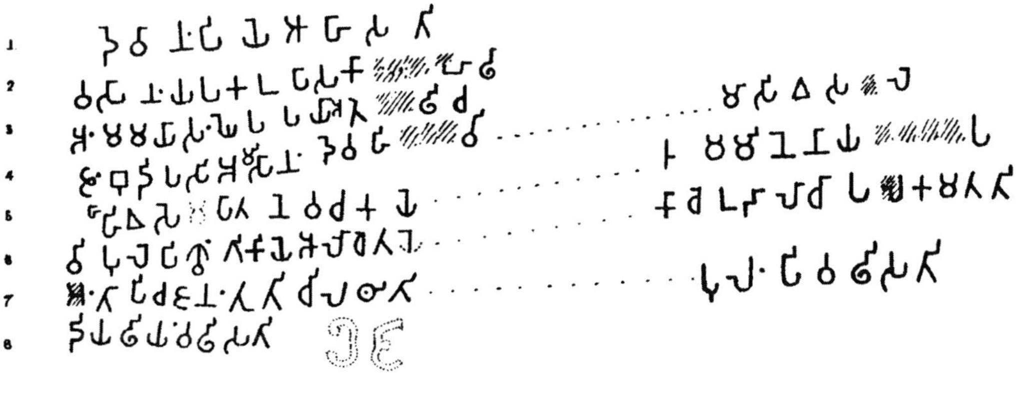

A. Cunningham, del. Photozincographed at the Surveyor General's Office, Calcutta.

ROCK AT BAIRÂT
near Jaypur.

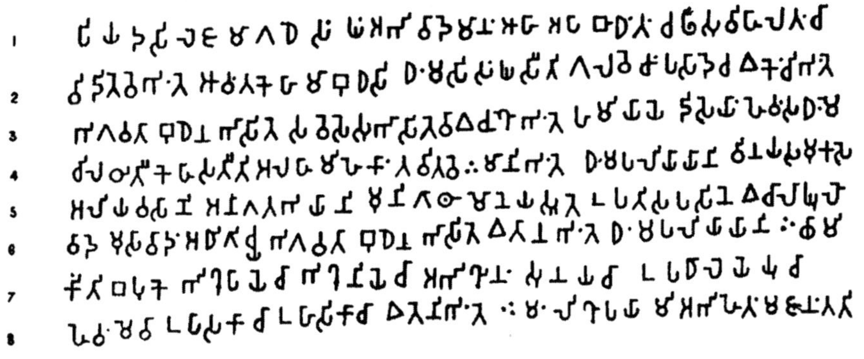

CAVES IN RÂMNÂTH HILL
near Sirguja.

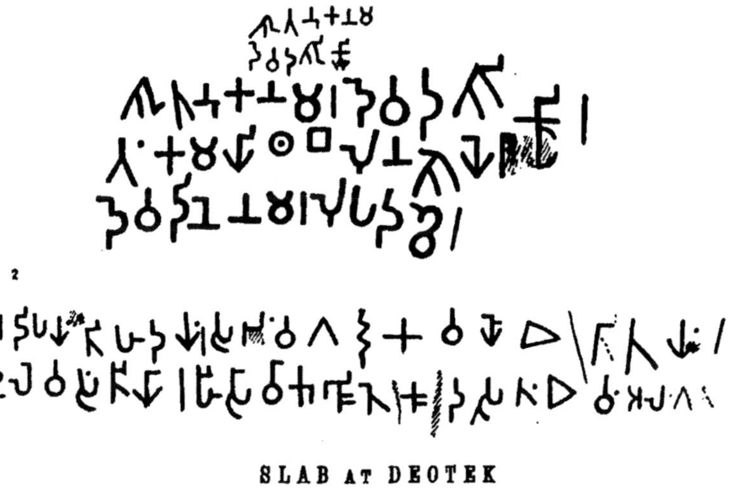

SLAB AT DEOTEK
near Nagpur.

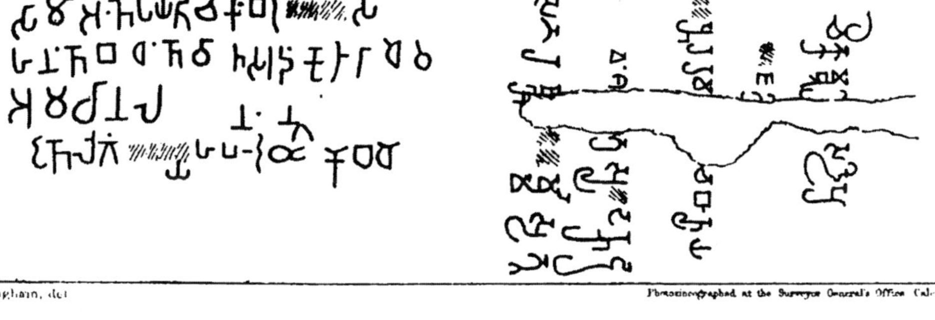

INSCRIPTIONS of ASOKA. PLATE XVI.

CAVES AT BARÂBAR.

1. Sudâma.

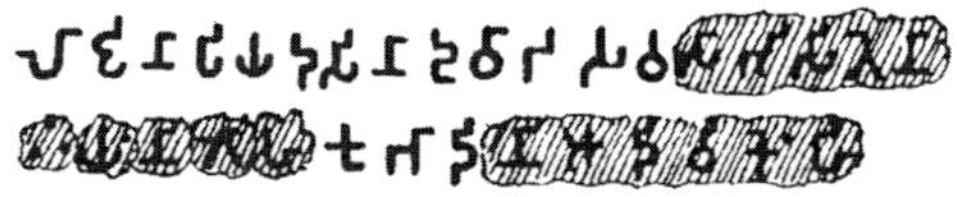

2. Viswa.

3. Karna.

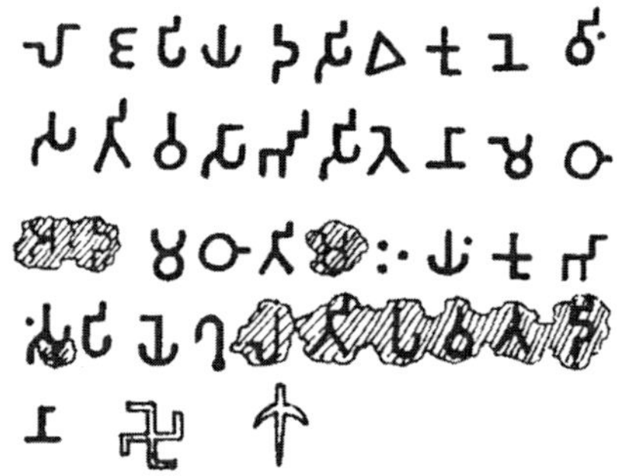

INSCRIPTIONS of DASARATHA.

CAVES AT NÂGÂRJUNI.

4. Vapiyaka.

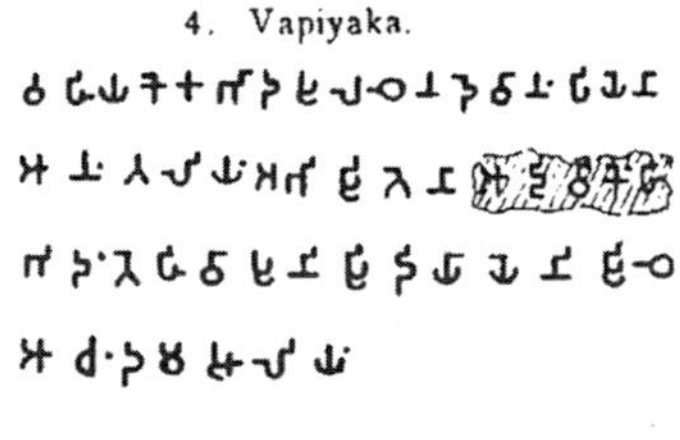

5. Gopika.

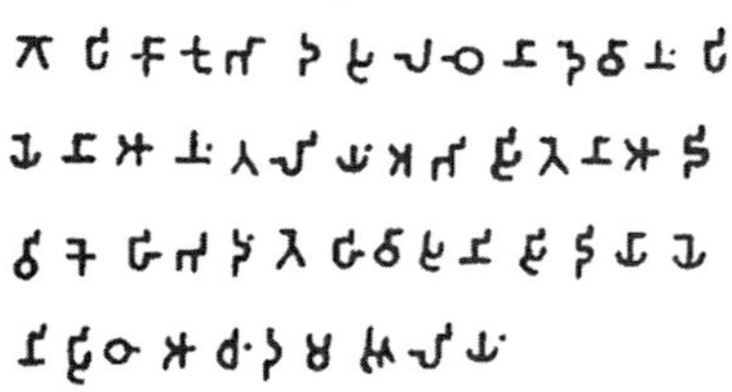

6. Vadathi.

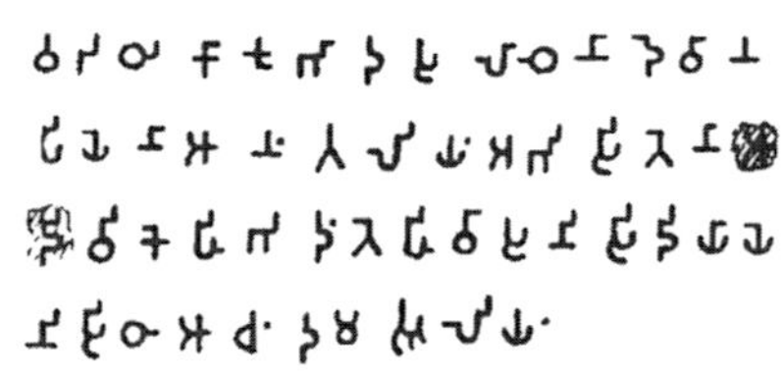

One-sixth of the Original.

A. Cunningham, del.

Photozincographed at the Surveyor General's Office Calcutta.

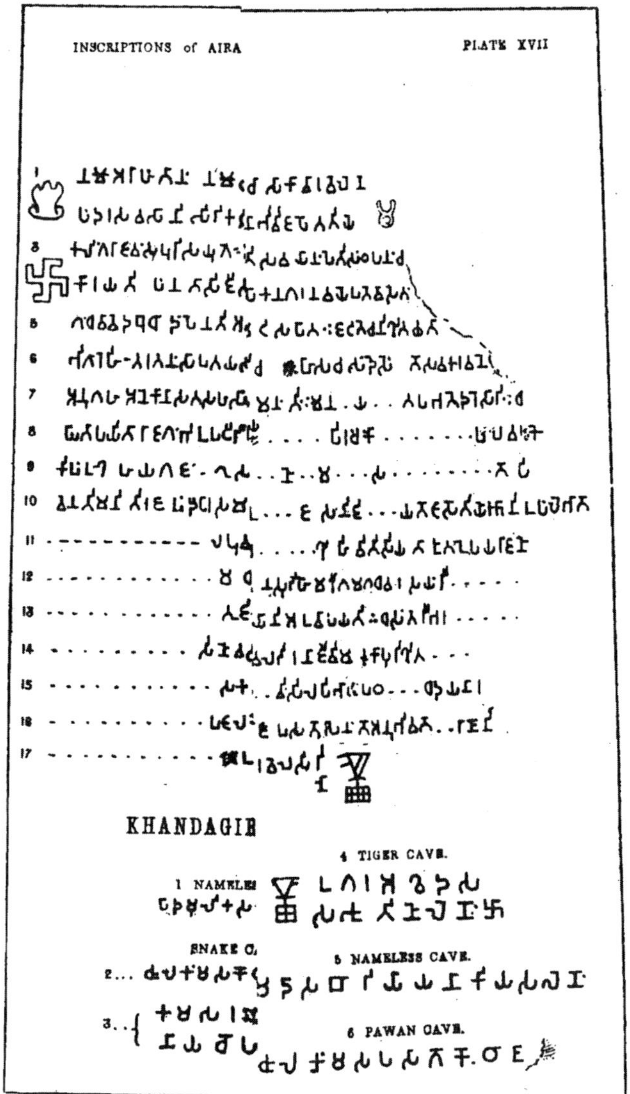

A. Cunningham, del.

Photozincographed at the Surveyor General's Office Calcutta.

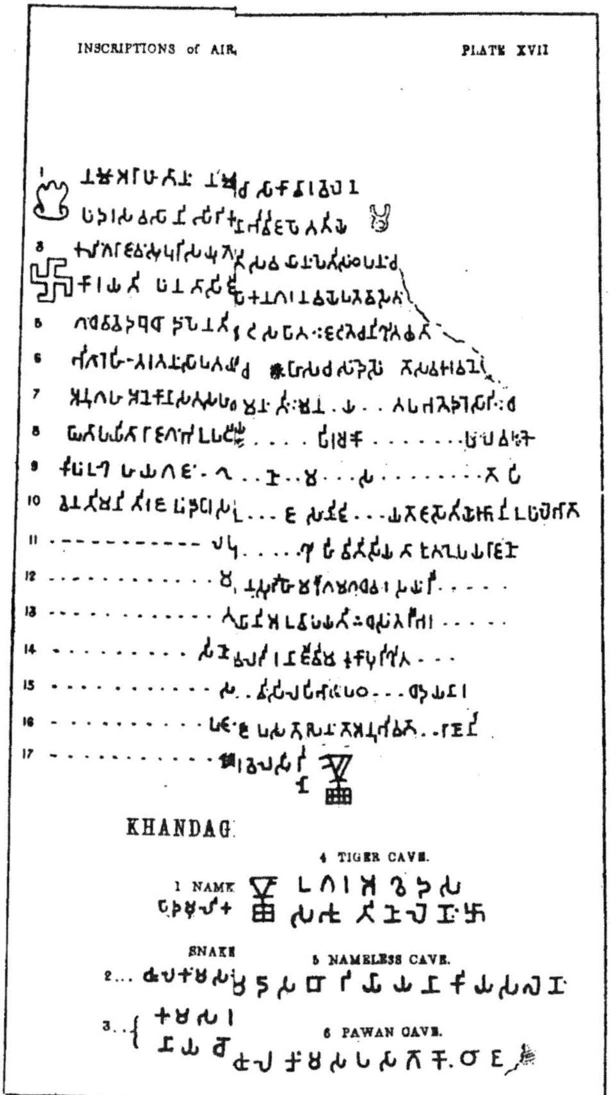

A. Cunningham, del.

Photozincographed at the Surveyor General's Office Calcutta.

INSCRIPTIONS of ASOKA. PLATE XVIII

DELHI PILLAR
From Siwâlik.
(Firoz Shah's Lât.)

NORTH WEST

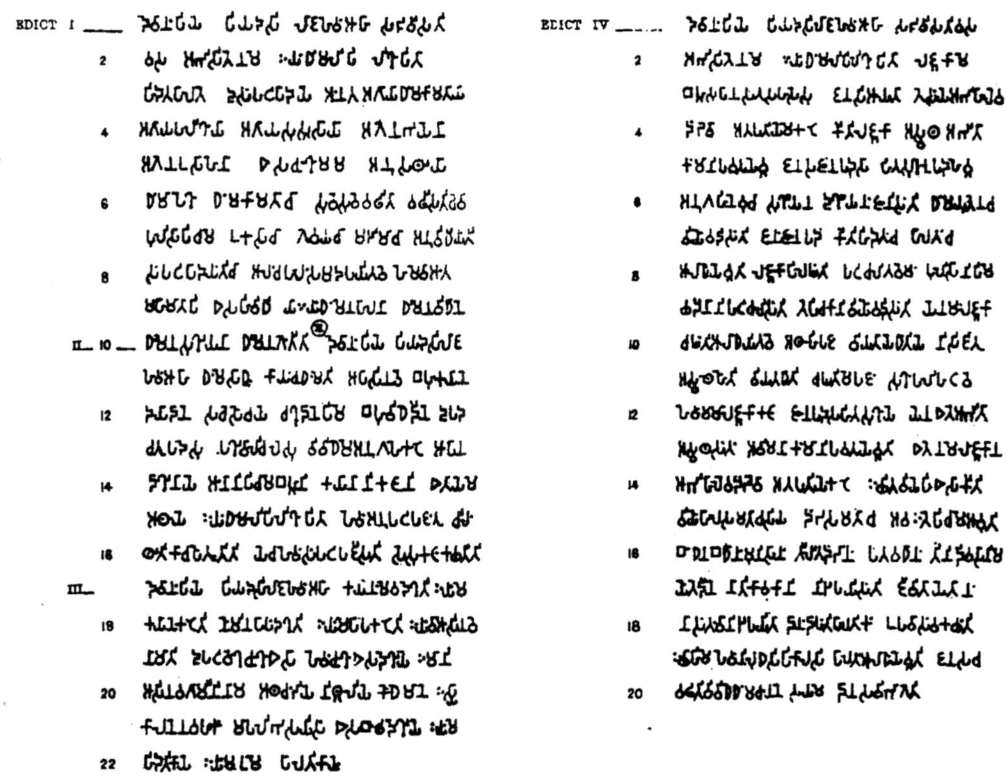

One-Tenth of Original.

A. Cunningham, del.

Photozincographed at the Surveyor General's Office Calcutta.

INSCRIPTIONS of ASOKA. PLATE XIX

DELHI PILLAR
From Siwâlik.
(Firoz Shah's Lât.)

SOUTH. EAST

EDICT V — EDICT VI — VII

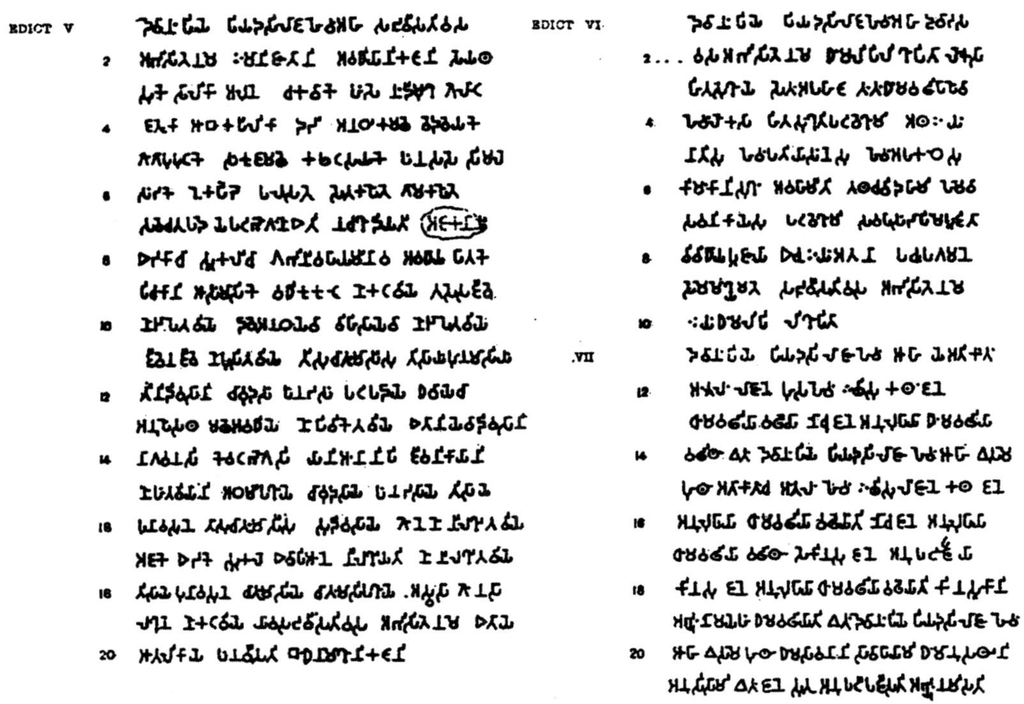

One-Tenth of Original.

A. Cunningham, del.

Photozincographed at the Surveyor General's Office Calcutta.

DELHI PILLAR
From Siwâlik.
(Firoz Shah's Lât.)

INSCRIPTION ROUND THE PILLAR.

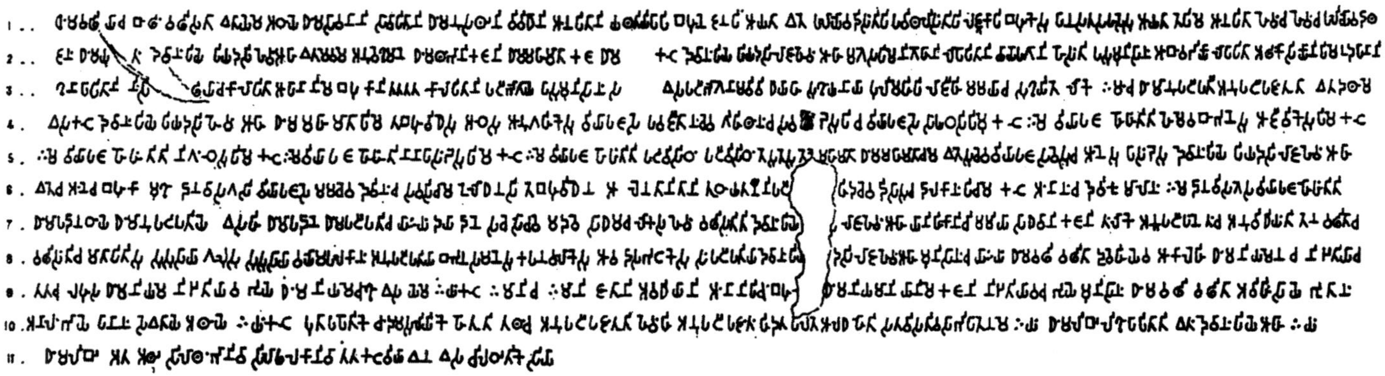

SANCHI PILLAR.

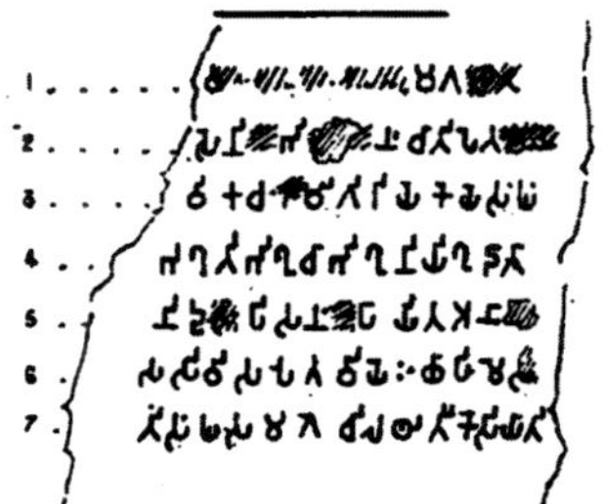

One-Tenth of Original.

A. Cunningham del.

Photozincographed at the Surveyor General's Office Calcutta.

INSCRIPTIONS of ASOKA. PLATE XXI

DELHI PILLAR
From Mirat.

Upper Part all peeled off

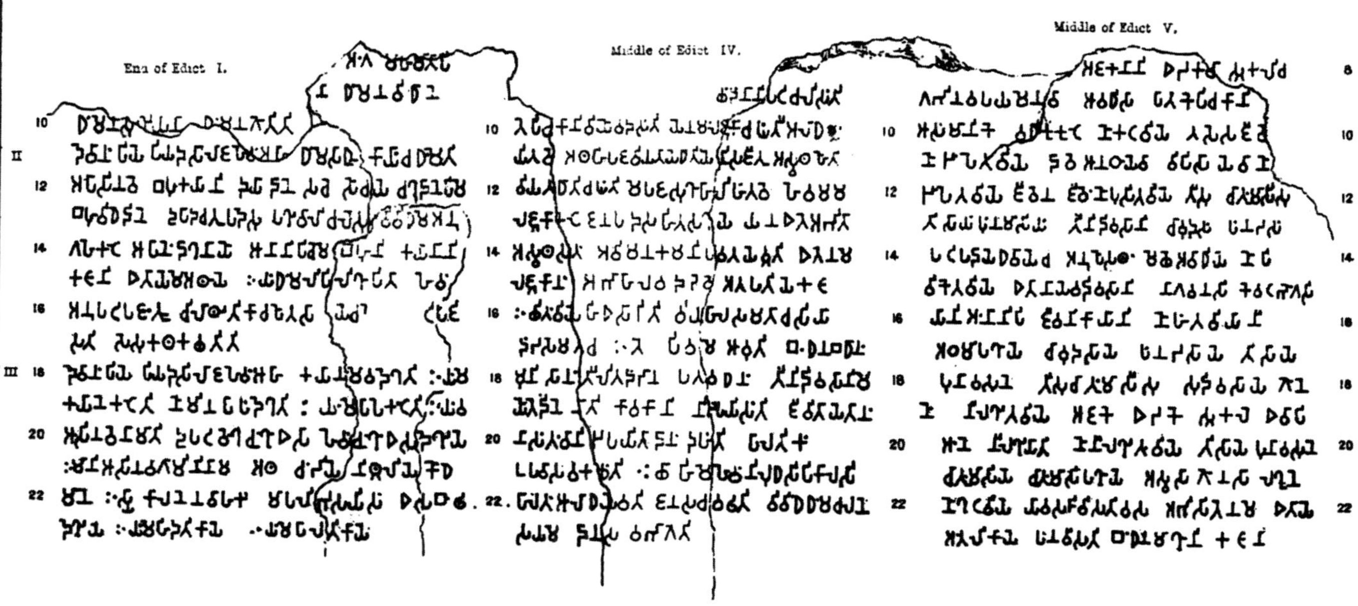

One-Eighth of Original.

A. Cunningham, del.

INSCRIPTIONS of ASOKA. PLATE XXII

ALLAHABAD PILLAR.

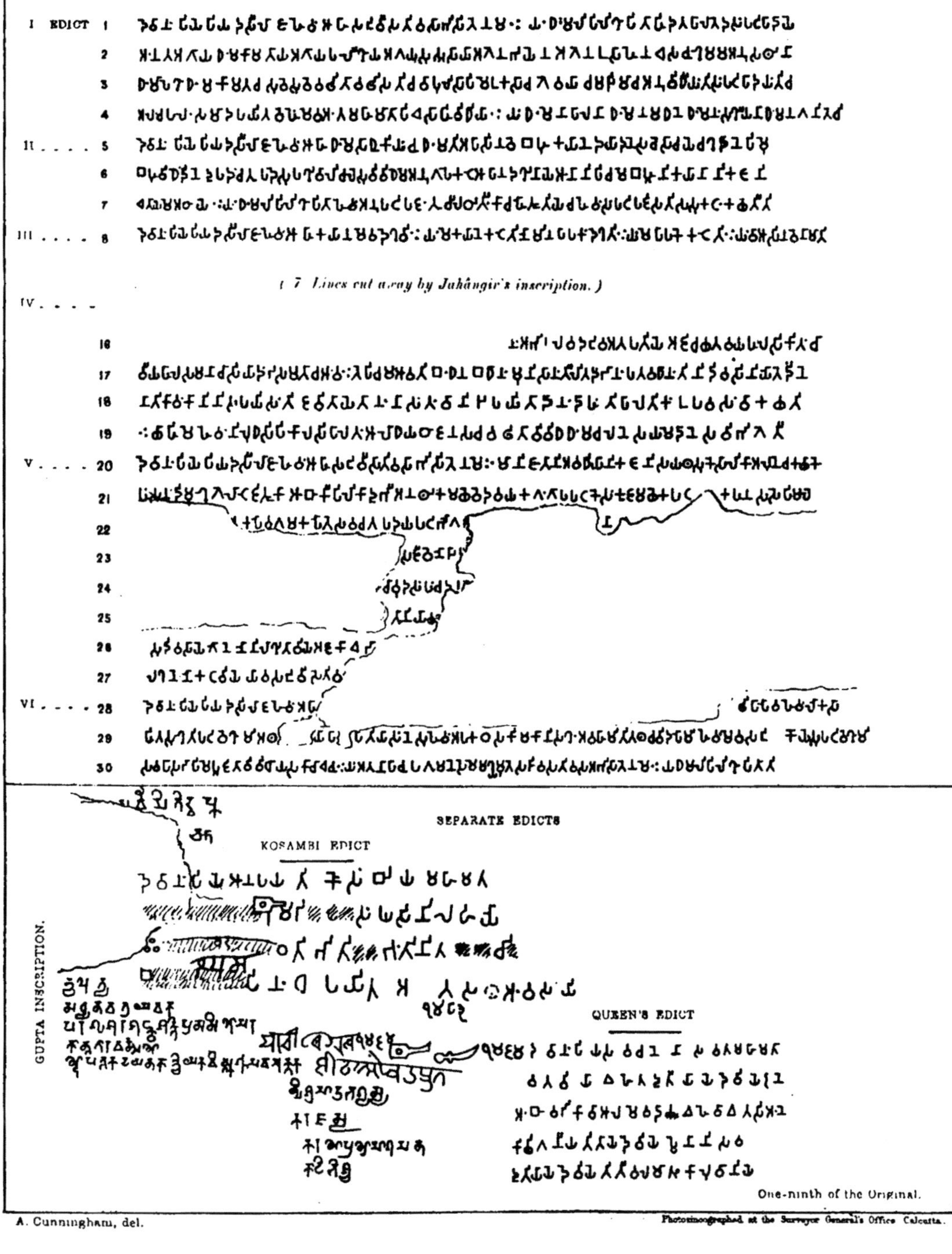

One-ninth of the Original.

A. Cunningham, del.

Photozincographed at the Surveyor General's Office Calcutta.

INSCRIPTIONS of ASOKA. PLATE XXIII.

PILLAR
AT
LAURIYA-ARARÂJ
(Radhia.)

SOUTH

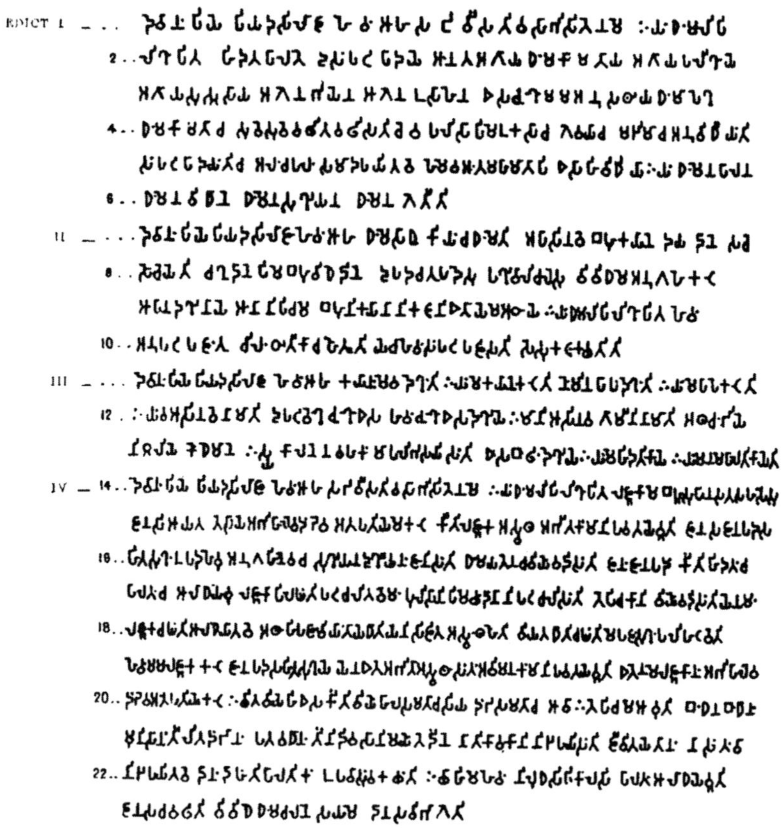

One-twelfth of the Original

A. Cunningham, del.

Photozincographed at the Surveyor General's Office Calcutta.

PILLAR

AT

LAURIYA-ARARÂJ

(Râdhia.)

NORTH

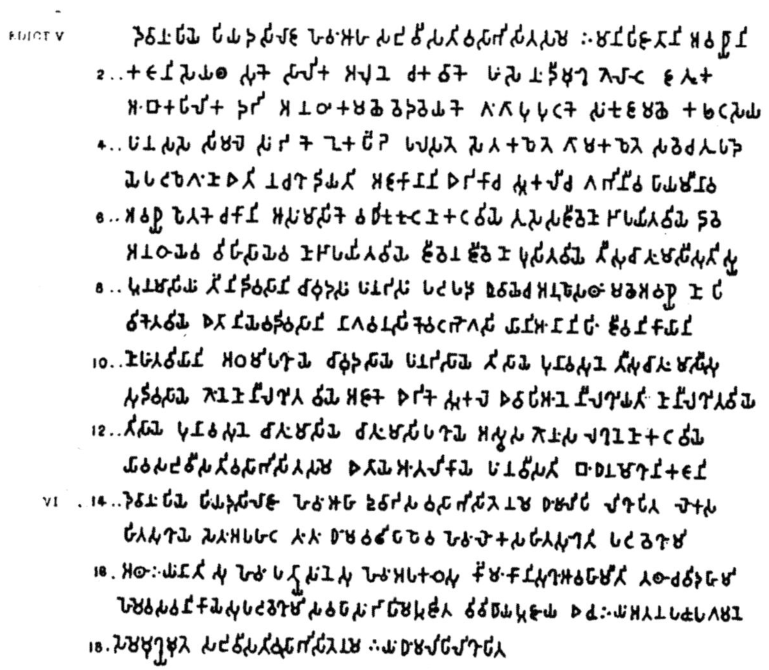

One-twelfth of the Original.

A. Cunningham, del.

Photozincographed at the Surveyor General's Office, Calcutta

INSCRIPTIONS of ASOKA. PLATE XXI.

PILLAR
AT
LAURIYA-ARARÂJ
(Râdhia.)

NORTH

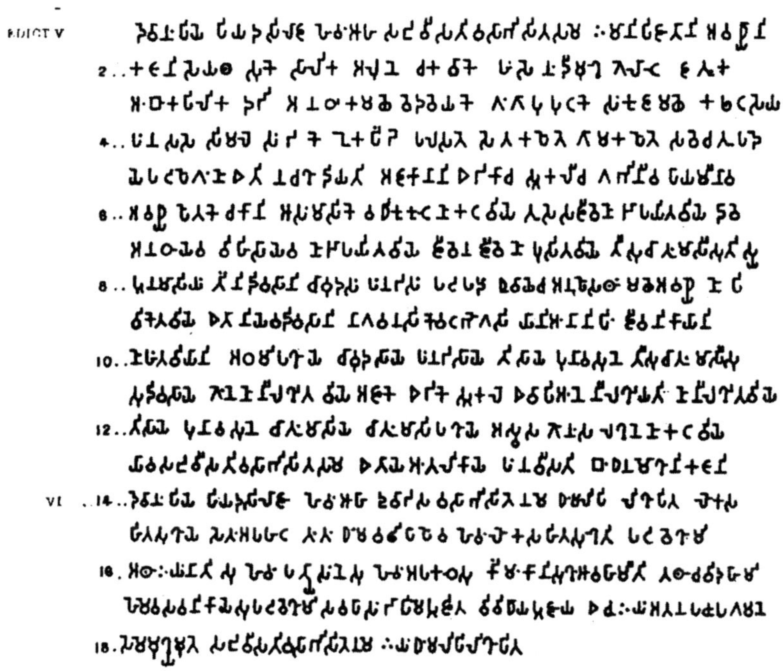

One-twelfth of the Original.

A Cunningham, del

Photozincographed at the Surveyor General's Office Calcutta

PILLAR
AT
LAURIYA-NAVANDGARH
(Mathia.)

EDICT I .... 2.. 4.. 6.. II — 8.. 10. 12.. III .... 14.. 16.. IV — 18.. 20.. 22.. 24.. 26..

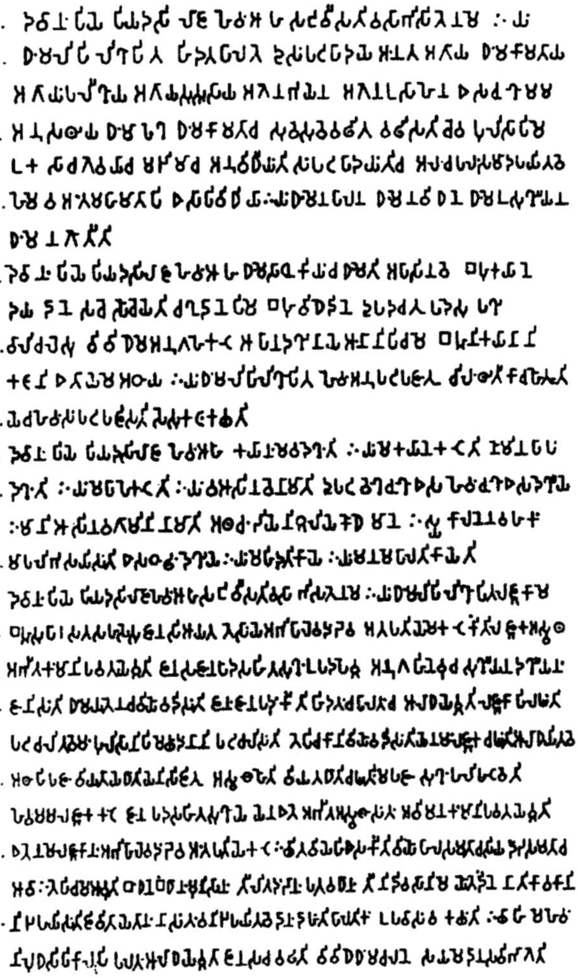

One-twelfth of the Original.

A. Cunningham, del.

Photozincographed at the Surveyor General's Office Calcutta.

PILLAR
AT
LAURIYA-NAVANDGARH
(Mathia.)

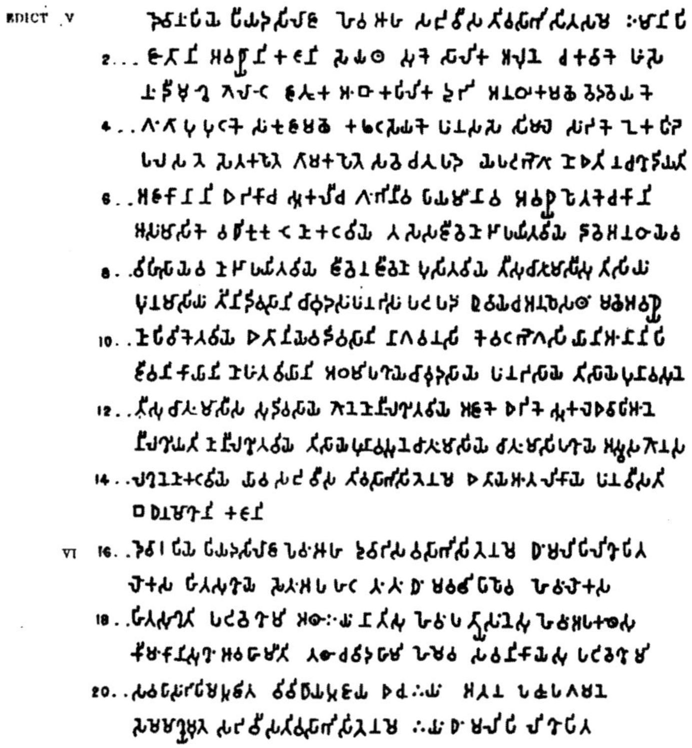

One-twelfth of the Original.

A. Cunningham, del.

Photozincographed at the Surveyor General's Office Calcutta

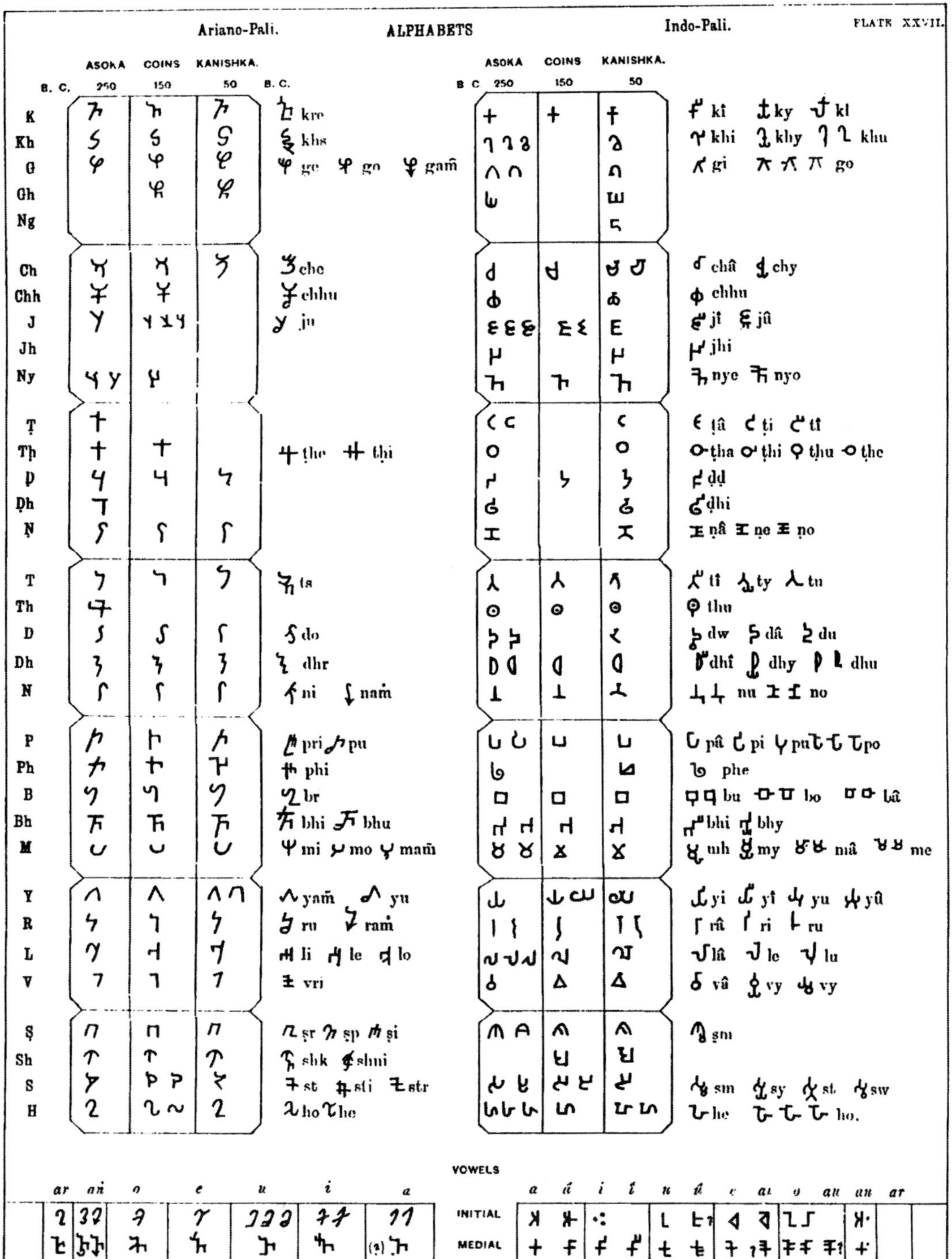

A. Cunningham del.

Lithographed at the Surveyor General's Office, Calcutta, January 1877.

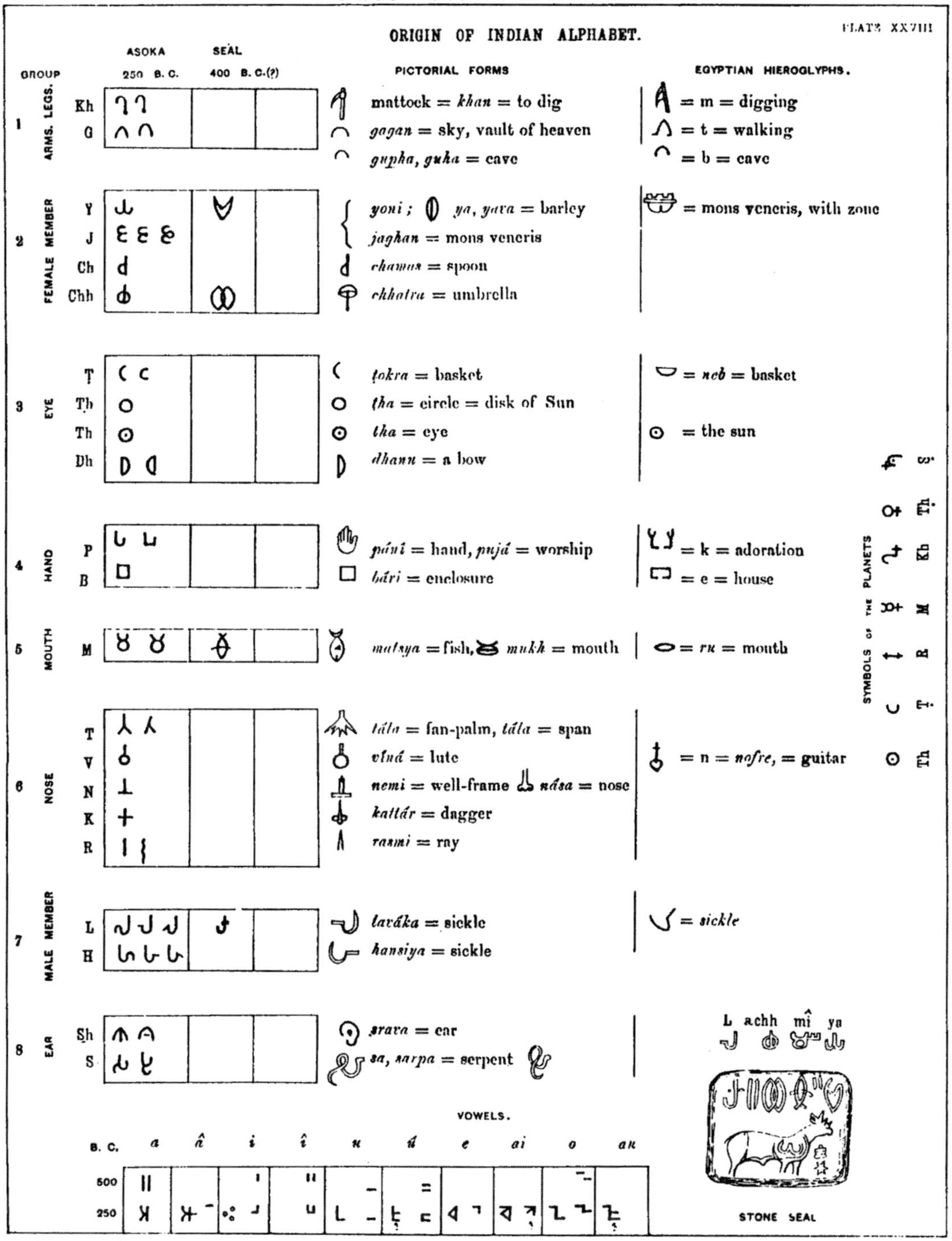

A. Cunningham del.

Lithographed at the Surveyor General's Office, Calcutta, January 1877.

INSCRIBED ROCKS PLATE XXIX.

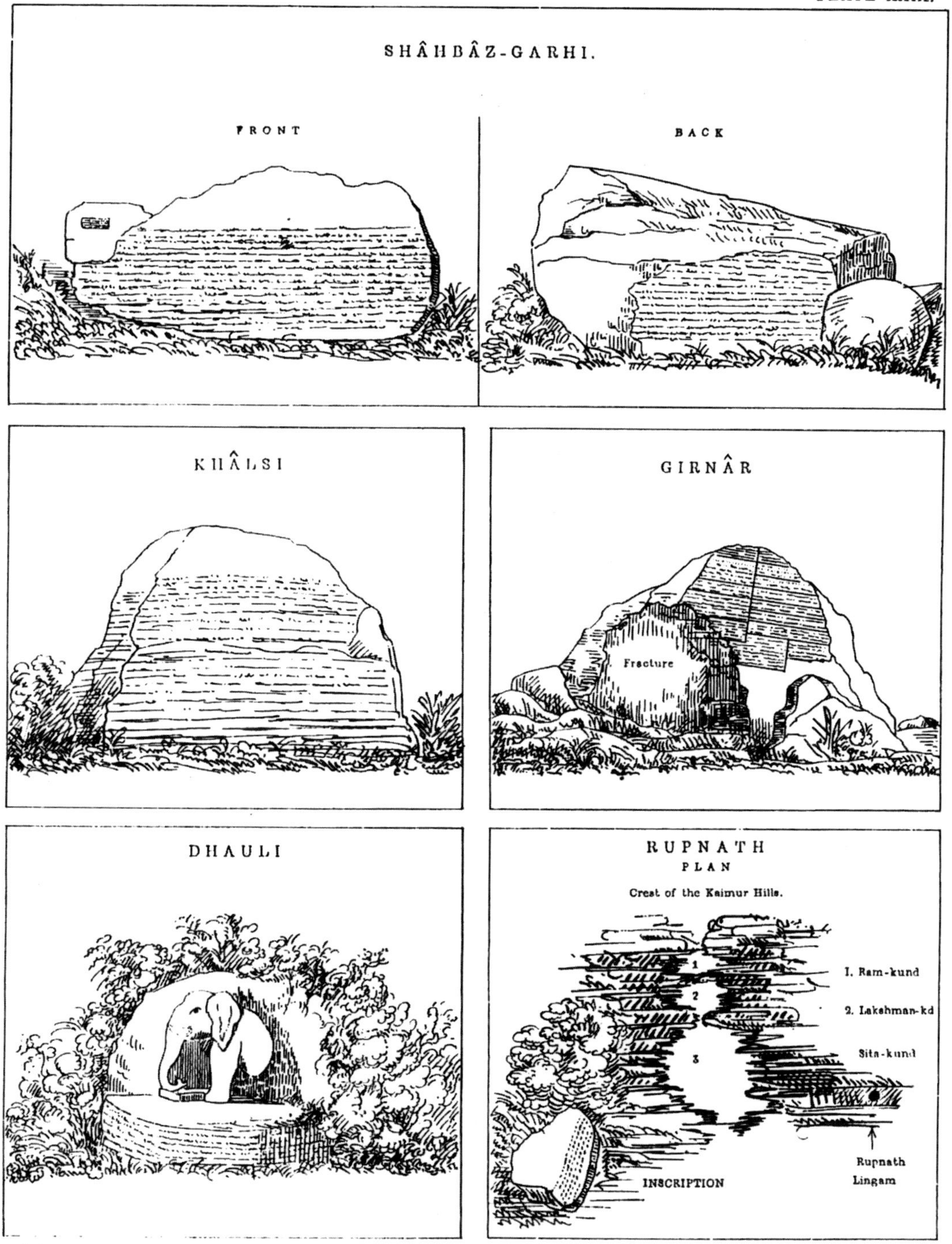

A. Cunningham, del.

Lithographed at the Survr. Genl's. Office, Calcutta, April 1876.

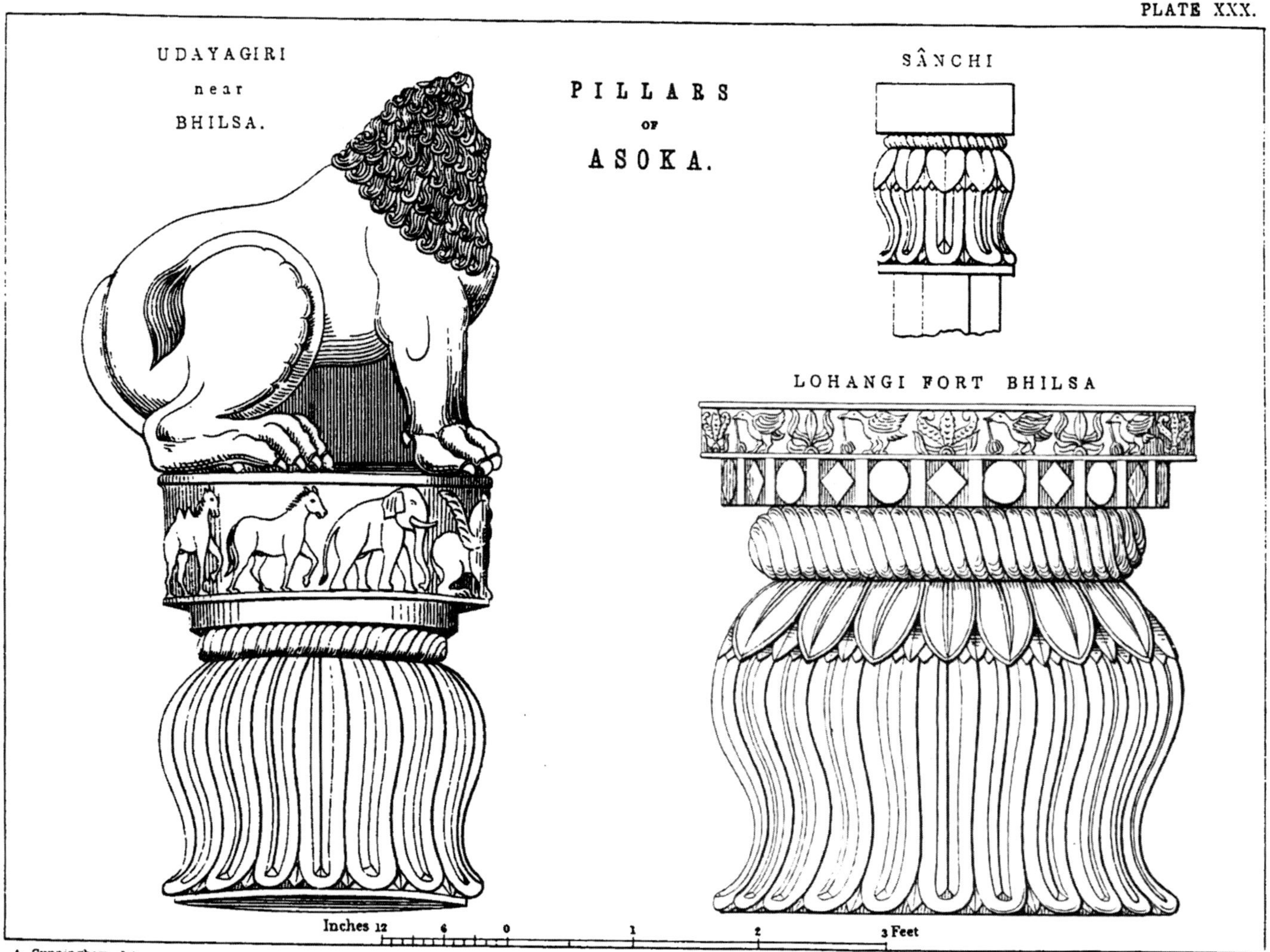

A. Cunningham, del.

Lithographed at the Survr. Genl's. Office, Calcutta, April 1876.